MENU PLANNING TIPS

There's probably a dish or two that you can whip up better than most anyone else. But a knack for cooking is not all there is to putting together a special meal. Making the menu is all important. And that takes time, practice, and above all, careful planning.

Starting Points

When you're planning the menu, there are several things to consider.

- Preplan your menu before you shop. Make a shopping list, but be flexible enough to take advantage of seasonal specials or weekend buys. While planning your menu, check your recipes and the groceries you have at home.
- Keep your cooking utensils and appliances in mind. Two dishes that require baking at different temperatures won't work in a one-oven kitchen.
- Choose the main dish first and select the other courses to complement it.
- It's wise to save more complicated dishes for the days when you have the time for them. Shorten your preparation time by choosing some recipes which can be partially or totally prepared ahead of time. This leaves you more free time just before the meal.
- Your meal will really stand out from the ordinary if you collect interesting recipes. Make sure that they offer a variety of textures, tastes, colors and shapes. Also, keep in mind that certain qualities go together; crisp goes with soft, bland or sweet with tart or zippy, hot with cold, light with heavy. When you don't have time to prepare a new dish, something as simple as an attractive garnish can help keep the meal from looking routine.

Preparation Tips

Learning how to organize your meals can save you from those horrible last minute flurries. The best way to keep things under control is to read through each recipe and make out a work schedule on paper. You can tailor the schedule for any meal if you follow these steps.

- Each dish needs to be assembled before it's ready to be cooked, so estimate the preparation time for each dish.
- Check the recipe for the cooking time of each dish.
- Add the preparation time and cooking time together to determine how long each dish will take. List these starting times in sequence, with the longest time first. Jot down what you will be doing during each.
- Working backwards from your scheduled serving time, figure when you should start the first dish. You will find that there will be extra time throughout your schedule to take care of miscellaneous tasks.

Careful planning can make your family reunion—or any special occasion—a success.

THE 1979

KRAFT

Family Reunion Recipes

From the March
TELEVISION SPECIAL
STARRING PEARL BAILEY

G8-829 Printed in U.S.A.

Illustrissimi

*Letters from
Pope John Paul I*

Illustrissimi

Letters from Pope John Paul I

ALBINO LUCIANI

Translated from the Italian
by WILLIAM WEAVER

Little, Brown and Company

BOSTON · TORONTO

LIBRARY OF CONGRESS CATALOG CARD NO. 78-73843

FIRST AMERICAN EDITION

T12/78

*Published simultaneously in Canada
by Little, Brown & Company (Canada) Limited*

PRINTED IN THE UNITED STATES OF AMERICA

Foreword

On 26 August 1978, Albino Cardinal Luciani was elected to the Chair of Peter and took the name Pope John Paul. Within five weeks he was dead. His reign as successor to Peter was the shortest in modern times and one of the shortest ever in the long history of the Church. Yet in the brief days given him by Divine Providence to guide the flock of Christ, Pope John Paul left his mark.

We cannot look to the structures of the Church to see what changes Pope John Paul made. He did not have the opportunity, if indeed he sought one, to alter much. Nor can we look at the initiatives of his pontificate to see in what direction he intended to guide the efforts of the Church. There was not time. To gauge the effect of Pope John Paul on our days we must turn to the few brief glimpses of him, the man who for one month walked in the shoes of Peter.

For most of us the glance into the life and spirit of Pope John Paul came through the handful of public audiences he had and the infectious smile that dominated his public appearances beginning with the day he stepped out onto the balcony of St. Peter's to greet the world for the first time as the Holy Father. In these all-too-few occasions, Pope John Paul was seen by us all as the happy, smiling preacher of the Gospel of Christ. On his lips the teaching of the Church seemed to be what it has been called since the days of the Apostles, the "Good News."

I submit that the secret of Pope John Paul's communicability lay not in his ability to smile but in the underlying reasons for so spontaneous and broad a smile. The Holy Father from Venice was a man of unshakable faith and was not ashamed of that faith in all its ramifications. He was therefore able to speak the truth of the Gospels in plain and clear terms, neither hesitant to preach to those who would not accept such doctrine, nor unsure himself where, as we say today, "the Church is going." It was this strong and uncluttered faith in the Lord and His Church that was the foundation for what was more obvious to the photographer and the TV camera — his joy.

Pope John Paul was a profoundly happy man. This became apparent to all the world when he beamed his broad smile together with his Apostolic Blessing from the loggia of St. Peter's Basilica in Rome minutes after being chosen Pope. His happiness permeated everything he did and said. It accounted for the smile — even when one might have reason to assume there was little to laugh about. I think it was the Holy Father's evident joy that caught up the world in interest at the humble man "used to small things and silence."

If we were to single out a new element or a refreshed received spirit especially needed in the Church at the moment, in the work of the Church and in the hearts, the minds, and all the being of those who do the work of the Church on whatever level in our days, there is one that we can see in the life and face of Pope John Paul. If we were to point out this element in terms of the world's hunger and the audible needs of mankind we can find it in the pages of his written word. That desperately needed spirit is the spirit so openly associated invariably with Pope John Paul. It is a quality heralded not only by the partisans of his smile who share his faith but by those who have become hardened to the Spirit in this life and cynical of any motive to rejoice in the prospects of a life to come. That virtue, that so badly needed quality, is the spirit of joy: joy in the work, joy in being alive to do the work, joy in having the ability to do it, joy in honestly recognizing one's lack of ability when it is absent, joy in the existence of God before we even begin to consider the multiplying motives for further joy in all His attributes, His mercy, His providence, His goodness, and, on occasion, His justice.

For we, the man and woman of today, have reached, as far as many are concerned, the heights of boredom produced by a highly technically advanced civilization that is also dangerously close to becoming totally sterile. Excitement is programmed. Anticipation eliminated and love packaged so that the spirit of man that is essentially and eternally free finds itself smothering under our own organizational skills.

If there is a virtue, I repeat, that is desperately needed in the life and the work of the Church today — as it is needed in the world today — that virtue is joy. In one of the bleakest developments of modern times, Christians have suddenly become a people seemingly without humor. By a singularly unhappy chance, followers of Christ in particular have lost, please God only momentarily, the gift of laughter. The world is faced more and more — in routine daily life, in the mass media, in our leaders — with sarcastic people, stridently indignant people speaking in glib phrases with a certain acid cleverness; but people without humor.

How this has happened to the family of the faith, I have no idea. It is one thing, I hope, that cannot be blamed on the Second Vatican Council. It would be an irony beyond acceptance if a period of Church history inaugurated by the radiant Pope John XXIII were to become one of continued, constant, morbid introspection.

Less than a generation ago, I found myself in a crowd tense and frightened by a problem facing the nation where I was a guest and by the spellbinder who was rehearsing the glory or doom that awaited his listeners. A man next to me in that mass of people turned and asked me and those within hearing: "What do you think would happen, if we all started to laugh?" The crowd did not laugh and history records the tribulation that faced that land and its inhabitants.

Within our own land, at the same time, sometimes in great poverty, in second-class citizenship and in the midst of other limitations, we Catholics were universally accredited with being lighthearted Christians. Now we appear to have become the grim ones, marked by an air of deadly earnestness and an appalling absence of the light touch. We seem almost overcome by the problems that face the world, the Church, and any Catholic alive and at work today.

The present almost pathological lack of joy shows up in every vocation and in every area of life. There already exist among us people who rejoice as little in the coming of children as once used to do only some of our neo-pagan neighbors. Among descendants of people who spoke, only yesterday, of the coming of a baby as a "blessed event," maternity is no longer thought joyful. A quick glance at the TV confirms a world view of the networks that is totally devoid of humor — unless by humor one is confined to double-meaning asides and ridicule of others.

The mood of Christian joy, I regret to say, is momentarily under a certain trauma or paralysis — an eclipse of some sort. It cannot possibly come back too soon for the sanity of civilization and the salvation of the Church.

It was in contradiction to this negativism and defeatism, that seem to be the source of the sourness afflicting so many of this generation, that Pope John Paul's smile takes on such significance. He was a happy soul. His talks, his writings radiate joy. He was a breath of fresh air and he succeeded in spreading his own quiet happiness in the face of a world full of difficulties.

Such joy in the Church is not at all inconsistent with full recognition of the suffering or privation that are the tragic aspects of the human condition. It does not render the devout insensible to these or unwilling to do their part in remedying them, but it does preserve them from the absurd air of personal offense which the reformers invariably bring to their reaction to evil in the universe or inadequacy in its inhabitants. The joy that the Church sings was the joy of Jesus Crucified. "Not mine to glory but in the Cross of Jesus Christ." That Cross, far from being the denial of the joy that must be restored to the Church and to the world, is essential to its very existence. It is the symbol of its exaltation, but, be it said with great care and no mere poetry, the source of its laughter. "And I think that Christ laughed when they took Him with staves the night before He died." Thus did Theodore Maynard sum up the place of the Passion and the Cross in the mood of the poets who wrote for us in the days when laughter, the laughter of Chesterton, the laughter of Belloc, the laughter of scores of others, greater and less, rang through our halls.

Certainly Saint Thomas More was no fool when he joked about his own death. He could afford to be joyful because he believed. He, as every believer should see, saw joy in creation, joy in being, joy in knowledge, joy in love, joy in beauty; and above all joy in that which sanctifies and ennobles and immortalizes these, joy in the Cross of Jesus Christ.

Pope John Paul brought all this back into focus with his gentle ways, winning smile, and joyful ease with people. He had the light touch. Nowhere does this become more apparent than in his book, *Illustrissimi*. Here he banters with figures of literature, great and small, real and fictitious, to teach, exhort, correct, and chat.

It would be a great mistake to see these charming essays that combine to make a delightful book as the diverting writings of an idle cleric. Cardinal Luciani was first and foremost a pastor of souls. His approach to literature reflects the ancient Christian maxim *"per verbum ad verbum."* One can reach the Word of God through the study of the written word. If Cardinal Luciani wrote to Mark Twain, Pinocchio, or Charles Dickens, it was to teach some point of the Christian ideal. Again and again this comes through clearly. Yet what endears the writer

to his reader is the light, confident, and happy manner.
Much as the warm smile reached out from the balcony
of St. Peter's to all kinds of people, friendly and not so
friendly, believer and nonbeliever, so Luciani's "letters"
to the illustrious figures of literature reach out to touch a
responsive chord in the hearts of many of us who look to
Peter as we look to the Lord for the face of our Father — a
Father who also smiles.

JOHN CARDINAL WRIGHT
Vatican City

Introduction

The fourth edition of *Illustrissimi* is about to be released as we mourn the sudden and unexpected passing of Pope John Paul I. It is uncanny that one of his final actions was to review and revise this present volume. Is it possible that he had a premonition that this would be the only document to contain his human, spiritual, and pastoral testament? We are deeply thankful to have this treasured inheritance and precious keepsake.

We who knew Pope John Paul I personally are still unable to believe that he is no longer with us. His smiling presence and loving concern had become such a part of our lives. His appearances before the television camera were simple and unpretentious. It almost seemed as if he were apologizing for being the heir of Jesus and Peter. Yet, we felt that he was our pastor, our father, friend, and confidant. No other pope before him had ever come so close to becoming one of us. Still, this did not alter his true identity as the Vicar of Christ on earth. Love made him one of us, though his mission to represent Jesus as "sweet Christ on earth" distinguished him from us. He so completely personified Christ as to enkindle in us the yearning to have lived in the time of Jesus, to have heard His voice, to have participated in His joys and sorrows, in His Passion and Resurrection. More than any other pope before him, he conveyed the image of "Jesus of today."

There was no exterior sign of his authority or power. His authority lay in his concrete love for God and for us: "Peter, do you love me more than these? . . ." This is the pope who movingly represented Christ to us, who made us feel the presence of Christ in the Church and in humanity. He shared the same attitude as Christ who, though being of a divine nature, did not consider His equality with God a treasure to be guarded jealously. Rather He lowered himself, assuming "the form of a servant, being born in the likeness of men."

In the month of his pontificate he carried out perhaps the greatest revolution in the history of the Church, as well as in the history of mankind. Authority of any kind, either religious or civil, is not, and must not be, dominion of man over man. Authority, which comes from God, is donation and service.

Pope John Paul I is a marvelous, moving figure in the history of humanity. Like Jesus, he attracted the crowds with his simple, captivating words, which were enlivened by examples, stories, "parables," and references to persons and happenings of today. He made the life and word of Christ real to all, not an abstract philosophy or theology, but livable and comprehensible to persons of all ages and extraction.

His serenity, his smile, his evangelic freshness, his winning manner, his humility, his human and spiritual depth, his whole unique personality remain a "sign," a "symbol" that has irreversibly altered the course of history. Like Jesus, Pope John Paul I told us, "I have given you the example. Do likewise!"

Neither pope nor politician can afford to contradict this example if he wishes to be credible.

Thank you, Pope John Paul, for having been the living presence of Christ in our midst.

Your benediction which arrived as a gift from Heaven is a source of comfort and encouragement to us to follow the example of your life.

Padova, 4 October 1978
The Feast of St. Francis of Assisi

FATHER ANGELO BEGHETTO
Director General of the *Messenger*
of St. Anthony

Contents

Foreword *by John Cardinal Wright*   v

Introduction *by Father Angelo Beghetto*   xiii

To Charles Dickens
We Are Running Out   3

To Mark Twain
Three John Does in One   9

To Gilbert K. Chesterton
In What Sort of World . . .   14

To Maria Theresa of Austria
Beautiful Without All This Nonsense   19

To Charles Péguy
We Are the Amazement of God   24

To Trilussa
In the Heart of the Mystery   29

To Saint Bernard, Abbot of Clairvaux
If You Govern, Be Prudent   33

To Johann Wolfgang von Goethe
Noblesse Oblige 44

To King David
A Requiescat for Pride 49

To Penelope
In Good Times and Bad 54

To Figaro the Barber
Revolution for Its Own Sake 60

To the Four Members of the Pickwick Club
Blunders and the Mohs Scale 66

To Pinocchio
When You Get a Crush on Someone 72

To Paulus Diaconus
Vacation Fever 81

To Don Gonzalo Fernandez de Cordova
The Bells of the Guerrillas 89

To Saint Bernardino of Siena
"Seven Rules" That Still Hold 96

To Saint Francis de Sales
On the Ship of God 103

To the Bear of Saint Romedio
Dirty Mouths 109

To Pavel Ivanovich Chichikov
The Time of Imposters 115

To Lemuel, King of Massa
King Lemuel and the Ideal Woman 121

To Sir Walter Scott
Nostalgia for Cleanliness   128

To the Unknown Painter of the Castle
Four Paintings in the Old Castle   134

To Hippocrates
The Four Temperaments   139

To Saint Thérèse de Lisieux
Joy, Exquisite Charity   146

To Alessandro Manzoni
The Only Aristocracy   153

To Casella, Musician
The Music of Reconciliation   160

To Luigi Cornaro
We're Old; Are We Falling Apart?   166

To Aldus Manutius
From the Times of the "Rialto Hunchback"   171

To Saint Bonaventure
Was He Also a "Big Gun"?   177

To Christopher Marlowe
The Devil's Most Successful Trick   184

To Saint Luke the Evangelist
Forbidden to Forbid   191

To Quintilian
Other Times, Another School . . .   198

To Guglielmo Marconi
You'd See Some Fine Things   205

To Giuseppe Gioacchino Belli
Words, Words, Words   213

To Felix Dupanloup
The Text Exists, But What about   220
   the Readers?

To Petrarch
Confession Six Hundred Years Afterwards   227

To Saint Teresa of Avila
Teresa, a Penny, and God   233

To Carlo Goldoni
The Feminists and the Beard   240
   of Saint Wilgefortis

To Andreas Hofer
The Call of the Iselberg   248

To Jesus
I Write in Trepidation   254

Illustrissimi
*Letters from
Pope John Paul I*

To Charles Dickens

We Are Running Out

Dear Dickens,

I am a bishop, and I have accepted the curious assignment of writing each month for the *Messenger of Saint Anthony* a letter to some illustrious figure.

Pressed for time, with the Christmas season upon us, I really didn't know whom to choose. But then, in a newspaper, I came across an advertisement for an edition of your famous *Christmas Books*. I promptly said to myself: I read them as a boy, and I enjoyed them immensely because they are filled with love for the poor and a sense of social regeneration; they are warm with imagination and humanity: I shall write to him. And so here I am, taking the liberty of disturbing you.

* * *

I mentioned earlier your love for the poor. You felt it and expressed it magnificently, because as a boy you also lived among the poor.

At the age of twelve, when your father was put into

CHARLES DICKENS, *English writer* (1812–1870). *A harsh childhood (his father was imprisoned for debt and Charles began working in a factory at the age of twelve) inspired his most famous works* (Oliver Twist, David Copperfield), *but they are also pervaded by a distinct humorous vein, as in* The Pickwick Papers. *Dickens's effective realism, charged with human warmth, even had social consequences (reform of the English laws concerning children).*

debtors' prison, you went to work in a blacking ware-house, to help support your mother and your brothers and sisters. From morning till night, your little hands prepared pots of blacking, under the gaze of a merciless employer. At night you slept in an attic. On Sunday, to keep your father company, you and your whole family spent the day in prison, where your childish eyes were wide with amazement, alert and moved, at the sight of dozens and dozens of pathetic cases.

This is why all your novels are populated by the poor, by people who live in distressing poverty: women and children pressed into labor in factories or in shops, with-out any choice, even under the age of six. There is no union to defend them, no protection against sickness or accidents, starvation wages, work continuing up to fif-teen hours a day, as with depressing monotony these delicate creatures are bound to the powerful noisy ma-chine, to the physically and morally unhealthy environ-ment, and driven often to seek oblivion in alcohol or to attempt an escape through prostitution.

These are the oppressed, and all of your compassion is poured out on them. On the other side there are the oppressors, whom you stigmatize, your pen driven by the genius of wrath and of irony, capable of shaping typ-ical characters as if in bronze.

* * *

One of these figures is the usurer Scrooge, protagonist of your *Christmas Carol.*

Two gentlemen turn up in his office, books and papers in their hands, to address him: "It is Christmas. At this festive season of the year . . . many thousands are in want of common necessaries, sir!"

Scrooge's answer: "Are the workhouses not in opera-tion? Are there no prisons?"

There are plenty of prisons, Scrooge is assured, and the workhouses are functioning, but "they scarcely furnish Christian cheer of mind or body" on the occasion of Christmas. The gentlemen are collecting funds "to buy

the poor some meat and drink, and means of warmth.
. . . What shall I put you down for?"

"Nothing. . . . I wish to be left alone. . . . I don't
make merry myself at Christmas, and I can't afford to
make idle people merry. I help to support the establishments I have mentioned — they cost enough; and those
who are badly off must go there."

"Many can't go there; and many would rather die."

"If they would rather die, they had better do it, and
decrease the surplus population. Besides . . . it's not my
business."

This is how you described Scrooge, the usurer: concerned only with money and business. But when he
speaks of business to his "kindred spirit," his late
partner in money-lending, Marley, the latter complains
mournfully: "Business! Mankind was my business. The
common welfare was my business; charity, mercy, for-
bearance, and benevolence were all my business. . . .
Why did I walk through crowds of fellow-beings with my
eyes turned down, and never raise them to that blessed
Star which led the Wise Men to a poor abode? Were there
no poor homes to which its light could have conducted *me!*"

* * *

Since you wrote these words, in 1843, over one
hundred and thirty years have gone by. You must be
curious to know *if* and *how* some remedy has been found
for the situations of poverty and injustice that you reported.

I will tell you at once. In your own England, and in in-
dustrialized Europe, the workers have greatly improved
their position. The only power they could command was
their numerical strength. They exploited it.

The old socialist orators used to say: "The camel was
crossing the desert; his hooves pounded the grains of
sand, and he said, in proud triumph: 'I am crushing you!
I am crushing you!'

"The little grains allowed themselves to be crushed,

but the wind rose, the terrible *simoon*. 'Come, you grains of sand,' it said, 'unite, join with me. Together we will lash the animal and will bury him under mountains of sand!' "

The workers, at first separate and scattered grains of sand, have become a compact cloud, in their unions and in the various forms of socialism, which have the undeniable merit of having been, almost everywhere, the chief cause of the workers' upward rise.

Since your day, they have advanced and achieved much in the areas of economy, social security, culture. And today, through the unions, they often manage to make their voice heard still higher, in the upper ranks of the government where, actually, their fate is decided. All of this cost great sacrifices; opposition and obstacles had to be overcome.

The union of workers in defense of their own rights was, in fact, first declared illegal, then it was tolerated, and finally it was recognized by law. The State at first was a "policeman-state," declaring labor contracts a completely private matter, forbidding collective bargaining; the boss had the upper hand; laissez-faire reigned without control. "Are two bosses after the same worker? Then the worker's wages will rise. Are two workers pleading with a boss for a job? Then wages will drop." This is the law, people said, and it leads automatically to a balance of power! But, on the contrary, it led to the abuses of a capitalism that was, and in some instances still is, a "wicked system."

* * *

And what now? Alas! In your time social injustices were all in one direction: against workers, who could point their fingers at the boss. Today, a vast array of people are pointing their fingers: farm workers complain that they are much worse off than workers in industry; here in Italy, the South is against the North; in Africa, in Asia, in Latin America, the nations of the Third World are against the well-to-do nations.

But even in these privileged countries there are many pockets of poverty and insecurity. Many workers are unemployed or fear for their jobs. They are not always sufficiently protected against accidents, and often they feel treated as mere tools of production and not as human protagonists.

Moreover, the frantic race for creature comforts, the exaggerated, mad use of unnecessary things, has compromised the indispensable things: pure air and pure water, silence, inner peace, rest.

It was believed that oil wells were like the well of Saint Patrick, bottomless; suddenly we realize that we are almost running out of oil. We were confident that when oil was exhausted, at some remote time, we could count on nuclear energy; but now they tell us that its production involves the risk of radioactive wastes, dangerous to man and to his environment.

Fear and concern are great. For many the desert animal to be attacked and buried is no longer only capitalism, but also the present "system," to be overturned with a total revolution. For others the process of overturning the system has already begun.

The poor Third World of today — they say — will soon be rich, thanks to its oil wells, which it will exploit for itself alone. The comfortable world of consumers, having only a thin trickle of oil, will have to limit its industries, its consumption, and will have to undergo a recession.

In this growing tangle of problems, worries, and tensions, the principles — broadened and adapted — that you, my dear Dickens, supported warmly, if a bit sentimentally, are still valid. Love for the poor, and not so much for the individual poor person as for the poor in general, who, rejected both as individuals and as whole nations, consider themselves a class and feel solidarity with one another. To them, unhesitatingly, the sincere, open preference of Christians must be given, following Christ's example.

Solidarity: We are all in the same boat, filled with peoples now brought closer together both in space and in behavior; but the boat is on a very rough sea. If we would avoid grave mishaps, the rule must be this: all for one and one for all. Insist on what unites us and forget what divides us.

Trust in God: With the voice of your Marley, you wished that the Star of the Wise Men might illuminate the houses of the poor.

Today the whole world, which has such need of God, is a poor abode!

February 1971

To Mark Twain

Three John Does in One

Dear Mark Twain,

You were one of my favorite authors during my adolescence.

I still remember the amusing *Adventures of Tom Sawyer*, which, after all, are your own boyhood adventures, dear Twain. I have repeated some of your witticisms hundreds of times: the one about the value of books, for example. The value is beyond calculation, you once said to a girl who had questioned you, but it varies. A book bound in leather is excellent for sharpening a razor; a small book, concise — the sort the French write so well — is wonderfully used when wedged under the short leg of a table; a thick book, a dictionary, for example, is an ideal projectile for throwing at cats, and finally, an atlas, with its wide pages, has the most suitable paper for keeping a pane of glass from rattling.

My pupils used to be delighted when I would announce: Now I'll tell you another Mark Twain story. But I fear that the members of my diocese are shocked. "A bishop who quotes Mark Twain!" Perhaps it should be first explained to them that, just as books vary, so there

MARK TWAIN (*pseudonym of Samuel Langhorne Clemens*), *American writer (1835–1910). Printer, pilot on Mississippi riverboats, journalist, he became, through his books, an interpreter of the myth of the new frontier. His masterpieces are* The Adventures of Tom Sawyer *and* The Adventures of Huckleberry Finn, *fast-paced and rich in humor.*

are various kinds of bishop. Some, in fact, resemble eagles, soaring in masterly documents, at the highest level; others are nightingales, singing the praises of the Lord in a wondrous way; others are poor wrens who, on the lowest branch of the ecclesiastical tree, attempt to express some notion on very vast subjects.

I, dear Twain, belong to the last category. And so, summoning my courage, I will recall how you once remarked, in effect, that man is more complex than he seems: every adult contains not one, but three different men. "What do you mean?" someone asked. And you said: Take John Doe. In him there is John the First, namely the man he thinks he is; there is John the Second, the man others think he is; and finally, John the Third, the man he really is.

*   *   *

How much truth, Twain, is contained in your joking remark! Take, for example, *John the First.* When we are shown a group photograph in which we posed, which is the likable, attractive face we look for at once? Sad to say, it is our own. Because we are vastly fond of ourselves, above all others. Loving ourselves so much, we are naturally led to enlarge our own merits, to play down our transgressions, to judge others by different standards from those used to judge ourselves. Enlarged merits? They are described by your fellow-writer Trilussa:

> The little snail of Vainglory
> Who had crawled up an obelisk
> Looked at its slimy trail and said:
> I see I'll leave my mark on History.

This is the way we are, dear Twain; even a bit of slime, if it is our own, and because it is our own, makes us boast, gives us a swelled head!

Play down transgressions? "I take a friendly drink once in a great while," a man says. Others insist, on the contrary, that he is a sponge, afflicted with a chronic dry throat, a true worshiper of Bacchus, forever bending his elbow. And the woman says: "I have sensitive nerves; at times I grow upset." Upset, indeed! People say she's tough, cantankerous, vindictive, an unbearable character, a harpy!

In Homer, the gods move about the world wrapped in a cloud that hides them from everyone's eyes; we have a cloud that hides us from our own eyes.

Francis de Sales, a bishop like me and a humorist like you, wrote: "We blame our neighbor for the slightest faults, and we condone the greatest ones in ourselves. We want to sell dearly, but buy cheaply. We want justice done in the home of others, but mercy in our own. We want our words to be taken kindly, but we are offended by those of others. If an inferior is not well-mannered with us, we are irked by whatever he does; but if we find someone agreeable, we excuse him, in any action. We firmly demand our rights, but we want others to be temperate in demanding theirs. . . . What we do for others always seems a great deal, what others do for us seems nothing."

* * *

That is enough about John Doe the First. Let us turn to *John the Second.* Here, my dear Twain, it seems to me that the situation is two-fold: John wants people to respect him or else he suffers because people ignore and despise him. Nothing wrong there; he should, however, try not to exaggerate in either direction. "Woe to you" — Our Lord said — "for you love the best seat in the synagogues and salutations in the market places . . . ," and all is done in order to attract attention. Today we would say . . . that, given the struggle for position, the pushing and shoving to achieve titles, through concessions and renunciations, you are trying to get your name in the papers.

But why "Woe to you"? In 1938, when Hitler visited Florence, the city was covered with swastikas and slogans. The writer Bargellini said to Cardinal Dalla Costa: "You see, Your Eminence, you see?" "Never fear!" the cardinal replied, "his destiny is already marked down in the thirty-seventh Psalm: 'I have seen a wicked man overbearing, and towering like a cedar of Lebanon. Again I passed by, and, lo, he was no more; though I sought him, he could not be found.' "

At times that "woe to" does not indicate divine punishment, but only human ridiculousness. It may be like the ass who covered himself with a lion's skin, and everyone said: "What a lion!" Men and animals fled. But the wind blew, lifted the skin, and everyone saw the ass. And then they came running back in a rage and gave the animal a sound, deserved beating.

Shaw said much the same thing: How comical truth is! In other words, we can't help smiling when we know how little there is behind certain titles and certain forms of celebrity!

And what if the opposite happens? What if people think evil, where good exists? Here another thing Christ said comes to our aid: "For John came neither eating nor drinking, and they say, 'He has a demon'; the Son of man came eating and drinking, and they say, 'Behold a glutton and a drunkard, a friend of tax collectors and sinners!' " Not even Christ managed to satisfy everyone. So we must not take it too much to heart if we fail, too.

* * *

John the Third was a cook. This is not one of your stories, Twain; it is Tolstoy's. Outside the kitchen door the dogs were lying. John slaughtered a calf and threw the entrails into the yard. The dogs fell on them, ate them, and said: "He's a good cook; he cooks well." Some time after that, John was shelling peas, peeling onions; he threw the husks into the yard. The dogs rushed over, but, sniffing scornfully, they said: "The cook is spoiled; he's worthless now." John, however, was not upset by this opinion; he said, "It is the master who must eat and enjoy my meals, not the dogs. The master's appreciation is enough for me."

Good for Tolstoy. But I ask myself: What are the Lord's

tastes? What does He like in us? One day, as He was preaching, someone said to Him: "Your mother and your brothers are outside, asking for you." He held out His hand toward His disciples and answered: "Here are my mother and my brothers! Whoever does the will of God is my brother, and sister, and mother."

This is the person whom He likes: the one who does His will. He likes us to pray, but He does not like prayers to become a pretext for avoiding the labor of good works. "Why do you call me 'Lord, Lord,' and not do what I tell you?" Do what He tells you!

This may be a moralizing conclusion. You — humorist that you are — would not have drawn it. I, who am a bishop, must; and I urge my faithful: If you happen to think again of the three Johns, the three Jameses, the three Franceses that are in each of us, pay special attention to the third, the one whom God likes!

May 1971

To Gilbert K. Chesterton

In What Sort of World...

Dear Chesterton,

On Italian television, these past months, we have seen Father Brown, that unpredictable priest-detective, a typical creation of yours. Too bad Professor Lucifer and the monk Michael did not also appear. I would have been happy to see them, as you described them in *The Ball and the Cross*, traveling in an "airship," seated side by side, Lent next to Carnival.

When the ship is over St. Paul's Cathedral in London, the professor hurls blasphemy at the Cross. And the monk says: "I once knew a man like you, Lucifer. . . . This man also took the view that the symbol of Christianity was a symbol of savagery and all unreason. His history is rather amusing. It is also a perfect allegory of what happens to rationalists like yourself. He said, as you say, that it was an arbitrary and fantastic shape, that it was a monstrosity, loved because it was paradoxical. Then he began to grow fiercer and more eccentric; he would batter the crosses by the roadside. . . . Finally in a height of frenzy he climbed the steeple of the Parish Church and tore down the cross, waving it in the air, and

GILBERT KEITH CHESTERTON, English writer (1874–1936). Converted to Catholicism in 1922, fertile novelist and brilliant polemicist, he dreamed of an ideal society without class conflict, a society based on common sense, religion, humor. His numerous works include Orthodoxy, The Ball and the Cross, *the* Father Brown *stories,* The Man Who Was Thursday.

uttering wild soliloquies up there under the stars. Then one still summer evening as he was wending his way homewards, along a lane, the devil of his madness came upon him with a violence and transfiguration which changes the world. He was standing, smoking, for a moment, in the front of an interminable line of palings, when his eyes were opened. Not a light shifted, not a leaf stirred, but he saw as if by a sudden change in the eyesight that this paling was an army of innumerable crosses linked together over hill and dale. And he whirled up his heavy stick and went at it as if at an army. Mile after mile along his homeward path he broke it down and tore it up. For he hated the cross and every paling is a wall of crosses. When he returned to his house he was a literal madman. . . . He broke his furniture because it was made of crosses. He burnt his house because it was made of crosses. He was found in the river."

Lucifer was looking at him with a bitten lip.

"Is that story really true?" he asked.

"Oh, no," said Michael, airily. "It is a parable. It is a parable of you and all rationalists. You begin by breaking up the Cross; but you end by breaking up the habitable world. . . ."

The monk's conclusion, which is also your own, dear Chesterton, is correct. If you take away God, what remains, what does mankind become? In what sort of world are we reduced to living?

But, it is the world of progress, I hear some say, the world of well-being!

Yes, but this vaunted progress is not everything that was hoped: it also brings with it missiles, bacteriological and atomic weapons, the current process of pollution: things which — if provision is not made in time — threaten to bring catastrophe on the whole human race.

In other words, progress with human beings who love one another, considering themselves brothers, children of a single God the Father, can be something magnificent. Progress with human beings who do not recognize God as a universal Father becomes a constant danger.

Without a parallel moral process, interior and personal, that progress develops, in fact, the most savage dregs of mankind, making the human being a machine possessed by machines, a number manipulating numbers, "a raving barbarian," Papini would have said, "who instead of a club can wield the immense forces of nature and of mechanics to satisfy his predatory, destructive, orgiastic instincts."

I know: many people think the opposite of you and of me. They think that religion is a consolatory dream: it is supposed to have been invented by the oppressed, imagining a nonexistent world where they later will recover what is stolen from them today by their oppressors; it is supposed to have been organized, entirely for their own advantage, by those oppressors, to keep the oppressed still under their heel, and to lull in them that instinct of class which, without religion, would impel them to struggle.

It is useless to point out that it was precisely the Christian religion that fostered the wakening of the proletarian consciousness, exalting the poor, announcing future justice.

Yes, they answer, Christianity awakens the consciousness of the poor, but then it paralyzes it, preaching patience and replacing the class struggle with faith in God and gradual reformation of society!

Many think also that God and religion, directing hopes and efforts toward a future, distant paradise, *alienate* man, prevent him from fighting for a more immediate paradise, to be achieved here on earth.

It is useless to point out to them that, according to the recent Council, a Christian, precisely because he is a Christian, must feel more committed than ever to fostering progress, which is for the good of all, and to supporting social advancement, which is meant for everyone. The fact remains, they say, that you think of progress for a transitory world, while waiting for a definitive paradise, which will not come. We want paradise here, as the end of all our struggles. We already glimpse its rise, while your God, by the theologians of *secularization*, is called "dead." We agree with Heine, who wrote: "Do you hear the bell? On your knees! They are carrying the last sacraments to God, who is dying!"

My dear Chesterton, you and I do indeed fall on our knees, but before a God who is more alive than ever. He alone, in fact, can give a satisfying answer to these three problems, which are the most important for everyone: Who am I? Where do I come from? Where am I going?

As for the paradise to be enjoyed on earth, and only on earth, and in a near future, as conclusion of the famous "struggles," I would like people to listen to someone much more gifted than I and — without denying your merits — also than you: Dostoevski.

You remember Dostoevski's Ivan Karamazov. He is an atheist, though a friend of the devil. Well, he protests, with all his atheist's vehemence, against a paradise achieved through the efforts, the toil, the sufferings, the torment of countless generations. Our posterity happy thanks to the unhappiness of their forebears! These forebears who "struggle" without receiving their share of joy, often without even the solace of glimpsing the Paradise emerging from the Inferno they are going through! Endless multitudes of the maimed, the sacrificed, who are merely the humus that serves to make the future trees of life grow! Impossible! Ivan says, it would be a pitiless and monstrous injustice.

And he is right.

The sense of justice that is in every man, of whatever faith, demands that the good done, the evil suffered, be rewarded, that the hunger for life innate in all be satisfied. Where and how, if not in another life? And from whom if not from God? And from what God, if not from the one of whom Francis de Sales wrote: "Do not fear God in the least, for He does not want to do you harm; but love Him greatly, because He wants to do you great good"?

The one that many are fighting is not the true God, but the false idea of God that they have formed: a God who protects the rich, who only asks and demands, who is envious of our progress in well-being, who constantly observes our sins from above to enjoy the pleasure of punishing them!

My dear Chesterton, you know as well as I, God is not like that, but is at once good and just; father also to prodigal sons; not wanting us poor and wretched, but great, free, creators of our own destiny. Our God is so far from being man's rival that He wanted man as a friend, calling him to share in His own divine nature and in His own eternal happiness. And it is not true that He makes excessive demands of us; on the contrary, He is satisfied with little, because He knows very well that we do not have much.

Dear Chesterton, I am convinced, as you are: this God will become more and more known and loved, by everyone, including those who reject Him today, not because they are wicked (they may be better than either of us), but because they look at Him from a mistaken point of view! Do they continue not to believe in Him? Then He answers: I believe in you!

June 1971

To Maria Theresa of Austria

Beautiful Without
All This Nonsense

Royal and Imperial Highness!

I know you only from books. A typical sovereign of the Enlightenment, you also governed like a concerned parent: you called yourself the "mother" of all your lands. It seems, however, that you were most anxious that the children of those lands should be obedient subjects of the empress.

There is nothing surprising about that. Not even a queen can be expected to foresee future times. After all, among the pack of sovereigns of the period, you are perhaps the one who comes off best: conductor of the governmental orchestra, without insisting on playing all the instruments!

You managed even better as a wife and mother. A husband loved, then sincerely mourned after his death (knowing that he had been unfaithful to you with various favorites!). "A glass house," where your subjects could observe their ruler's flawless behavior. Sixteen children, including the famous Joseph II, called by the neighboring

MARIA THERESA OF HAPSBURG (1717–1780), empress of Austria after 1740. An "enlightened" sovereign, she governed in a paternalistic fashion. She was an exemplary wife and mother. With the sensitivity of a woman and mother, she wrote to her unhappy daughter Marie Antoinette, queen of France, some letters, which survive, about questions of dress.

king of Prussia the "sacristan-king," and the unhappy Marie Antoinette, first dauphine, then queen of France.

To the latter, with the sensitivity of a woman and mother, you wrote letters, which still survive, about the proper style of dress.

They murmur in Paris that the dauphine pays scant attention to elegance. You hear the rumor in Vienna, promptly take up your pen, and warn her: "They tell me that you dress badly and that your ladies-in-waiting do not dare point this out to you."

On becoming queen, Marie Antoinette goes too far in the other direction and sends you a portrait in which, on her head, she is wearing a monumental catafalque made up of fruit, flowers, feathers, and a good ten yards of cloth. You write her again: "I do not believe that the sovereign of a great nation should dress in this way. One must follow fashion, but not exaggerate it. A pretty queen does not need all this nonsense on her head!"

There is a wise maxim: A woman's beauty can be seen without any need for so much nonsense.

* * *

Your Majesty, can you believe this? There is a colleague of mine, a bishop, who seems even more understanding than you. Saint Francis de Sales, in fact, is full of smiling indulgence toward the eternal little human weaknesses that drive women especially to seek and change ornaments, hair styles, and clothes; he is particularly broad-minded in considering the coy elegance of young girls. "They feel," he writes, the "innate need to be pleasing to others." And he continues: "It is quite licit for them to wish to please many, though they do so with the sole purpose of catching one, in marriage."

Bishop though he is, he must moderate the zeal of the baroness de Chantal, overaustere supervisor of her daughters' dress; and he writes: "What would you have them do? The girls must be a bit pretty, after all." When necessary, however, he knows how to reject gently the little (they were little in those days!) audacities of the girls in his own family. One day, when Françoise de Rabutin appeared before him with a bodice cut somewhat too low, he offered her some pins, with a smile.

The same moderation is shown toward fashions among men and older ladies. Madame Charmoisy's son is a young man who is uncomfortable because all his friends *"sont beaucoup mieux que lui,"* they are better dressed than he, that is. This will not do, the saint writes: "For, as we live in the world, the rules of the world must be followed, in everything that is not sinful." Madame Le Blanc de Mions, on the contrary, has scruples: can she — devout as she is — powder her hair, as is the fashion? "Ah, *mon Dieu,"* Francis replies, "go ahead and powder your hair *hardiment* [boldly]: even pheasants preen themselves!"

In writing like this, Francis de Sales thought to give sound, Christian advice, leaving to devout life all the roses without removing any thorns. He ran into trouble, Your Majesty. The great Bossuet wrote to him that, in this way, he did nothing but "place pillows under the elbows of sinners." A monk, moreover, actually spoke from the pulpit against the *Introduction to the Devout Life,* a book in which the saint had dwelt on the ideas mentioned before; at the end of the sermon, the monk had a lighted candle brought to him with great solemnity, and then pulled the book from his sleeve and set fire to it, scattering the ashes to the four winds.

*   *   *

Your Majesty, let me make this quite clear: I am not on that monk's side! I am with you and with Francis de Sales, in the moderate, just position of those who understand and encourage everything that is beautiful in a healthy way, including fashions.

But I am with you also in condemning nonsense. And how much nonsense there is nowadays! In dress and in what is inevitably connected with dress: expense, behavior, amusement! I will not mention the beach and the way some people act there.

Your own Marie Antoinette wore ten yards of cloth on her head, while a great deal more cloth went into her dress and train. Now, the opposite happens: there are women who wear almost nothing, and go about everywhere in this condition, even wanting to enter churches this way.

At your court, Pietro Metastasio, moving among periwigged gentlemen and powdered ladies, wrote librettos. In one of them he wrote:

> The fidelity of lovers
> Is like the Arabian Phoenix;
> Everyone tells us that it exists,
> But no one knows where it is.*

This is the most he dared write, sentimentally speaking. Now everything is dared: in dress, in songs, in writing, in photography, in shows, in behavior.

In your time, here in Venice, Margherita in Goldoni's *Il campiello* (The Little Square) said: "My mother took us to the opera, or else to the play, and bought her key to a box, and spent her money. She made a point of going where the comedies were good, so she could take her daughters, and she came with us, and we enjoyed ourselves. We went sometimes to the Ridotto, a bit to the Liston, and a bit to the Piazzetta to see the fortune-tellers, the puppets, and once or twice to the fair. Se we were seldom at home, but there we had our conversation. Relatives came, friends came, also some young men: but there was no danger."

And now? Some girls from good families stay out for whole days. Where do they go? A girl may go with "her" boy, alone in a car, alone to a hotel with him, over the roads of the world.

This sometimes happens: an invitation to a party arrives, and on the note there are letters: WTL (without troublesome luggage, i.e., parents!).

Translator's note: Metastasio's sentiment — and his words — were later borrowed by Lorenzo Da Ponte for the libretto of Mozart's *Cosi fan tutte*.

We can also read in the papers about the male workers in certain firms, who reduce considerably the pace and the quality of production because they are too busy "meditating" at length on the Lilliputian skirts or shorts of their female co-workers. Or else we read that a certain government, to prevent the increase of automobile accidents, has put up signs to remind drivers not to let themselves be distracted — while at the wheel — by girls in miniskirts, seen through the windshield or the side window.

Your Majesty, what you wrote is correct: a woman does not require much to be pleasing to others. It is simply a matter of knowing whom you wish to please and for what purpose. Please everyone? This is not, in itself, bad; it can be bad to want to please *in that particular way*. I think, however, that a woman must try to please first her parents, brothers, sisters, and especially, her husband, the man who will choose her as his wife, who will be the father of her children.

Now all these men want, naturally, a woman to be elegant and beautiful, but within a framework of modesty, which makes her even more beautiful and morally fresh.

* * *

Your Majesty, forgive me for unburdening myself to you, but you approve these ideas. Mind you, even today there is no lack of women who also appreciate them. But there are other women who consider them old, outdated. You know, on the contrary, that they are eternal, always timely because they reflect the thought of God, who inspired Saint Paul to write also that "women should adorn themselves modestly and sensibly in seemly apparel."

July 1971

To Charles Péguy

We Are the
Amazement of God

Dear Péguy,

Your enthusiastic spirit, your passion as an inspirer and leader of souls have always appealed to me; I am less sure about your literary excesses, sometimes bitter, sometimes ironic, sometimes overimpassioned in the battle fought against the erring men of your time.

In your pages there is an occasional passage which is poetically (I will not say theologically) happy: for example, the one where you introduce God to speak of hope.

Men's faith does not amaze me — God says — it is not surprising: I shine so in my creation that, not to see me, these poor people would have to be blind. Men's charity does not amaze me — God says — it is not surprising: these poor creatures are so unhappy that if they do not have hearts of stone, they cannot but feel love for one another. But hope: that is what amazes me!

I agree, dear Péguy, that hope is amazing. I agree with Dante that it is an *attender certo*, a waiting with certitude.

CHARLES PIERRE PÉGUY, *French writer (1873–1914). A fervent Catholic, he died in battle at Villeroy in 1914. Editor of the* Cahiers de la Quinzaine, *author of vast religious poems, including* The Mystery of the Charity of Joan of Arc. *He made his works an instrument of Christian witness and hope.*

I agree with what the Bible says about those who hope.

Abraham did not really know why God had ordered him to kill his only son; he could not see from where, with Isaac dead, the numerous posterity that had been promised him could come, and yet he awaited with certitude.

David, advancing against Goliath, knew very well that five stones, even hurled by a hand expert in the use of the slingshot, were too few against an ironclad giant. And yet he awaited with certitude, and warned the armored colossus: "I come to you in the name of the Lord of hosts. . . . This day the Lord will deliver you into my hand, and I will strike you down, and cut off your head."

Praying with the Psalms, I also, dear Péguy, feel myself transformed into a man who awaits with certitude: *"The Lord is my light and my salvation; whom shall I fear? . . . Though a host encamp against me, my heart shall not fear; though war arise against me, yet will I be confident."*

* * *

How wrong, dear Péguy, are those who do not have hope! Judas made a great mistake the day he sold Christ for thirty pieces of silver, but he made an even greater one when he thought his sin was too enormous to be forgiven. No sin is too big: a finite wretchedness, however immense, can always be covered by an infinite mercifulness.

And it is never too late. God is not merely called Father: He is the Father of the prodigal son, and sees us when we are still far off, and is moved and, running, comes to throw His arms around us and kiss us tenderly.

And no tempestuous past should frighten us. The storms, which were evil in the past, become good in the present if they drive us to remedy, to change; they become jewels, if they are given to God to afford Him the consolation of forgiving them.

The Gospel recalls, among the ancestors of Jesus, four women, three of them not entirely commendable: Rahab had been a courtesan; Tamar had borne a son, Perez, by her own father-in-law, Judah; and Bathsheba had committed adultery with David. It is a mystery of humility that these relatives were accepted by Christ, included in his genealogy, but also — I believe — in God's hand, a means to reassure us: you can become saints, whatever your family history may have been, the temperament and blood inherited, your past situation!

My dear Péguy, it would, however, be wrong to wait, to postpone continually. He who takes the road of *later* ends then on the road of *never*. I know some people who seem to turn life into a perpetual waiting room. The trains come and go, and they say: "I'll leave another time! I'll make a confession on my deathbed!" Visconti-Venosta said of the "hero Anselmo":

> A day goes by, and then another,
> But the hero Anselmo never returns.

Here we have the opposite: an Anselmo who *never sets out*.

The matter is not without risk. Suppose, dear Péguy, that the barbarians are invading Italy; they advance, killing and destroying. Everyone flees. Planes, cars, trains are assailed. "Come!" I cry to Anselmo, "there's still a place on the train. Come aboard at once!"

And he says: "But is it actually certain that the barbarians will kill me, if I stay here?"

"Of course not, they might spare you, it might even happen that, before their arrival, another train could come by. But these are remote possibilities, and your life is at stake. To wait further would be an unforgivable imprudence!"

"Can't I convert later?"

"Of course, but it will perhaps be more difficult then than now: repeated sins become habits, chains that are harder to break. Now, at once, please!"

* * *

You know this, Péguy. Waiting is based on the goodness of God, which shines especially in the behavior of Christ, called in the Gospel "friend of sinners." The dimensions of this friendship are well known: when a sheep is lost, the Lord goes seeking it until He finds it. Having found it, He puts it, joyfully, around His neck, carries it home, and says to all: *There will be more joy in heaven over one sinner who repents than over ninety-nine righteous persons who need no repentance.*

The Samaritan woman, the woman taken in adultery, Zacchaeus, the good thief on the cross, the man sick of the palsy, and we, too, are sought, found, and treated like this. And this is yet another amazement!

* * *

But there is another still: *the waiting with certitude of future glory*, as Dante says. It is amazing that this *certitude* is set next to the *future*, the hazy distance. And yet, Péguy, this is the situation of us who hope.

We are with Abraham, who, having received from God the promise of a very fertile land, obeyed, and "set out," the Bible says, "without knowing where he was going," but sure nevertheless and given over to God. We are in the condition described by John the Evangelist: We are already children of God, but what we will be has not yet been made manifest. We find ourselves, like the Napoleon of Manzoni, "directed on the blossoming paths of hope," even if we do not clearly know the region to which those paths lead.

Do we know it at least vaguely? Or was Dante merely indulging in fantasy when he tried to describe it as light, love, and happiness? "Intellectual light," because our mind, up there, will see very clearly what it had only glimpsed here below: God. "Love of true good," because the good that we love here is only *one* good, a drop, a crumb, a fragment of good, while God is goodness. "Happiness that transcends all sorrow," because there is no comparison between that happiness and the sweets of this world.

Augustine agrees, for he calls God "beauty ever ancient and ever new." Manzoni agrees: Up there ". . . is silence and shadow of the glory that passed." Isaiah agrees in the famous dialogue: " 'Cry!' And I said, 'What shall I cry?' All flesh is grass, and all its beauty is like the flower of the field. The grass withers, the flower fades."

With these great men we also agree, dear Péguy. Will some people call us "alienated," poetizing, impractical? We will answer: We are the children of hope, the amazement of God!

August 1971

To Trilussa

In the Heart of the Mystery

Dear Trilussa,

I have reread that melancholy and autobiographical poem in which you tell of being lost, at night, in the middle of the woods, where you meet an old blind woman, who says to you: *If you don't know the road, I'll go with you, because I know it!* You are surprised: *I find it strange that someone who cannot see can guide me.* But the little old woman brusquely takes your hand and orders you: *Walk.* This is faith.

I agree with you partly: faith is truly a good guide, a dear and wise old woman who says: Set your foot here, take this ascending path. But this happens later, at a second stage, when faith has already put down roots in the mind, as a conviction, and from there directs and guides the actions of life.

Before that, however, the conviction must be formed and planted in the mind. And here, my dear Trilussa, lies the difficulty today, here the journey of faith proves to be not the pathetic walk along the path in the woods, but a journey at times difficult, at times dramatic, and always mysterious.

TRILUSSA (pseudonym of Carlo Alberto Salustri), Roman poet (1871–1950). His satire, often light-hearted and good-natured, at times becomes biting sarcasm against the hypocrisies, the maliciousness, and the egoism of the modern world. His best-known works are Fables (1922) *and* Jove and the Animals (1932).

It is already difficult, for that matter, to have faith in others, accepting their assertions on trust. The student hears the teacher say that the earth is 148 million kilometers from the sun. He would like to check this, but how can he? He summons his courage and, with a volitive act of faith, he accepts: "The teacher is honest and informed: let's trust him!"

A mother tells her son about her remote years, of sacrifices made to protect him, to cure him, and she concludes: "Do you believe me? And will you remember how much I have done for love of you?" "How can I not believe you?" the son answers. "And I will do everything I can to be worthy of the love you have borne me!" This son must create in himself not only faith in his mother, but also tenderness and love toward her; this is the only way that he can feel an impulse of dedication and commitment to life.

Faith in God is something similar: it is a filial *yes* said to God, who tells us something about His own intimate life: *yes* to the things narrated and, at the same time, to Him who narrates them. He who proclaims it must not only have faith, but also tenderness and love, and feel himself a little son, admitting: I am not the type who knows everything, who has the last word on everything, who checks everything. Perhaps I am used to arriving at scientific certitude with the most rigorous laboratory controls; here, on the contrary, I must be satisfied with a certitude that is not physical, not mathematical, but based on good common sense. And more: Trusting in God, I know I must agree that God may invade, direct, and change my life.

* * *

In his *Confessions*, my dear Trilussa, Augustine is far more impassioned than you are in describing his journey toward faith. Before saying his total *yes* to God, his soul shudders and writhes in painful conflicts. One one side there is God, inviting him; on the other, his old habits, his former "friends," who "tug gently at his clothing of flesh" and whisper to him: "You dismiss us? Remember: the moment we leave you, that certain thing will no longer be allowed you, nor will that other — forever!"

God urges him to hurry and Augustine pleads: "Not at once, just another moment!" And he goes on for weeks, in a state of indecision, inner turmoil, until, assisted by a powerful thrust from God, he summons his courage and makes up his mind.

As you see, Trilussa, in the human drama of faith there is a mysterious element: the intervention of God. Paul of Tarsus experienced it on the road to Damascus and describes it in this way: that day, the Lord "appeared also to me": "by the grace of God I am what I am."

Here we are in the heart of the mystery. What, in fact, is this grace of God, and how does it operate? It is so difficult to say!

Suppose, Trilussa, that the unbeliever is a sleeping person; God wakens him and says to him: Get out of bed! Suppose he is sick; God puts the medicine in his hand and says to him: Take this! The fact is that the incredulous person, all of a sudden, without having thought of it, finds himself reflecting at a certain point on problems of the soul and of religion, and thus is potentially available for the faith.

After this intervention, which happens "without us," God performs others, but "with us," that is to say, with our free collaboration. To wake us from our sleep, He was the only one; getting out of bed is up to us, even if, to do so, we need further intervention on His part. The grace of God, in fact, has force, but does not mean to force us; it has a holy violence, but intended to make us fall in love with the truth, not to violate freedom. It can happen that, once wakened, invited to rise, taken by the arm, some may instead roll over on the other side, saying: "Let me sleep!"

In the Gospel we find cases of this sort. "Come follow me," Christ says, and Levi rises from the banquet and follows Him; another, however, though invited, answers: "Lord, let me go first and bury my father," and never shows up again. These are people — Christ reflects sadly — who put their hand to the plow, then turn back. This explains how there is a whole range in belief, going from those who have never had faith to those who have it to an insufficient degree and finally to those who have a faith that is fervent and productive.

But this explains only up to a point, my dear Trilussa. Why do some of us not believe? Because God did not give us His grace. But why did He not give us His grace? Because we did not correspond to His inspirations. And why did we not correspond to them? Because, being free, we abused our freedom. And why did we abuse our freedom? This is the hard part, dear Trilussa; this is where I fail to understand. Here, instead of the past, I like to think of the future, and I decide to follow the invitation of Paul: "We entreat you not to accept the grace of God in vain" (in the future).

* * *

Dear Trilussa! Manzoni describes as a "joyous miracle and a banquet of grace" the return of the Unnamed to the faith. Manzoni knew what he was writing about; he also had "returned."

The banquet table is always laid, open to all. As for me, I try to take daily advantage of it, erecting again today the life of faith knocked down by the sins of yesterday. I wonder if Christians who, like me, feel themselves sometimes good, sometimes sinners, will agree to be "good dinner guests" with me?

September 1971

To Saint Bernard, Abbot of Clairvaux

If You Govern, Be Prudent

To the Abbot of Clairvaux,

You were a great monk and, in quite an original way, a great statesman. There was a moment when Clairvaux was more important than Rome: emperors and popes turned to you, kings, feudal lords, vassals. You initiated a Crusade: an action much debated today, but then part of the system.

On the other hand, in your outspoken defense of the Jews, you were, prophetically, opposed to the anti-Semitism of the time. You did not mince words! To a pope you wrote: "For you I do not fear the sword or poison, but the pride of ruling." And to the king of France, who named an abbot to the post of seneschal (that is to say generalissimo), you wrote: "Now what will happen? Will the new seneschal say Mass with helmet, cuirass and iron greaves, or will he lead the troops wearing surplice and stole?"

Others in the Middle Ages had led Europe by wielding a sword. You, by wielding your pen, with letters that

BERNARD DE CLAIRVAUX, saint and Doctor of the Catholic Church (1090–1153). A monk at Citeaux, in 1115 he founded the monastery of Clairvaux. He had a very great influence on emperors, popes, feudal lords, and vassals of his time. Ascetic and mystic, he wrote treatises on spirituality which influenced considerably trends in Western asceticism.

were sent off in all directions and of which, unfortunately, only a part survive today: about five hundred.

Most of these deal with ascetic matters. But there is one, the twenty-fourth in the *Collected Letters*, which contains a synthesis of your Christian view of government; this letter became a classic under extraordinary circumstances.

There was a Conclave in progress. The cardinals were vacillating among three candidates, one favored because of his holiness, the second because of his great learning, the third because of his practical sense.

One cardinal put an end to the indecision, quoting, in fact, your letter. "It is futile to hesitate any more," he said; "our situation is already contemplated in the twenty-fourth letter of the *Doctor mellifluus*. We have only to apply it and everything will proceed as smooth as silk. Is the first candidate saintly? Very well, *oret pro nobis*, let him say some Paternosters for us poor sinners. Is the second candidate learned? This delights us. *Doceat nos.* Let him write some erudite book. Is the third prudent? *Iste regat nos*, let him govern us, let him become Pope."

In view of all this, dear abbot, why not resume your old profession and write some letters, with the charity of useful advice, to me, a poor bishop, and to other Christians who face numerous difficulties in serving the public? A monk's voice, from the depths of the Middle Ages, resounding in the complicated dynamism of modern life! It is a possibility of doing good. Exploit it, please, Father Abbot!

Yours,

Albino Luciani

* * *

To the Patriarch of Venice,

I accept, and I begin by reversing my own sentence.

"If he is prudent, let him govern!" I wrote then. "If he governs, let him be prudent!" I write now. That is to say:

Let him bear firmly in mind certain basic principles and let him be able to adapt them to the circumstances of life.

What principles? I will mention some, at random. An apparent success, even sensational, is in reality a failure if it is won by trampling underfoot truth, justice, charity. He who is above is at the service of him who is below: both are masters and subjects. The greater the responsibility, the greater the need of God's help. Your Metastasio says much the same thing:

> In achieving great feats
> Art helps and sense has a share,
> But art and sense are vain,
> When Heaven is unfriendly.

But great principles must fit into the life of men, and men are like the leaves of a tree: all similar, but none perfectly identical to another. To us they appear different, one from the other, according to their culture, temperament, background, situation, mood.

So be alert to circumstances, moods: if they change, you must also change, not your principles, but the application of those principles to the reality of the moment. Christ, once, withdrew and fled the people who had come to "take Him by force to make Him king." When the circumstances had changed, however, on the eve of the Passion, He Himself prepared the modest triumph of His entry into Jerusalem.

I do not, however, call prudence an excessive nonchalance in changing. The good tactic of proper dosage and adjustments is not the same as opportunism, flattery, turning against those out of favor, fencing with one's own soul and with principles. The cabinet minister falls, the mayor is dismissed, how many times people bustled about them, and then, suddenly, the void! And how many times do we see the turncoat!

I cite the classic, though remote, case of the *Moniteur*, the official French newspaper. In 1815 the paper reported on Napoleon's activities in the following terms: the *bandit* has escaped from the Island of Elba; the *usurper* has reached Grenoble; *Napoleon* enters Lyons; the *Emperor* arrives in Paris this evening! A really insouciant *crescendo!* Not to be taken for prudence! Any more than prudence means the attitude of those who stubbornly refuse to face evident realities and fall into excessive rigidity and integralism, becoming more monarchist than the king, more papist than the pope.

This happens. There are those who, having mastered an idea, bury it and continue to preserve it, to defend it jealously for their whole lives, never reexamining it, never checking to see what it has become after so much rain and wind, after the storms of events and changes.

Those who travel in the stratosphere run the risk of not being prudent, and, crammed with purely bookish learning, they cannot once move away from what is written, real nitpickers always intent on analyzing, taking to pieces, always in search of hairs to split.

Life is quite another thing. Lord Palmerston observed rightly that, to cut the pages of a book, a bone paper cutter was much more useful than a sharp razor. Clemenceau, the tiger, was of the same opinion, when, in expressing a view of two ministers of the cabinet he headed, he stated: Poincaré knows everything, but understands nothing! Briand knows nothing, but understands everything!

I would say: Try both to know and to understand. As I said before: Possess principles and apply them to reality! This is the beginning of prudence!

Yours,

Bernard de Clairvaux

*   *   *

To the Abbot of Clairvaux,

Thank you for your letter. I particularly appreciate the stimulus to check, to reexamine, to avoid letting situations stagnate, to initiate necessary reforms. This applies to the Church, as it applies to the State and to the community.

You know what once happened? a mayor asked me. A town councillor, just nominated, sees a municipal guard keeping daily watch over some benches in the park. A waste, the official thinks. It would be explicable if he were guarding the Bank of Italy, but not a dozen humble benches! He decides to investigate, and he discovers . . . what? Years before, the garden benches had been freshly painted. To keep people from getting stained with fresh paint, a guard — by municipal order — was stationed in that place. The council then forgot to withdraw that order. The paint dried, and the policeman remained there, guarding . . . nothing!

To return to the prudence of those who govern, do you not feel, Father Abbot, that it must be something dynamic? Plato called prudence the charioteer of the virtues; well, the driver tries to reach his destination, sparing the life of the horse if he can; but if necessary, he uses his whip and even destroys the horse in order to arrive, and to arrive on time. In other words, I would not like prudence to be confused with inertia, laziness, somnolence, passiveness. It excludes blind zeal and insane audacity, but it demands straightforward, decisive action, bold when necessary. Now it acts as brake, now as accelerator; now it urges restraint, now generosity; now it represses the tongue, hopes, anger; now, carefully considered, it allows them to explode.

In the years when Cavour's envoys were at work in Romagna, the dramatist Paolo Ferrari came to Turin and said to him: "Count, back there we no longer know whom to believe: Buoncompagni preaches prudence; La Farina preaches audacity. Which of the two interprets your thoughts, which is your true representative?"

"Both," Cavour answered, "because we need a prudent audacity and an audacious prudence!"

I await further explanations.

Yours,

Albino Luciani

*   *   *

To the Patriarch of Venice,

Though I have some reservations about the seriousness of Cavour's answer, I find it right that prudence should be dynamic, that is, it should inspire action. But there are three stages to be considered: deliberation, decision, execution.

Deliberation means seeking out means to the desired end: it is based on reflection, advice asked, careful examination. Pius XI often said: "Let me think first." The Bible admonishes us: "A wise son hears his father's instruction." Folk sayings put all this more colorfully: "Four eyes see better than two." "Marry in haste, repent at leisure." "The hasty cat bore blind kittens."

Decision means picking out one of the various possible means after having studied them. "I choose this, it is the most suited, or the only one that can be carried out!" Prudence is not an eternal vacillation, which keeps everything in suspense and tears the soul with uncertainty, nor does it mean waiting for the ideal, before deciding. It is said that "politics is the art of the possible"; in a certain sense, this is true.

Execution is the most important of the three stages; here prudence is associated with strength in not allowing discouragement in the face of difficulties and obstacles. This is the moment when one is proved a leader, a guide. This is the moment Philip of Macedon was referring to when he said: "Better an army of timid deer led by a lion than an army of strong lions led by a deer!"

Monk that I am, I want particularly to point out that prudence is, above all, a virtue; therefore it serves only noble causes and adopts only licit means.

According to Plutarch, Alcibiades was obsessed by the need of popularity; he wanted people to be concerned with him, no matter the cost. When public interest in his affairs was languishing at a certain point, what did he do? He had a very handsome dog, which had cost him the considerable sum of seventy minas. He cut the dog's tail off, and thus all Athens had reason to talk about Alcibiades, about his wealth, about his expensive caprices.

This is an example not of prudence but of slyness, which I see repeated in your world by other means: photographs in the papers, press officers, carefully contrived speeches, artfully circulated rumors. If you then add dishonest forms of cleverness, I can picture you at the school of the fox, of Ulysses, of Machiavelli.

The clever man speaks, and his words are not a vehicle of thought, but a screen, making the false seem true and the true, false. He achieves results, at times. Usually, however, they do not last. In the fur business, the furs of foxes are more numerous than asses' hides. When the sly march in procession, it is the devil who carries the cross at their head!

Forgive my frankness.

Bernard de Clairvaux

*   *   *

To the Abbot of Clairvaux,

According to your last letter, there are some pseudoprudences, such as slyness and dishonest cleverness, which you described. It is undeniable, however, that the life of public men is difficult at times without recourse to some sly practices. Just think of political candidates, who must persuade voters to choose them against dozens of rivals; and of the elected, who must cultivate their electoral garden, in view of future reelection.

Do you know that, right in your native France, a little volume (*Pigeon vole*) came out some time ago, to answer this need? First of all, you will find in it a treatise on *blah-blah-blah*, that is to say the art of talking on and on and on until you have found something to say. Second, there is an explanation of the art of presenting statistics, percentages, numbers, particularly useful in interpreting election results. On the subject of numbers, the book says: "Democracy is not commanded only by the law of numbers, but also by the law of *figures!*" Third, there is an autopsy of phrases that sound fine, but which mean nothing.

And now, to avoid all problems of this sort, another book has appeared, a true *vademecum*, for speeches and discourses of politicians. Imagine! It contains, ready-made, thirty-two different formulas for commemorating the dead, thirty-seven for condolences to the family, eighteen for proposing toasts, and fourteen for accepting them! Some rules are suggested for toasts: they must be uttered with glass in hand, and the length of the little speech should vary according to the degree of the orator's inspiration, the importance of the person being honored, and the quality of the liquor. There are rules also for speeches of praise: do not praise too much, praise sufficiently, praise tastefully, do not damn with faint praise.

In short, a manual which teaches small and almost innocuous tricks similar to the "witty inventions" of Goldoni's Lelio. These must, after all, be allowed, do you agree?

Yours,

Albino Luciani

* * *

To the Patriarch of Venice,

I see that, in your last remarks, you want to joke. I am in favor of correctness and coherence in public men. Also because their behavior determines the education (or lack of it) in the young. For that matter, they can help themselves with means far more allowable than those you mention. *Wisdom*, for example. The wise man does not let himself be dazzled by appearances and by flattery: he senses the temperament, the ambitions of another person from the face, from gestures; they urge him to act at once, but he feels that the time is not yet ripe; they tell him it is better to wait, but, with a sixth sense, he feels that, on the contrary, he should act fast, and events, later, prove him right.

Another help is *methodicalness:* it leads us to put the end before the means, we connect our means one to the other, and to each we give the importance it deserves. The norms that it prompts are better than those of *Pigeon vole,* which you mention. Here they are:

1) In deliberation consider only authenticated facts. I say *facts,* not opinions, not gossip; I say authenticated, not only certain, because, if I am a public administrator, it is not enough that evidence be satisfactory for me; I need evidence satisfactory for everyone, which can be displayed tomorrow and which is bombproof. The English say that a fact is like the Lord Mayor of London; it alone, in other words, has true, indisputable dignity.

2) Bear in mind an epiphonema that was used a great deal in the Middle Ages: *Distingue frequenter!* At the court of the Sun King a lady was capable of greeting, with a single bow, as many as ten people; the bow was single, but her eyes sent various, multiple flashes, to give each person — whether he was a duke, marquess, or count — his due. Distinguishing, the glances said: This matter is important, I will give it absolute precedence; this other business is less important, I will give it a secondary place. The famous "preferential choices!"

3) You may find useful also the *divide et impera* of the Romans. Here, however, it is a question of dividing actions into various stages and not separating some people from others. The motive? You cannot do well more than one thing at a time!

The *divide* principle, therefore, should be applied also to work; to divide, distributing tasks among various collaborators. But then, they must be used, these collaborators. It must not happen, as in the days of the Triple Alliance, when it was said: The Triple is the Two-faced, i.e., Bismarck. It seems that, with the democratic atmosphere reigning where you are, Bismarcks today do not have a great appeal!

Yet another aid? *Foresight.* Napoleon, in 1800, before leaving Paris for Italy, stuck a pin at a point on the map between Alessandria and Tortona, saying: Here, probably, the Austrians will concentrate their forces. He was a prophet. That is exactly where they gathered: at Marengo.

Not all of us are granted such a prophetic finger; but we must all try to see at a distance the effects of our actions and calculate in advance the efforts and the sums that will be required for a given initiative. Your minister Sonnino set an example for prudence also, when it came to remaining silent. Once a friend ran into him, thoughtful, pensive, and said to him: "I bet you are thinking about what you must say to the Chamber tomorrow!"

"Oh, no!" Sonnino answered, "I'm thinking of what I must not say!"

Luzzati said of him: At Versailles, Orlando speaks all the languages he does not know, and Sonnino is silent in all the languages he knows!

It can happen, however, that, despite every precaution, the enterprise works out badly. The public man prepares himself also for this eventuality with the proper measures. The farmer thinks hail may come, and he takes out insurance. The general arranges everything for the victory; but he also keeps something in readiness, against the hoped-against eventuality of a defeat or a withdrawal.

Plutarch says that Diogenes one day went and begged alms from a marble statue. Naturally he was not given a single penny, but he kept on begging.

"Isn't this a waste of time?" someone asked him.

"It's not a waste of time," he answered. "I'm learning to accept refusals."

This, too, is prudence!

A final piece of advice. Never be too discouraged! "For years I have worked and sweated for the city government. I've given my all, I've even neglected my family and my personal interests, shortening my life with serious, constant worries. And now what? They freeze me out, they pull the rug from under my feet, they attack and destroy me. So let them do as they please; I'm giving up, retiring!" The temptation is strong, but it is not always prudent to succumb to it. It is true that rotation is necessary, but it is also true that the public weal sometimes demands that the beginner should serve an apprenticeship, and that the man who has experience and gifts should remain. While it is right to ponder just criticism (no one is infallible!), we must also remember that not even Christ was able to satisfy everyone. When you work for the public, you must not dream too much of recognition and applause, but must prepare yourself for indifference and the criticism of the very people in your charge, who have a curious psychology.

Aristide Briand, several times premier of France, has described this psychology. In a shop — he said — a madman enters, with a club in his hand; he wields it furiously at the china and smashes everything to pieces. People stop, others rush up from all sides; they admire his exploits. A few hours later, a little old man turns up at the shop with a box of glue under his arm; he takes off his overcoat, puts on his eyeglasses, and with saintly patience — in the midst of all those shards — he starts mending the broken pots. You can be sure that none of the passersby will stop to watch him!

Yours,

Bernard de Clairvaux

October 1971

To Johann Wolfgang von Goethe

Noblesse Oblige

Most illustrious poet,

The recent Venice Film Festival (1971), which aroused immense debate of all sorts, has made me think of you, for some reason or other. It may be a question of impressions, emerging from my subconscious mind, stimulated by words read these days in the papers, which cite you, aesthete, artist, and critic of art.

You were a great aesthete because you were able to perceive at once, intensely, and on a wide scale the "natural beauty" that is scattered through the world, from the phenomena of nature to the intense passions of the human spirit. You were a great artist because you were able also to express powerfully for others both the beauty perceived and the spiritual state in which you had perceived it. You were an eminent critic of art because you examined with understanding and passion the artistic creations of others.

Did not Germany admire you for twenty-five years as director of the theater at Weimar? Did you not call your "second birthday" the day when you set foot in the

JOHANN WOLFGANG VON GOETHE, German poet (1749–1832), one of the greatest figures in Western literature. Romantic and classical at once, he reproduced during the Enlightenment the vast world of knowledge the Renaissance had yearned for. Art, in his view, can narrate, depict, describe everything, including evil. His greatest work is Faust, *on which he worked for sixty years.*

Rome of ancient monuments? Did you not faint with joy in contemplating the Apollo Belvedere? A pity you were not able to "contemplate" the films of the festival, nor was I able to observe your reactions. I will try, therefore, to intuit them.

* * *

As an aesthete, you would have found at the festival a host of beautiful things new to you. Cinema itself, composed as it is of light, movement, colors, music, and action, is a thing of beauty.

You sit down in front of the screen. If the film has been skillfully cut, a rapid pace will sweep you along with the events, and the hours will seem minutes to you. The close-ups, filling the screen with a single face, will bring the characters extraordinarily near to you, showing spirits overwrought by deep emotions, creating a great intimacy between you and the actors. The powerful perspectives that you admired in Mantegna and Caravaggio, you will see here amplified, thanks to the "angle," which, depicting — let us say — a scoundrel from below, distorts him with sinister shadows and makes him appear menacing and terrifying to you. These are just some of the technical aspects.

Will you also find "artistic beauty" in films? I believe so. The "critic of art" in you should, however, prepare for some surprises. You were accustomed to transcendent contemplations, to classical fervors, listening to a language that reached you from architecture, from marbles, frescoes, from illuminated miniatures. You judged, individually, the architect, the painter, the actor-interpreter.

In cinema, on the contrary, the artists can be numerous: producer, script-writer, director, actor, each working in agreement and understanding with the others, to produce a single film. It is, however, difficult to establish what was the true "creative moment" of the work: this varies from one film to another. Art can exist there — I repeat — and of the highest quality. But, if it is there, it cannot easily be included in this or that category, it prefers instead to roam and range through all categories. Art *sui generis:* they call it the "Tenth Muse."

As far as influence is concerned, it has become the "Fifth Estate," after Parliament, the Cabinet, the Magistrature, and the Press. But its range is so vast that at times it can be designated the "First Estate": experts have calculated, in fact, that some films — over the course of the years — have influenced millions of spectators. Thus the cinema can condition people!

But it, in turn, is conditioned, because it is bound to industry, to commerce, and therefore to money. The director, the actors often would like to produce works on a high artistic level, which would enable them to reveal their talents. But the producer, who must put up the money, thinks differently, and he wants films that are successful, that are "box office." If some wizard existed — your Doctor Faust, for example, or even Mephistopheles in person — who, with a stroke of a magic wand or with philters and spells, could guarantee in advance the success of an artistic film, the producer would make the artistic film.

But since such a wizard does not exist, the producer seeks assurance in other ways. Which? Terence, in his day, had the bitter surprise of seeing audiences walk out on his artistic plays to go split their sides laughing at clowns and mimes, who had come to perform in the neighborhood of the theater.

The phenomenon is repeated: the producers tend to turn out movies appealing to the less noble tendencies of the audiences, who go to movie theaters as a rule not to be elevated, but to be amused.

Here, then, is something that would perhaps have saddened the critic of art Goethe at the recent festival: the observation that there were the means and the people to achieve masterpieces but the discovery in their work at times of only mediocre things, due to the prevalent economic concerns.

*   *   *

Another phenomenon might have happened there: you might have found, in some film of genuine artistry, an admixture of equally genuine immorality. Here, perhaps, you are amazed that I should admit the existence of immoral works which, at the same time, are artistically beautiful.

The fact is that the adjective "artistic" refers to the surface of the work; the adjective "immoral," on the other hand, refers to the creation of the artist as man and Christian. Certain immoral novellas of Boccaccio are artistically beautiful; Boccaccio, however, in writing them, committed a morally ugly action, which harmfully affects some categories of readers.

You know something about this yourself, for, after you wrote *The Sorrows of Young Werther,* you felt uneasy and upset, aware of the corroding effect the book had on the weaker, more impressionable young Germans.

* * *

But I am daring to criticize that Goethe who wrote, referring to one of his critics: "Like every rose, every artist has his own insect: I have Tieck!" Well, now you have also me, an admirer of your genius, who still does not accept some of your ideas. This one, for example: that, since the province of art is all reality, the artist can legitimately and very freely narrate, depict, describe everything, including evil.

The artist can indeed portray evil, but in such a way that it appears an evil to flee, that cannot be believed good, that is not beautified and does not inspire others to repeat it or imitate it.

In Sophocles' *Oedipus the King* the central theme is incest: it is described there with crudely powerful sentences, but, from the beginning to the end, the deploration of it is so evident, the punishments which fall on the guilty are so terrible, that the reader, when he has finished reading, remains anything but enthusiastic about incest.

I wrote: "from the beginning to the end." *Pour cause.*

There are, in fact, directors and critics who believe they can redeem an entire pornographic film with a final moralistic sequence or speech, added like a sprinkle of holy water, as exorcism and counterspell.

It takes more than that!

*   *   *

Another idea that must be rejected: that the man of genius is virtually a semi-god — a *"divo!"* — above common morality. You expressed this thought especially at the time when, studying Spinoza with Frau von Stein, you sought God in the "Great All," reflecting that the intelligent man, raising himself ever higher through culture, could be absorbed, a bit at a time, by God, mingling with Him, becoming a law unto himself.

Today a number of people share this idea. Wrongly! Man's destiny and his possibilities are, true, great, but those of every man, even the poor, ignorant, suffering. God wanted us all to be His children, and wanted all of us to have, in a sense, His own destiny. But this is an elevation that is achieved with His help and with the observance of His law, which governs everyone, great and small, including artists.

You, a great poet, today's artists with their works at the festival, and we, ordinary people in the street, less endowed with natural gifts, are all equal before God, in this respect. If some have received the gift of art, of celebrity and wealth, they have, if anything, a deeper obligation to show their gratitude to God through a good life.

To be one of the "great" is also a gift of God, which must not give anyone a swelled head, but should, on the contrary, lead him to modesty and virtue.

Once again, *noblesse oblige!* Nobility is an obligation!

December 1971

To King David

A Requiescat for Pride

Illustrious sovereign, poet, musician!

People see you from a thousand different points of view.

Artists, for centuries, have depicted you with your harp, or with your slingshot facing Goliath, or on your throne holding your scepter, or in the cave of Engedi, cutting up Saul's cloak.

Children love your fight with Goliath and your exploits as a bold and generous leader.

The Liturgy recalls you especially as an ancestor of Christ.

The Bible presents the various components of your personality: poet and musician, brilliant officer, a shrewd king, sometimes involved — alas! not always happily — with women and in harem intrigues with the consequent family tragedies; and, nevertheless, a friend of God, thanks to your notable piety, which kept you always aware of your insignificance in the face of God.

This last note I find particularly likable, and I am happy when I encounter it in the brief Psalm 131, which you composed.

You say in that Psalm: *Lord, my heart is not lifted up.* I

DAVID, king of Israel from about 1010 B.C. The Bible presents the various elements of his personality: musician and poet; brilliant warrior; shrewd king, involved in affairs with women; but, nevertheless, friend of God, thanks to the notable piety which kept him aware of his own smallness.

try to follow you closely, but, unfortunately, I must confine myself to praying: Lord, I wish my heart not to pursue thoughts of pride! . . .

Too little for a bishop! you will say. I know, but the truth is that I have conducted my pride's funeral a hundred times, convinced I was burying it six feet underground with a proper requiescat, and a hundred times I have seen it rise again, more sprightly than ever: I have realized that I still dislike criticism, while I like praise, on the other hand, and I am concerned about what others think of me.

When I am paid a compliment, I must compare myself with the little donkey that carried Christ on Palm Sunday. And I say to myself: If that little creature, hearing the applause of the crowd, had become proud and had begun — jackass that he was — to bow his thanks left and right like a prima donna, how much hilarity he would have aroused! Don't act the same! . . .

When criticisms come, I must, on the other hand, place myself in the situation of Manzoni's Fra Cristoforo who, when others made ironic remarks or snickered at him, remained calm, saying to himself: "Monk, remember that you are not here for yourself!"

The same Fra Cristoforo, in another context, "going back two steps, putting his right hand on his hip, raises his left hand, the forefinger pointed at Don Rodrigo" and *he turns two blazing eyes on his face.* The gesture pleases today's Christians immensely, as they demand "prophecies," sensational accusation, "blazing eyes," "lightning-bolt orbs" Napoleon-style.

I prefer the way you write, King David: "My eyes are not raised too high." I would like to be able to approach the sentiments of Francis de Sales, who wrote: "If an enemy were to put out my right eye, I would want to smile at him with the left; and if he put out both my eyes, I would still have a heart to love him!"

You continue, in your Psalm: "I do not occupy myself with things too great and too marvelous for me." A very noble spiritual position, when you compare it to what

Manzoni's Don Abbondio said: "That is the way men are made: they want always to climb higher and higher." Unfortunately I fear Don Abbondio is right: those who are higher attract us, we want to overtake them, putting our equals below us and leaving those below still farther behind.

And we? We would like to shine, to be in first place, through recognition, advancement, promotions. Nothing wrong with that, so long as it is a matter of healthy emulation, of moderate and reasonable desires, which stimulate one to work, to seek.

But if it becomes a kind of illness? If, to get ahead, we trample others underfoot with acts of injustice, with denigration? If, also to get ahead, we join the "pack," with the most specious pretexts, but actually to block the way for other "packs," also endowed with "more advanced appetites"?

And for what satisfactions then? High positions, seen from the distance, have one effect, before we reach them; and another from close by, when they have been won. This idea was expressed very well by someone madder than you, but a poet like you: Jacopone da Todi. When he heard that the monk Pier di Morone had been made pope, he wrote:

> What will you do, Pier di Morone? . . .
> If you are not good at fencing,
> You will sing a sad song! . . .

I say to myself often, amid the concerns of my episcopal office: "Now, my dear friend, you are singing the sad song of Jacopone!" But you said the same thing to yourself, in Psalm 52, against the "deceitful tongue." This, according to you, is like a "sharp razor" which, instead of beards, cuts off good names.

Very well. But, when the razor has passed, after a little while, the beard sprouts again, spontaneously, amply. Even assailed honor and tarnished reputation grow again. So for this reason it can be wise at times to remain silent, to have patience: little by little, everything returns spontaneously to its place!

* * *

To be an optimist, in spite of everything. This is what you meant, when you wrote: "Like a child quieted at its mother's breast . . . quieted is my soul." Faith in God must be the mainspring of our thoughts and of our actions. When you think about it, in fact, the chief characters of our life are two: God and ourselves.

Looking at these two, we will always see goodness in God and wretchedness in ourselves. We will see divine goodness well disposed toward our wretchedness and our wretchedness the object of divine goodness. The opinions of fellowmen should be kept somewhat at a distance: they cannot heal a guilty conscience nor can they wound an upright conscience.

Your optimism at the end of the little Psalm explodes in a joyous cry: "O Israel, hope in the Lord, from this time forth and for evermore." In reading you, I do not find you at all a timid man, but a brave, strong man, who drains faith in himself from his soul in order to fill it with faith in God and with God's strength.

Humility — in other words — goes hand in hand with magnanimity. To be good is a great and beautiful thing, but difficult and arduous. So that the spirit will not aspire to great things in an excessive way, there is humility; so that it will not be afraid in the face of difficulties, there is magnanimity.

I think of Saint Paul: contempt, flagellation, pressures never depress this magnanimous man; ecstasies, revelations, applause do not swell up this humble man. Humble, when he writes: "For I am the least of the apostles." Magnanimous and ready for every risk, when he declares: "I can do all things in Him who strengthens me. . . ." Humble, but at the right time and place, he knows how to be proud: "Are they Hebrews? So am I. . . . Are they the servants of Christ? I am a better one — I am talking like a madman. . . ." He places himself below all, but, in his duty, he does not allow himself to be bent by anything or anyone.

The waves hurl the ship carrying him against the rocks; vipers bite him; pagans, Jews, false Christians drive him away, persecute him; he is beaten with staves and put into prison; he is made to die every day; they think they have frightened him, annihilated him, and he leaps forth, fresh and dewy, to reassure us: *non angus-tiamur*, I am not in despair; and then he stands up and hurls the challenge of Christian certitude: "For I am sure that neither death, nor life . . . nor things to come, nor powers, nor height, nor depth, nor anything else in all creation, will be able to separate us from the love of God in Christ Jesus Our Lord."

This is the fulfillment of Christian humility. It does not end in pusillanimity, but in courage, in enterprising work, and in abandonment in God!

February 1972

To Penelope

In Good Times and Bad

Princess,

Television has revived the story of Dido, who ruled at Carthage during the years when Your Highness was the wife of Ulysses, king of the rocky island of Ithaca. A pathetically human story.

Saint Augustine, who was bishop quite near Carthage, wept over the story as a boy, and we also heard it again with emotion.

Poor Dido! She swears fidelity to the ashes of Sychaeus, she makes an effort to deny her growing feeling for Aeneas, then she abandons herself trustingly to love.

But tragedy comes: the loving woman sees Aeneas preparing to leave Carthage; in vain she begs her beloved hero to stay, in vain she accuses him of ingratitude and betrayal. Aeneas leaves, and the abandoned woman cannot bear her grief. The flames of the pyre, on which she kills herself, are seen by the Trojan ships bound for Italy.

Your Highness was more exemplary, and more fortunate! The wise Ulysses, the man with a multiform mind, carried you to his palace, after he had built the matrimo-

---

PENELOPE, wife of Ulysses, mother of Telemachus. She warded off her suitors during her husband's absence by promising to make her choice among them after she had finished weaving a cloth, which she wove during the day and unraveled at night. Symbol of the woman "indissolubly faithful in good times and bad."

nial bed squarely on the most flourishing olive tree. You bore him Telemachus, a treasure of a son.

It is true that Ulysses left almost at once for the long Trojan war, and at its conclusion (due especially to the famous horse that he built), he was forced to roam the seas of half the world.

But despite his wanderings, he had the good fortune to return to his Ithaca and to your love. Which, in the meanwhile, had been kept intact, fresh. Those tiresome suitors, installed in your house, feasting merrily at your expense, certainly urged you to choose a new husband from among them; but you held firm! They feasted below, and you, in the upper rooms, with your hand-maidens, wove your famous web during the day and unraveled it at night, to keep them at bay and to defend the fidelity of your love.

Your heart, your dreams every night told you that your husband would return. Who, then, could the bold man be, who insisted on sleeping on the pillow of Ulysses, drinking from his cup, commanding his now-grown son, riding his horse, calling his dog?

The suitors were all shot, your fidelity was rewarded, the family reunited, conjugal love renewed.

* * *

Such a love, Princess, which was sacred for you, is even more sacred for us Catholics. And those who joke about it are doing wrong.

Montaigne, for example, presented marriage as a kind of painted, gilded cage: the birds outside strive to get in, those on the inside would do anything to get out.

Vatican Council II, on the contrary, observes with plea-sure that "many people in our time assign great value to the love between husband and wife."

Among the biblical passages that the Council mentions marginally there is the following one, which seems writ-ten especially for your returned Ulysses: "Rejoice in the wife of your youth, a lovely hind, a graceful doe." And think no more of the sorceress Circe, who trapped you in her palace for a full year with banquets and festivities; think no more of the charms of Nausicaa, the girl first glimpsed on the banks of the river; if it were necessary, have yourself tied again to the mast of the ship so as not to be enchanted by the song of the sirens!

For Your Highness, on the other hand, there is another suitable passage from the Council, which speaks of a conjugal love "indissolubly faithful in good times and bad, both for the body and the spirit, alien to all adultery and divorce." A goal that you reached by practicing a "virtue beyond the ordinary," "the greatness of soul and the spirit of sacrifice" mentioned by the Council, and by overcoming the numerous obstacles that stand in the way of conjugal love.

And the first obstacle is this *poor heart* of ours, so fickle and unpredictable! The prudent husband or wife knows it must be kept under control. It can still happen that one mistakenly believes this surveillance may at times be relaxed, allowing some "distraction." And the partner says: "It's only for a moment! I won't leave my yard; I will only take a glance over the closed gates, just a glance to see what life is like outside!" It so happens, however, that the gates are accidentally open, that the moment becomes an hour, and the hour becomes betrayal.

"What do you mean to do?" Saint Francis de Sales wrote: "Arouse love, isn't that it? But no one deliberately arouses it, without remaining, necessarily, caught by it; in this game, the catcher is caught. . . .

"I want to have a bit of it, someone will say to me, but not too much. Alas . . . the fire of love is more active and more aggressive than it seems; you think you can receive only a spark of it, but then you will be amazed, seeing that in a flash it will have burned your heart, reduced your intentions to ashes and your reputation to smoke."

* * *

Second obstacle: *monotony*. Every day the couple is occupied with the prosaic needs of the house and the job.

He is afraid his male friends will think him weak if he gives up the football game to keep his wife company; she believes she is wasting time if she leaves her chores to chat a bit with him; and so they come to admit that in their affective life everything, more or less, has been said, and that as far as love is concerned it is enough to relegate its manifestations to the past, to their memories. In this situation there are risks: those of the forties, which Paul Bourget analyzed so profoundly in his novel *Le Démon de Midi.*

Venus appears, or Adonis, in the form of a fellow-employee at the office, and you find you have more ideas in common with him or her than with your spouse.

Or else a foolish curiosity arises: "I want to see if I am still attractive as ever." Once this has been ascertained, it is almost impossible not to be swept further.

Or else, as healthy convictions fall to pieces, one is overpowered by the fashions of the day: "Everybody does it!" "Betray a husband, a wife? Those are operatic expressions; it's a much simpler matter: it's just a question of seizing an opportunity, of plucking a rose!" "The partner's vocation to fidelity? Yes, but to a multifidelity: if I go with this girl, it doesn't take anything away from the tenderness I feel for the mother of my children, the woman who brings them up, keeps the house, does the daily shopping, cooking, etc."

Are there remedies against this kind of danger? Yes: the sense of our dependence on God; prayer, which supplies what our weakness lacks; the art of renewing one's own love: let the husband continue to pay his wife some court; and let the wife try always to flatter the husband, with attention and kindness.

Francis de Sales writes: "Love and fidelity, joined together, generate always intimacy and trust; this is why married saints, of both sexes, exchanged many caresses in their conjugal state.

"Thus Isaac and Rebekah (the most chaste married couple of ancient times) were glimpsed through the window, caressing each other in such a way that, though there was nothing indecent about it, Abimelech realized they could only be man and wife.

"The great king Saint Louis was almost reproached for going too far in such . . . little attentions demanded for the preservation of conjugal love."

* * *

Third obstacle: *jealousy,* which does not ennoble love — as is sometimes believed — but humiliates and corrupts it. "It is a foolish way of flaunting love, choosing to exalt it through jealousy; jealousy is, yes, an index of the greatness and power of love, but not of its goodness, purity, and perfection. In fact, he who has perfect love is sure the beloved is virtuous and faithful; he who is jealous suspects the fidelity of the beloved." So writes Saint Francis de Sales, who continues: "Jealousy ends by spoiling the substance of love, because it produces disagreements and arguments."

And these *arguments,* these *disagreements* represent a fourth obstacle to conjugal love. Even the best of husbands and wives have their moments of weariness and bad humor, for which a remedy must be found without destroying the peace of the home. Is he dark and frowning? This is the moment for her to be radiant with sweetness. Are her nerves on edge, is she tired? Now it is his turn to remain calm, waiting for the moment to pass. The important thing is that his nerviness should not occur at the same time as hers, should not overlap it; otherwise there is a short circuit, sparks fly, words slips out, sometimes words all too true, with that sad truth that produces disappointments, bitterness, secret wounds.

Fairness would demand — if these nasty moments simply cannot be avoided — that each of the two should have a turn to be ill-humored. Unfortunately it sometimes happens that one of the two has the monopoly! In this case . . . the other partner can only summon up his or her courage and try to hold the monopoly on patience!

* * *

Princess, I realize I have brought together and made coincide practice and theory, superimposing on what you, a non-Christian, achieved with your innate sense of honesty and delicacy everything taught by the bishop Francis de Sales, enlightened by the Bible and supported by great psychological introspection.

Can all this be of some help to the couples of today, who find themselves in the midst of undeniable difficulties?

I hope so.

March 1972

To Figaro the Barber

Revolution for Its Own Sake

Dear Figaro,

You're back! I saw your *Marriage* on the tiny screen. You were a son of the people, who in the old days dealt as an equal with the members of the privileged class, keeping your hat on your head. With your Susanna, you stood for youth, which struggles to achieve recognition of its right to life, to love, to the family, to just freedom.

In the face of your enterprising "artistic air," your aggressively and youthfully devilish vigor, the nobility cut a sorry figure, a frivolous, decrepit class, in a process of decay!

I heard again your famous monologue. From the stage, you said, more or less: "Well then, who and what am I, for example, I, Figaro, against all these nobles with their coats of arms, these bewigged bourgeois, who are and do everything, whereas, substantially, they are no better or worse than I? Barber, marriage-broker, adviser of pseudodiplomats, yes, ladies and gentlemen, whatever you like! But I also am — and feel that I am — for all of them, something new, strong. They demand that I alone

FIGARO, protagonist of the successful plays of the French writer Beaumarchais (1732–1799), The Barber of Seville and The Marriage of Figaro. Symbol of youth, fighting for the recognition of its right to life, love, family, and freedom.

be honest in a world of cheats and rogues. I do not accept. I rebel: I am a *citizen!*"

That evening, in Paris, the theater was in an uproar. The groundlings applauded, but the nobility, shocked, covered their ears. The king, for his part, covered your mouth, putting you in prison. In vain: from the stage, from prison, you leaped into the public square, shouting: "Ladies and gentlemen! The play is over, and the revolution is on the march!"

And you really did initiate the French Revolution.

* * *

Coming back now, you will discover that millions of young people are doing, more or less, what you did two centuries ago: they are comparing themselves with society and, finding it decrepit, they rebel and rush into the squares.

Over in England, in a basement in Liverpool, there is a plaque that says: "This is where the Beatles were born! It all began here!" In case you have not heard of them, they were four long-haired young singers, who had the same "artistic air" as you; but the queen did not cover their mouths; she awarded them a high decoration.

They sold millions of records and made a pile of money. They were applauded in halls far more vast than your theater; they have inspired throughout the world the formation of "groups" in which, accompanied by drums and electrical guitars, young singers writhe in the very violent light of powerful lamps, arousing spectators, overheating them psychologically, and leading them to collective acts of paroxysmal participation.

* * *

Look around you! Many of these young men wear a pigtail as you did and worry about their hair with almost feminine seriousness: with shampoos of every description, and waves, curls, even "sets" at the beauty parlor. And all these beards! And sideburns and muttonchops!

And the variety of dress! A real mixture of old and new, of feminine and masculine, or Orient and Occident! At times, only a pair of blue jeans with a T-shirt or a sweater or a leather jacket. At other times Renaissance-style breeches, jackets resembling those of Napoleonic officers, with eighteenth-century laces, and shoes with ecclesiastical buckles. At times shorts and trousers of gaudy colors, floral patterns, and in addition gypsylike cloaks. At times purposely tattered clothes, which suggest a mythical city of Hoboville. For the girls, miniskirts, shorts with maxi- and midicoats, and other concoctions.

How do you judge these phenomena? For myself, I am incapable of judging, an outsider, just a bit amused and curious, but also critical. They call it "young music"; I see, however, that the record industry makes millions by the carload for shrewd older people!

They invoke the name of spontaneity, nonconformity and originality; actually, canny "clothing industrialists" manipulate the field, undisturbed sovereigns! They call themselves revolutionaries, but the overscrupulous attentions devoted to their hair and their dress risk creating merely effeminates. The girls, dressing in minimal clothing, think of elegance and fashion; I do not wish to be a Manichaean or a Jansenist, but I think sadly that these clothes are no help to the virtue of the young.

Naturally these young people are on the side of the "revolution," considered a means to stop man's exploitation of man.

Some feel that reforms are inadequate, counterproductive; and these young people justify the revolution as the only means toward social justice.

Others, on the contrary, want courageous and rapid social reforms; they accept violence as an extreme means, and only in exceptional, very grave cases.

Others cast aside all scruples. "Violence," they say, "is justified in itself and *revolution must be made for the sake of revolution!*"

Mao Tse-tung said to the Chinese: "Let us set up the

cultural revolution, wiping out the bourgeois ideology that has remained in Marxism!"

The French writer Regis Debray said to the South Americans: "Your revolution cannot be the kind carried out elsewhere, led by a party; the *guerrilla* of all the people — that is your true revolution!"

From Mao and Debray they have moved to Fidel Castro, to Giap, and to the French students of May '68: "The aim of the student revolution," said Cohn-Bendit, "is not to transform society, but to overturn it."

Obviously, dear Figaro, they go further than you and follow your epigones — Castro, Ché Guevara, Ho Chi Minh, Giap — and dream of becoming *guerrilleros* and *desperados*. With good intentions, mind you; but, meanwhile, they are manipulated by others; meanwhile, they do not realize that it is utopian to divide radically and without appeal good from bad, loyalty from deceit, "progress" from "conservatism"; they do not perceive that disorder, in the "spiral of violence," most of the time retards progress, sowing discontent and hatred.

* * *

And yet, both from you and from them something can be learned. This, for example: that parents, teachers, employers, authorities, priests, all of us must admit that we have not been perfect in our methods and in our concern for the young. That we must begin again in the spirit of humility and true service, preparing ourselves for a long, minute, unobtrusive labor.

A lunatic took a club and shattered a shop window and some objects in it. The street was immediately filled with curious bystanders, who watched and made comments. A little later an old man arrived at the shop with a box under his arm: he removed his coat, took glue, string, and tools from the box and with infinite patience began piecing together broken glass and shards. He finished his job many hours later. But, this time, no one stopped in the street; none of the curious bystanders was interested in his work.

Something similar happens with the young. They make a racket, demonstrations; everyone watches and talks. Very slowly, with great toil and patience, parents and educators put things back together, fill gaps, rectify notions; no one sees or applauds.

* * *

It would be best for us to show that we are very open and understanding toward the young and toward their mistakes. Mistakes, however, must be called mistakes; and the Gospel must be presented *sine glossa,* without altering it to court popularity. "Woe to you," says the Lord, "when all men speak well of you, for so their fathers did to the false prophets." The young, for that matter, like to be told the truth and they sense the love that lies behind frank, if admonishing, words.

We must also allow the young to be different from us older people in their way of judging, of behaving, of loving and praying. They also have — as you, Figaro, had — something to say worth listening to, worth the world's respect.

We must share with them the task of making society progress. With one warning: that they press more on the accelerator, while we press more on the brake. In any case, the problem of the young must not be separated from the problem of society; their crisis is, in part, a crisis of society.

* * *

Figaro! You were very acute in perceiving abuses and weaknesses, but less acute in proposing remedies. Despite exaggerations, your diagnosis of society is accurate; but the therapy is wanting.

And yet, for the young of today and of all times, the therapy exists: to have them perceive that the right answer to the problems that torment them, more than by Marcuse or Debray or Mao, was given by Christ.

Is it fraternity they want? Christ said: You are all brothers! Do they thirst for authenticity? Christ strongly condemned all hypocrisy. Are they against authoritarianism and despotism? Christ said that authority is service. Do they contest formalism? Christ contested prayers recited only mechanically, alms given only for show, charity that was selfish. Do they want religious freedom? Christ, on the one hand, wanted "all men . . . to come to the knowledge of the truth," and, on the other, He imposed nothing through force, did not prevent propaganda against Himself, allowed the abandonment of the Apostles, the denial of Peter, the doubting of Thomas. He asked and asks to be accepted both as man and as God, true, but not until we have checked and seen that He was to be accepted, not until we make a free choice!

* * *

What do you say to this? The *protest* of Figaro, plus the *proposal* of Christ — can they not, united, help both the young and society? I believe so, with faith.

April 1972

To the Four Members
of the Pickwick Club

Blunders and the Mohs Scale

You have always been favorites of mine, dear sirs!

You, President Pickwick, as gallant as Don Quixote, always with that merry, loyal youth Sam Weller at your side, full of ingenuity and as wise as Sancho Panza. And you, Snodgrass, Tupman, and Winkle, with your amusing eccentricities! I've always found you likable!

While I was reading, your figures would spring live from the pages to make me smile and, up to a point, I realized how it was once possible for a dying reader to ask of God, as a special grace, another ten days of life: long enough to receive and read the last installment of the book that immortalized you.

But here you are, President Pickwick, kneeling before a carved stone on the ground near the door of a house.

"Good heavens!" you exclaim, and you rub the stone with your handkerchief; you discern some letters on the surface; you have the immediate, distinct sensation that this must be a very ancient antiquarian find; and you buy the stone from the owner of the house for ten shill-

---

PICKWICK, *Snodgrass, Tupman, and Winkle are the bizarre protagonists of* The Pickwick Papers, *a well-known, humorous work by the English novelist Charles Dickens (1812–1870). A famous blunder on their part serves Pope John Paul I as point of departure in a discussion of those who, in good faith or bad, attack the Church only on the basis of prejudices.*

ings, then carry it off, like a relic, to the inn where your three friends are to be found.

Set on the table, the stone is "devoured" by all eyes, shining with joy. Carried religiously to the headquarters of the club, at a general meeting specially called, it is discussed by various oracles, who make the most ingenious and subtle conjectures as to the inscription.

You yourself, Mister President, with the erudition that distinguishes you, write a pamphlet offering twenty-seven different readings of the inscription! A rightly rewarded labor: seventeen learned societies, national and foreign, elect you honorary member, in recognition of your discovery.

But then what? Doesn't an envious antagonist turn up in the form of the member Blotton? He carries out a field trip, questions the man who sold you the stone, and reports to the club. The stone, true, is very ancient, but the inscription is recent, made by the very man who sold the stone: he declares that he meant to write this and only this: BILL STUMPS HIS MARK. As all can see!

The club's reaction is immediate: Blotton is ejected for his presumption and his defamation; gold-rimmed spectacles are voted and offered to President Pickwick as a mark of approbation and esteem; a motion of censure is passed by the seventeen societies against Blotton.

Now, however, between ourselves, we can say it: the stone was not an "archaeological find" but a banal, common rock; you made a colossal blunder, Mister President; and, in good faith, you caused your three friends, the whole club, and the seventeen other societies to commit the same blunder.

These things happen. And precisely because they do happen, and in order that they may happen as little as possible, Saint Thomas, a Doctor of the Church, has written a special little work on blunders, entitling it *De falla-cis*. May I enjoy a few points in it with you? I may? Thank you!

*   *   *

Your blunder, Mister President, is what Saint Thomas would call a "paralogism," that is to say, a false argument, but one expounded in good faith.

There are some today; it happens, for example, to me, to hear often the paralogisms of those who oppose the Church in good faith. On the one hand, I suffer at them because of my love of truth; the Church, in fact, is quite a different thing from what they believe. On the other hand, I console myself a bit: I see that often they are not so much opposed to the Church as to the idea they have formed of the Church.

As a rule, these blunders in good faith, or "paralogisms," derive from prejudices that are in the air and are circulated through propaganda, with catchy slogans. For example: "Church of the poor," "Treasures of the Vatican," "Church on the side of power" are concepts that today make a number of people hostile to the Church, people who, until yesterday, loved and respected the Church without reservations.

If these people are asked what they mean by "Church of the poor," perhaps they cannot say clearly. Having heard that the famous "treasures" have no commercial price, that an annual income, and a sizable one, is necessary for the Holy See to deal with a thousand problems and needs, also and especially those of the poor, these same people give in to some extent and agree.

But so it goes: the propaganda continues, prejudices leave their mark, the "blunders" cannot be avoided. God, fortunately, will judge men one day after having weighed their thoughts and will save them — I hope — in spite of their involuntarily twisted notions!

* * *

Not all, however, in arguing falsely, have your own good faith, Mister President; there are those who deliberately set out to deceive with their words; then we are no longer dealing with a paralogism, but with a "sophism," and nasty human passions come into play. Which ones?

I put in first place the spirit of contradiction, characteristic of the so-called professional objector. You affirm; he feels the need to deny. You deny, then he has to affirm. You converse with him; as you speak, he thinks only of how to contradict you, refute you, and enforce his position.

On the narrow bridge, linking the banks of a little stream, a mule had stopped and had firmly planted his hooves. Men tried pulling him away by the halter, beating his ribs with a stick; there was no way of making him move. On either side of the bridge people were impatiently waiting.

"I'll deal with it!" a man said, one who deserved to belong to the Pickwick Club. He came up, took the tail of the mule and gave it a yank. Feeling that they wanted him to move back, the animal darted forward like an arrow, leaving the bridge free.

This is how we are at times, dear Mister President! We do what others want us not to do; we will not do what others wish of us. Behaving in this way, we are not serene and upright in our thought and speech.

* * *

Have you ever heard of Mohs, Mister President?

He was a scientist, who died in 1839, just two years after the publication of the last of the "papers" of your club. He is the creator of the "Mohs Scale," which measures, in ten ascending degrees, the hardness of minerals; from *talc* and from *chalk* it moves, from one hardness to the next, all the way up to *diamond*.

Well, Mister President, you should tell Mohs that certain hard heads seem harder than diamond: they never give in, they cling to a mistaken opinion in the teeth of all evidence to the contrary. "Give a nail to a stubborn man," the axiom goes, "and he'll drive it home with his head!"

Into other heads hypercriticism has entered; some men always find a hair to split, always discover a flaw, are never satisfied with anything or with anyone.

Others are dogmatists: having read some magazine or

traveled or had some experience, they think they can teach everyone and they consider the tip of their own nose the hub of the universe. One of them said:

> Town Hall? I built it.
> Parliament? I run it.
> God? I made Him!

Obviously, the stubborn, the hypercritical, and the dogmatic have more than a tendency, an inclination, toward sophism. On the other hand, modest self-opinion and the desire also to hear others lead one to speak the truth.

This good spiritual attitude was characteristic of Mochi, our Florentine ethnologist and a contemporary of yours, Mister President, who had traveled widely and used to say: "Paris? Yes, I've seen it; it's like a larger Florence. As soon as Florence ends, another Florence begins, then another. . . . Several Florences, put together, make Paris. Massaua? Yes, I've seen it: it's like a smaller Florence, without monuments, without the Viale dei Colli, and without the *Nuovo Giornale*." Very modest, as you see, and all to the good, for the less proud one is, the more one is insured against insincerity and error.

*   *   *

But then, beyond personal pride, there is also group pride, which can beget sophisms. Take the party, the class, the country: you risk espousing a certain idea not because it is recognized as true, but because it is the idea of the group, of the party. The errors of racism, of nationalism, of chauvinism, of imperialism, embraced by millions of people, stem from here.

From here also come the sophisms produced by opportunism. Out of laziness, out of self-interest, people go passively where the others go, feathers borne by the wind, wisps in the power of the current. You fell into this, too, Mister President, in your famous electoral meetings, when "blue" and "buff" candidates of the town of Eatanswill faced one another.

Having got out of the stagecoach with your friends, you found yourself surrounded by an excited group of "blues," who immediately asked you to support their candidate, Slumkey. I quote the proceedings of the club:

"Slumkey for ever!" roared the honest and independent.

"Slumkey for ever!" echoed Mr. Pickwick, taking off his hat.

"No Fizkin!" roared the crowd.

"Certainly not!" shouted Mr. Pickwick.

"Hurrah!" and then there was another roaring, like that of a whole menagerie when the elephant has rung the bell for the cold meat.

"Who is Slumkey?" whispered Mr. Tupman.

"I don't know," replied Mr. Pickwick in the same tone. "Hush. Don't ask any questions. It's always best on these occasions to do what the mob do."

"But suppose there are two mobs?" suggested Mr. Snodgrass.

"Shout with the largest," replied Mr. Pickwick.

Alas, Mister President! You said more with this last sentence than with an entire volume. Alas! When you reach the point of shouting with those who shout loudest, all errors can happen. And they are not always easily repaired. You know it: it takes only one madman to fling a valuable bracelet down a well; twenty sane men, perhaps, are not enough to draw it out.

You know and would God that all were equally convinced, then no one would act foolishly!

May 1972

To Pinocchio

When You Get a
Crush on Someone

Dear Pinocchio,

I was seven years old when I read your *Adventures*
for the first time. I can't tell you how much I liked them
and how many times I have reread them since. The fact is
that, in you, I recognized myself as a boy, and in your
surroundings I saw my own.

How many times you dashed through the woods,
crossed the fields, ran to the beach, along the highroads!
And with you ran the Cat and the Fox, the poodle Me-
doro, the children of the battle of the books. They
seemed my dashes, my playmates, the roads and the
fields of my village.

You went to see the carnival wagons when they came
into the square; so did I. You balked, pursed your lips,
stuck your head under the covers rather than drink the
glass of bitter medicine; I did also. The slice of bread but-
tered on both sides; the candy with a liqueur inside; the
"little ball of sugar," and, on certain occasions, even an

*PINOCCHIO. Immortal character from the novel of the same name by the
Florentine writer Collodi, pseudonym of Carlo Lorenzetti (1826–1890). When
today's Pinocchios (today's children) have grown up they will have to deal
with the problems of love. On this score some people propose a broad permissiveness, but the young must not accept it: their love must be beautiful as
a flower.*

egg, even a pear, even the pear's peelings, represented a radiant "summit" for you, greedy and always hungry; the same was true of me.

I also, going to and from school, was involved in "battles": snowballs in the winter season; blows and punches and the like in every season of the year. Sometimes I was on the receiving end, but I also gave a few, trying to balance the ledger and not to whine to those at home, because, if I complained, perhaps they would have given me my "change!"

Now you have come back. You have spoken no longer from the pages of the book, but from the television screen; you have remained, however, the boy you were before.

I, on the contrary, have grown old. I find myself — if this is the right expression — now on the other side of the barricade. I no longer recognize myself in you, but rather in your advisers: Master Geppetto, the Talking Cricket, the Blackbird, the Parrot, the Firefly, the Crab, the Marmot.

They tried — alas, unheard, except for the case of the Tunny — to give you some suggestions for your life as a child.

I will also try to give some to you for your future as a boy, as a young man. Mind you, do not even think of flinging your usual hammer at me; I am not prepared to suffer the end of the poor Talking Cricket.

*   *   *

Have you noticed that, among your advisers, I haven't listed the Good Fairy? I don't like her methods very much. Pursued by the murderers, you knock desperately at the door of her house; she looks out the window, her face as white as a wax image; but she doesn't open the door and she lets you be hanged.

She frees you from the oak later, it's true, but then she plays the mean trick of allowing into your sickroom those four rabbits black as ink, who carry a little coffin on their backs.

And that's not all. When you have miraculously escaped the frying-pan of the Green Fisherman, you come home, numb with cold; the night is dark; rain is pouring down in buckets. The Fairy has the door locked against you, and after your long and desperate knocking, she sends the Snail to you, who takes nine hours to come down from the fourth floor and to bring you — half-dying of hunger as you are — some bread made of plaster, a cardboard chicken, and four alabaster apricots painted to look real.

Well, this is not the way to behave with little boys who make mistakes, especially if they are entering or have entered the age known as *precious* or else, equally, as the *difficult age,* which goes from thirteen to sixteen years, and which from now on will be your age, Pinocchio.

You will experience it: a *difficult* age, both for you and for your educators. No longer a child, you will avoid, in fact, the company, the books, the games of the little ones; not yet a man, you will feel misunderstood and virtually rejected by adults.

Victim of the strain of your rapid physical growth, you will suddenly find mile-long legs attached to you, arms like those of Briareos, and a strangely altered, unfamiliar voice.

You will feel, overpoweringly, the need to affirm your *ego.* On the one hand, you will be in disagreement with your family and school environment; on the other, you will plunge headlong into the solidarity of a "gang." On the one hand, you insist on independence from the family; on the other, you hunger and thirst to be "accepted" by those your age, to be dependent on them.

How frightening to be different from the others! Where the gang goes, there you want to go. Where the gang stops, there you want to stop. The jokes, the language, the hobbies of the others become yours. What they wear, you wear. One month, all the boys are wearing T-shirts and blue jeans; the next month all have leather jackets, colored slacks, white laces for black shoes. In certain things, nonconformist; in other things, unawares, one-hundred-percent conformists.

And of changeable humor! Today calm and docile as you were when you were ten; tomorrow as sharp as a bilious old man of seventy. Today planning to become a pilot, tomorrow determined to be an actor. Today bold and carefree, tomorrow timid and almost anxious. How much patience and indulgence and love and comprehension Master Geppetto must have with you!

And there is more: you will become introspective, you'll begin looking into yourself, that is, and you will discover new things: melancholy will afflict you, the need to daydream, sentiment and also sentimentality. It may be that, already in the seventh or eighth grade, you will get a "crush" — not a soft drink in this case, but a feeling that came over David Copperfield, who says:

"I adore Miss Shepherd. She is a little girl, in a spencer, with a round face and curly flaxen hair. [In church] I cannot look upon my book, for I must look upon Miss Shepherd. . . . I put her among the Royal Family. At home, in my own room I am sometimes moved to cry out, 'Oh, Miss Shepherd!' . . . Why do I secretly give Miss Shepherd twelve Brazil nuts for a present, I wonder? They are not expressive of affection . . . yet I feel they are appropriate to Miss Shepherd, and oranges innumerable. . . .

"Miss Shepherd being the one pervading theme and vision of my life, how do I ever come to break with her? Whispers reach me . . . of Miss Shepherd having an avowed preference for Master Jones. . . . One day Miss Shepherd makes a face as she goes by, and laughs to her companion. All is over. The devotion of a life . . . is at an end. Miss Shepherd comes out of the morning service, and the Royal Family know her no more."

It happened to Copperfield, it happens to everyone, and it will also happen to you, Pinocchio!

* * *

But how will your "advisers" help you?

For the "growing-up phenomenon," your new Talking Cricket should be old Vittorino of Feltre, a pedagogue who loved children your age and who, in educating them, attached great importance to exercise in the open air.

Riding, swimming, jumping, fencing, hunting, fishing, racing, archery, song. He meant — also through these means — to create the serene atmosphere of his "Joyous House" and give a useful release to the physical exuberance of his young pupils. He would gladly have said, as Parini was to say later:

> What can a bold spirit not do
> If it lives in strong limbs?

Your friend the Tunny, then, who carried you safe and sound on his back to shore, the moment you escaped from the Dog-fish's belly, could help you — calm and persuasive as he is — in the forthcoming, above-mentioned crisis of self-affirmation.

Today the dream of you young people is not the *auto*mobile, you all dream of a parking space for a whole series of moral *autos: auto*-choice, *auto*-decision, *auto*-government; recently, some young people in Bolzano actually tried to run an *auto*-school, on their own!

"Right enough," the wise Tunny would say in his calm fashion, "to arrive at *auto*-decision. But a little at a time, by easy stages. You cannot pass abruptly from the total obedience of the child to the full *auto*nomy of the adult. Nor can one use today completely the strong method of the past. As you gradually grow in age, Pinocchio, see — with the external help of good educators — that the proper awareness of your rights and duties also grows; let your sense of responsibility grow, to make good use of the autonomy you so desire."

Listen to how, more than a century ago, the Visconti-Venosta brothers were educated. One, Giovanni, became a man of letters; the other, Emilio, a political figure in our Risorgimento. "One of my father's methods of education was to spend as much time as possible with his sons, to demand boundless trust from us, which was abundantly reciprocated, and to consider us as persons slightly above our age; thus he inspired in us a feeling of responsibility and of duty. We were treated like little men, a method which greatly flattered us; and so we were profoundly determined to keep ourselves on that level."

* * *

In the journey toward autonomy, like almost all young people between seventeen and twenty, dear Pinocchio, you too will perhaps come up against a tough obstacle: the problem of faith.

You will breathe, in fact, antireligious objections the way you breathe the air at school, in the factory, at the movies, etc. If your faith is a pile of good grain, there will be a whole army of mice to attack it. If it is a suit of clothing, a hundred hands will try to rip it off you. If it is a house, the pickax will want to dismantle it, piece by piece. You must defend yourself; today, you preserve only as much faith as you defend.

For many objections there is a persuasive answer. For others, a total answer has not yet been found. What to do? Do not throw away faith! Ten thousand difficulties, as Cardinal Newman said, do not yet make up one doubt.

And bear in mind two things.

First: Every certitude must be respected, even if it is not mathematically evident. The fact that Napoleon, Caesar, Charlemagne existed is not as certain as $2 + 2 = 4$, but it is certain with a human, historical certitude. In the same way it is certain that Christ existed, that the Apostles saw Him dead and then resurrected.

Second: Man needs the sense of mystery. "We know all about nothing," Pascal said. I know many things about myself, but not everything; I don't know precisely what my life is, my intelligence, the degree of my health, etc.; how can I insist on understanding and knowing everything about God?

The most frequent objections you will hear concern the Church. Perhaps a remark reported by Pitigrilli can help you. In London, at Hyde Park, a preacher is preaching in the open air, but he is interrupted every now and then by a disheveled, dirty character. "The Church has existed for two thousand years," the character shouts at a certain point, "and the world is still full of thieves, adulterers, assassins!" "You're right," the preacher replies. "But for two million centuries there has been water in the world, and look at the condition of your neck!"

In other words: there have been bad popes, bad priests, bad Catholics. But what does this mean? That the Gospel has been applied? No, that, on the contrary, in these cases the Gospel has not been applied!

My dear Pinocchio, there are two famous remarks about the young. I commend the first, by Lacordaire, to your attention: "Have an opinion and assert it!" The second is by Clemenceau, and I do not commend it to you at all: "He has no ideas, but he defends them with ardor!"

* * *

May I go back to David Copperfield? The story of Miss Shepherd is some years past; he has reached the age of seventeen when he falls in love again; this time he worships Miss Larkins. He feels happy even if he can only bow to her slightly in the course of a day. He feels no relief except when he puts on his best clothes, has his shoes cleaned constantly. He dreams: "Oh! if tomorrow morning Mr. Larkins came to me and said: 'My daughter has told me all. Here are twenty thousand pounds. Be happy!' " He dreams of his aunt relenting, blessing the marriage; but as he dreams, Miss Larkins marries a hop-grower.

David is downcast for two weeks: he removes his ring, wears his worst clothes, no longer uses bear's grease, doesn't have his shoes cleaned!

Later it is love at first sight with Dora: "She was a more than human to me. She was a Fairy, a Sylph, I don't

know what she was — anything that no one ever saw.
. . . I was swallowed up in an abyss of love in an instant
. . . I was gone, headlong, before I had sense to say a
word to her."

These quotations are transparent: through them you
can glimpse the problems of love and engagement, for
which you too must prepare yourself, dear Pinocchio.

On this score, some people today argue in favor of a
broadly permissive morality. Even admitting that in the
past there was too much severity on some points, the
young must not accept this permissiveness; their love
must be with a capital *L*, beautiful as a flower, precious
as a jewel, and not vulgar like a paste diamond.

It is opportune for them to agree to impose some sacrifices on themselves and to keep their distance from people, places, and amusements which are, for them, occasions of evil. "You don't trust me," you say. "Yes, we
trust you, but it is not distrust to point out that we are all
exposed to temptations; and it is love to remove from
your path at least the unnecessary temptations!"

Look at motorists: they encounter traffic cops, traffic
lights, white lines, one-way streets, no-parking areas —
all things that seem, at first sight, nuisances and limitations *against* the driver whereas they are actually *in favor*
of the driver, because they help him proceed with greater
security and pleasure!

And if you were one day to have a fiancée — whether
Shepherd or Larkins or Dora — respect her! Defend her
against yourself! Do you want her to keep herself intact
for you? This is right, but you do the same for her, and
pay no attention to certain friends who tell of their "exploits," boasting and believing themselves "smart"
thanks to their conquests. "Smart" and strong is the man
who knows how to conquer himself and who joins the
throng of the young, who are the aristocracy of souls. As
long as you are engaged, love should procure not so
much sexual pleasure as spiritual and sensitive joy, man-
ifested in an affectionate way, of course, but correct and
worthy!

Similar advice is given on the other side, assuming that the girl knows how to tolerate "sermons."

"Dear Dora [or Miss Larkins or Shepherd or whatever]," her mother says to her, "allow me to remind you of a biological law. The girl, as a rule, has more control over herself than the boy, in sexual matters. If the man is stronger physically, the woman is stronger spiritually: it would even seem that God decided to make man's goodness depend on woman's. Tomorrow the soul of your husband and of your children will depend somewhat on you; today it is the souls of your friends and your fiancé. So you must have enough good sense for two and know how to say no in certain situations, even when everything seems to urge you to say yes. Your fiancé himself, if he is good, in his best moments will be grateful to you and will say to himself: 'My Dora was right: she has a conscience and she obeys it: tomorrow she will be faithful to me!' The overeasy fiancée, on the contrary, does not afford the same guarantee and runs the risk, with facile acquiescence, of sowing dangerous seeds, from which her husband's jealousy and doubts could grow in the future."

I will stop here, Pinocchio, but don't say now that it was out of order to speak of Dora. My boy, you had the Fairy, first as sister, then as mamma. When you are an adolescent and a young man, the Fairy at your side can only be a finacée and a wife. Unless you become a monk!

But I don't see the vocation in you!

June 1972

To Paulus Diaconus

Vacation Fever

Illustrious writer and historian,

The imminent National Eucharistic Congress, which will be held in Friuli (August 1972), has made me think of you, who, though of Lombard extraction, were born in Friuli, and wrote of your people with filial affection.

The Lombards who came into Italy — twelve centuries have now gone by — amounted to a few hundred thousand. You describe them advancing along the Via Postumia and to you they seem an anthill on the march.

What if you were to return now? What if one Saturday or Sunday in July or August, seated at the Fadalto pass, you started counting the cars, Italian and foreign, coming down toward Caorle, Jesolo, and Venice, or climbing up toward Cadore? Or what if you sat at the Brenner or other Alpine passes, even more congested with tourists?

What if I were to tell you that just during our mid-August holiday weekend a million Milanese leave Milan, a million Romans leave Rome, and there is an endless

PAULUS DIACONUS, eighth-century monk and historian of the Friuli region. He was educated in Pavia at the court of King Ratchis. He was tutor to the daughter of Desiderio Adelpaga. After the fall of the Lombards, Paulus Diaconus was taken to France, where he knew Charlemagne and remained for a long time at his court as teacher. Besides many poems, he wrote a His-tory of the Lombards which has made his name live in the history of the high Middle Ages.

procession of vehicles in all directions, on all the roads of Italy?

I can foresee your amazement and the question: "But where are all these people going?"

"They are going to the sea, to the mountains, to visit monuments, natural phenomena; they are looking for cool air, green areas, sand, air with ozone or resin in it; they are looking for escape!"

"And where will they stay?"

"Everywhere, more or less: in hotels, in pensions, in tents or tourist villages, in 'holiday houses,' in motels, in camps. You see that thing with four wheels, being drawn by a car? That is a trailer, a little traveling house."

In your day, you reined in your horse and tied it to a tree; in ours, they stop the car and the trailer wherever there is a clump of grass and a flowing stream; they take out a tank of compressed gas with portable stove and refrigerator, they prepare the food, they eat supper sitting on the ground, enjoying the rustle of the leaves stirred by the wind, the buzz of bees and dragonflies, the odor of the grass and the flowers, the color of the sky, the immediate contact with nature, which intoxicates them and calms them at the same time; in the trailer, among the hundred other things, the folding beds are ready, with foam rubber mattresses; at evening they unroll them, sleep on them all night, waiting to be waked by the birds' song; in short, they want, at least for a brief time, to bathe in nature, drowning their usual troubles and forgetting the city of cement and bricks that engulfed them and will engulf them again for long months.

I can almost see you, your head in your hands, and I seem to hear you say: "Here everything is changed! There is more racket than in the old invasions! Men have become like snails and they drag their homes after them: sometimes it is a house on wheels; sometimes it is the little white cloth first rolled up behind the seat of the motorcycle, then unrolled, unfolded, and raised like a room; sometimes it is that other tent, blue, with a veranda, electric light, supplied with radio and television and lined up with other tents, inhabited by people of every race and every tongue. It is another Babel! I give up any idea of writing about it!"

Lucky you! I, a shepherd of souls, on the contrary, cannot give up the idea; I must say at least a word on some of the problems of conscience inherent in this movement, this wandering or traveling that they call, depending on the circumstances, weekend, short holiday, vacation, tourism, summer season. Be so kind as to follow me out of the corner of your eye while I address the readers.

* * *

For us Italians, an early, classical example of the tourist is Petrarch, who was also a mountain-climber and journeyed as much as was feasible in those times, both inside Italy and out, "in search of dear places, of dear friends, of dear books." Traveling went well with his curiosity and his thirst for new knowledge, but not with his finances, so that his steward, Monte, often grumbled and said to him: "You do nothing but move about, and you will always have empty pockets."

Here a first reflection is called for: Is there not, at times, also an unjustified waste of money in traveling in a certain way, without proper limitations? These are not rare cases; "vacation fever," in those who spend beyond their means, can be found today as it was in the times of Goldoni. Often duties of conscience are sacrificed and so are family virtues such as economy, self-control, frugality.

* * *

Another reflection: It is said that one travels to learn, to broaden one's culture, to be able, at the right time, to carry on a conversation honorably, to extend one's spirit with foreign beauties of art and nature. All this is true, provided the journey is made calmly, with opportune rests, with the necessary preparation, with an eye alert to examining useful, essential elements. There is, indeed, a way to improve morally, to feel oneself smaller in a world so vast and beautiful, to be more grateful and closer to God, more united to our fellowmen.

There are certain travelers, however, who are carried away by trivia, like those who, on coming back from Rome, can talk only about a certain wine from the Castelli or certain dishes of the Trastevere cuisine . . .

There are those who seem completely without feeling for the history of places, like the guide who accompanied Fucini to see Sorrento. "And now," the writer said, "while I have a bite to eat, go find out where Tasso's house is!" The guide went, found out, and reported back: "Sir, that gentleman doesn't live there anymore!" There is also the boasting tourist who exaggerates, invents, dazzles, as if he were a Marco Polo, a Pigafetta, or a Cabot . . .

*   *   *

Vacation means rest, relaxation. But some people know how to rest and some don't. It's like dusting: some housewives think they have dusted when they have really only shifted the dust from one place to another.

The family that — to follow the fashion — arrives at a very popular resort on the big holiday weekend, when the hotels are full, so all must crowd into one room, or on makeshift beds, which can even be billiard tables or deck chairs, is not resting at all, but exchanging one fatigue, one boredom, for another.

A gentleman, on Sunday, drives a hundred miles to reach Cortina or Jesolo, along a road jammed with cars; after Mass, a stroll, lunch, a chat; then he drives back, the car joining an endless line of other cars, attempting or performing one complicated pass after another, grazing bumpers, taking difficult curves; if he arrives safe and sound at his house, he must thank the Lord. And he can say that he has made a big trip, different from his usual movements; he must not say he has rested.

How many return from their holidays tired and bored, because they have chosen too social or too noisy a place or they have not been able to limit their excursions or have joined the "crowd," which has drawn them into entertainments, talk, discussions, exciting but tiring!

I mentioned jammed roads and cars, curves and passing. This, too, is a serious spiritual problem. Curiously, no driver ever says in the confessional: "Father, I endangered my life and the lives of others!" No one says: "I was unwise, I was vain in my driving."

And yet there are many who, having barely glimpsed a car from a distance, say — and virtually vow — at once: "I'll pass it!" Even if it is a sports car, on an uphill stretch! They always have to pass, all of them, to pass into history for their passing. And sometimes they take the wheel after they have had plenty to drink or when they are too tired, depressed, with serious personal or family concerns. The fifth commandment is at stake; we can never sufficiently underline the grave responsibility of the driver of today's powerful cars on yesterday's poor, narrow, winding, crowded roads.

The fifth commandment does not contemplate only the damage done to the body but also that done to the soul by setting a bad example. The holiday-maker or tourist is observed with an admiring or at least curious eye, especially by those who are poorer and younger. As a rule the traveler thinks: "Now that I am away from my usual surroundings, I will allow myself greater moral liberties."

He should reverse this line of reasoning: "Away from home, I am more observed and therefore I will be even more correct than I am at home."

The fact that people keep their eyes open around tourists was also confirmed by the Tuscan writer Renato Fucini, as a tourist in Sorrento. The guide, whom I have already mentioned above, boasted that he could always tell where visitors came from. "You, for example," he said, "are Piedmontese, as I knew right away."

"No, no, I'm Tuscan. How could you have failed to realize that?"

"Your Excellency, you haven't said any bad words, you

haven't taken the holy name of God in vain. How could I have thought you are Tuscan?"

There, from this point of view, I would wish tourists to be "Piedmontese." And, vice versa, I hope that they choose their holidays in places so Christian — in spirit, in tradition, in daily life — that we could almost say of them what the first North American–born saint, Elizabeth Seton, wrote of a little Tuscan village, where she had stayed for a short time: "I assure you that my becoming a Catholic [previously she had been a Protestant] was a simple consequence of having gone to a Catholic country."

Besides the fifth, also the Lord's sixth commandment is involved. I am thinking of such things as manner of dress, mixed tourism among the young, improper amusements offered at many holiday places, long automobile excursions of young couples alone, whether engaged or not.

They say, about dress: "Everybody dresses like this now!" It is not true, not everybody does, though one must admit, ruefully, that apparently good families are inexplicably giving way on this point. Even if it were true that many or "everybody" does it, a bad thing remains bad.

They also say: "It's hot!" But there are available on the market various kinds of material so light that they are suited for the heat even if the dress is lengthened a few inches. As for companions, for solitary drives in the car, it is no mystery to anyone that these are occasions of evil. "My daughter is a good girl, she knows how to control herself!" a lady said to me. "Your daughter is weak like all of us and she must be protected against her own weakness and inexperience, by keeping her far from danger. Original sin, unfortunately, is not a myth, but a painful reality!"

After the sixth, comes the seventh commandment. A German bishop, some years ago, urged that tourists not be exploited wrongfully. This injunction is appropriate. I have been told that a chamber of commerce in a mountain locality has enriched the landscape with an inflated rubber cow. Seen from the distance, white against a green meadow, with a big bell (also fake), the cow lends a touch of color and serves as an attraction.

If true, this display would be more a naïveté than a fraud. It is true, however, that in certain tourist centers, the prices rise sharply at the peak season. It is true that some people consider holiday-making visitors only from the commercial point of view: they are the ones who "bring in money," who "have money" and "can spend." It is not always remembered, however, that these are people who have worked all year in factories, in offices, in damp and foggy cities; people who have barely two or three weeks' break, with a real need for rest, air, sunshine. Not always and not sufficiently do others remember that they are brothers, to whom all owe an obligation of sincere charity and cordial hospitality.

Saint Peter strongly urges us Christians to be *hospitales invicem* and adds: *sine murmuratione.* "Show hospitality to one another without grumbling and without . . . fleecing!"

* * *

A final thought: Though we may go on vacation, the Lord does not take a holiday.

His day is Sunday. He wants it kept, not profaned in any case, both for His own external respect and for our own interest. When I say "His day," I don't mean only that fragment of a day spent hearing Mass. The Christian Sunday is a whole day, which includes a complex of things: it means Mass or divine sacrifice with active participation (not just heard passively); it means the care of one's own soul in calm, in reflection, in approaching the sacraments; it means religious instruction, through listening to the word of the priest and reading the Gospel or some other good book; it means making contact with the whole parish family; it means the practice of charity toward the poor and the sick, toward children; it means good example given and received; it means the reward and the guarantee of our good life.

If we are able to live Sunday well it is almost certain, in fact, that we will live well for the rest of the week. This is why it means so much to the Lord; this is why we have to do everything to keep Sunday from degenerating. Tourism or not, holiday or not, our soul above all and before all!

*   *   *

I come back to you again, Paulus Diaconus. What do you think of my conclusion?

Is it old?

It is old, but true and wise. It helps us to become or to remain good; this is what matters!

July 1972

To Don Gonzalo
Fernandez de Cordova

The Bells of the Guerrillas

Dear Don Gonzalo,

All I know about you is what Manzoni writes in
The Betrothed.

You were Spanish governor of the State of Milan, the
Milan of the Casale war, of the plague of 1630. On your
coat of arms a Moorish king chained by his throat was
prominent. It was in front of this coat of arms that
Renzo, at the Tavern of the Full Moon, blurted out: "I
know that heretic's face, with the rope around its neck.
That face means: Let him who can, give the orders; and
those who want, obey them."

Poor Renzo! He got himself into trouble: a few hours
later the police had their hands on him, and after he
managed to escape, you had him sought for with great
uproar as a rogue, a public thief, a promoter of looting,
in a word, as a seditionist and revolutionary!

Today it would be different. For that remark Renzo
would be raised to the rank of prophet, charismatic,
theologian. You, dear Don Gonzalo, for the mere fact of

*GONZALO FERNANDEZ DE CORDOVA was Spanish governor of the
State of Milan during the Casale war and the plague of 1630. He was por-
trayed by Manzoni (1785–1873) in his novel* The Betrothed *because of the
Milanese sedition against the governor's commissioner of supply. Manzoni's
Renzo was involved in this sedition, as a protestor who soon finished in the
hands of the police.*

wanting to issue some decrees, would be a repressor, filled with lust for power, a trampler on dignity and human freedom.

Milanese sedition against your commissioner of supply would have been called an insignificant abortive revolt, a trifle compared to the true revolution, which means overturning the whole *system*.

The bells of certain "philosophy" and "theology" seem today to toll grimly for the death of authority, and ring festively for freedom and revolution. They would have made Bossuet, that genius who was almost your contemporary, say: "Where all do what they want, no one does what he wants; where no one commands, all command; where all command, no one commands!"

* * *

But who pays any attention to Bossuet? The luminary to whom large groups of students especially turn is Mao, who has said to them: "Wipe out all that is bourgeois with the cultural revolution! The culture of the past serves only to create divisions: 'making the revolution,' on the contrary, is the only culture worthy of the name." He has been taken at his word also here, in our country. The "new students" proclaim: "We are the fuse that will blow up present society. No more selective school, class school, favoring only the bourgeois, who have already received a certain type of education at home! Enough of the class-oriented meritocracy that wants to measure at school with the same yardstick those who can come by car and those who must come by foot."

And they mean business: they occupy the schools, they deny that there is any difference between Dante Alighieri and Bertoldino. They have learned the methods of urban guerrilla warfare, Marxist analysis of bourgeois society, the use of drugs; they paralyze the nonrevolutionaries with ridicule; they dominate with terrorism the silent student majorities; and they penetrate even the circles of Catholic students.

A curious phenomenon, these "fifth columns," accepted, applauded, theologized. Mao is the new Moses, who leads the people to a new Promised Land. So-called Western democracy is now a useless wreck. Even Soviet Communism is out of date.

The third way, the way of Mao, is the one that will liberate the world, because — they say — it is the way of the Gospel. How is this? We must realize — they say — that Palestine, in the time of Jesus, was a theater of guerrilla warfare; the guerrillas — zealots — were fighting a bloody battle against Rome; the reprisal against them was crucifixion; so the cross, even before it became a Christian symbol, was a sign connected with *guerrilla* fighting. Jesus, deprived of His rights as a citizen by the rulers from Rome, an oppressed Jew, could not help but find Himself among the revolutionaries.

This is not clear from the Gospels — they go on to say — which were written when the revolt against Rome was finished. Saint Mark, moreover, writing for the Romans, edulcorated the contents of his Gospel out of regard for them; also Saint Paul, a Roman citizen, allowed himself to be influenced by Rome.

The Gospels and Paul, as they stand, are therefore not reliable; they have to be reinterpreted.

It is written: "Render therefore to Caesar the things that are Caesar's." This must be replaced with: "It is forbidden to give Caesar anything, because in Palestine everything belongs to God." It is written: "Blessed are the peacemakers"; "go and be reconciled to your brother"; "forgive"; "he who lives by the sword dies by the sword"; "love your enemies." These would seem pacifist texts; but they aren't. Read in the pacifist sense, they sound absurd and cowardly to people under Roman oppression, yearning for political independence. So they must be "reinterpreted" as follows: "You must not have enemies: this is possible only when you have overturned power through revolution and have destroyed the demons of human nondignity, of economic disparity, of the disparity of power, which means oppression."

The real Christ — they conclude — is revolutionary, a

guerrilla; the one who armed His hand against the money-changers in the temple, who entered into conflict with the synagogue. To follow Him, one must become a revolutionary against power, both governmental and ecclesiastical, in the name of freedom, of corresponsibility, of dialogue, of charismata.

* * *

What can be said? Christ, though He is not inferior to anyone, not even to the Father, is a model of respect toward human authority! In Nazareth He is "obedient" to Mary and Joseph; at Capharnaum He actually provides a miraculous catch of fish in order to have the shekels necessary to pay the tax of the temple.

The position of Christ with regard to the synagogue cannot remotely be compared to that of some of us toward civil or ecclesiastical authority. Christ was "the master of the Law" and the Son of the Father, superior to the law; the synagogue was the consignee of the law. In clashing then with the synagogue, Christ did not invoke any right of His to rebel, but rather His duty of obedience to the Father. Even His driving the money-changers from the temple is a carefully calculated, pondered religious act. Christ in the temple, in fact, does not wound or kill anyone, He does not burn down the temple; He merely overturns the tables of the money-changers and scatters the animals of the merchants, to whom He causes not so much damage as temporary disturbance in view of His own foreseen aim: to teach respect for the house of the Father.

The Council underlined the fact that the Church is the people of God, community before it is hierarchy. Founding it, Christ had first in His thoughts the people, the souls to be saved. To serve the people He wanted Apostles and bishops endowed with special powers. To keep the bishops united, He wanted the pope. Pope and bishops are therefore not above, but within and at the service of the people of God.

They can perform that service, however, only by exercising the powers received, which, therefore, cannot be eliminated. The Council says: "The bishops govern the individual churches entrusted to them as vicars or envoys of Christ through counsel, persuasion, example, but also through authority and sacred power . . . thanks to which they have a sacred right and the duty to judge before the Lord and to regulate everything concerning worship and their apostolate."

It is difficult to exercise this authority in the proper manner, true. It is also true that the hierarchy has in the past been wanting and can also be wanting now. When the Fathers speak of a "leprous Church" and of a "lame Church," they are touching on an open wound.

But the wound is connected with human finiteness; it can be treated, cured in part, but not completely eliminated. The laymen and the priests who sometimes protest out of sincere love for the Church should bear this in mind. One must know how to build on what exists: often it is wise to be satisfied with what one has, aiming, however, at further conquests, without destroying through protest the existing germs of a future evolution.

— Respect for persons? Of course, but out of respect for individual persons, bishops cannot neglect the general good, allowing lack of discipline and anarchy to take over. Saint Augustine said: "We bishops govern, but only if we serve." And he added: "The bishop who does not serve the public is only a scarecrow set in the vineyards so that the birds will not peck at the grapes."

— More spirit, more charismata, and fewer institutions? But some institutions go back to Christ and cannot be touched without changing the very essence of the Church: they include the Primacy of the Pope, the Episcopal College, the episcopacy, the ministerial priesthood.

Other institutions are human, they must be changed when they prove out of date and counterproductive, but the change must follow the law of history. This law says to the bishops: nothing human is unchangeable, not even the Catholics' way of obeying. But it adds: subjects must not think that the course of history can be hastened with an impatient rebellion! Bertoldino also was in a hurry for his baby chicks to hatch: he drove away the hen and took her place, personally sitting on the eggs, but all he got was an omelet stuck to the seat of his pants!

— More freedom, less legalism? Right. Christ proclaimed the inner life, He condemned the legalism of the Pharisees. Saint Paul also exalted the freedom of the spirit and the code of love. But there is also the obverse of the coin: Christ handed down precepts, enjoining His followers to observe them, and He wanted the Church to have authority. Paul also warned: You have been called to freedom; only, this freedom must not become an excuse for the flesh.

— Corresponsibility? Let all shepherds remember: they have not been "set up by Christ to assume by themselves the weight of the redeeming mission of the Church"; "in decisive battles the most effective measures are often conceived at the front." In their turn, laymen must take care not to limit their corresponsibility to all-too-easy protest: they must add practical proposals, capable of being carried out; and above all they must collaborate in carrying them out. And more: They must remember that their contribution to the good of the Church must not happen in a disorderly way, but "under the leadership of the sacred guide," whose own charisma must be recognized and authenticated.

— Dialogue? The Council documents speak of it about fifty times. It must then be effected with goodwill on both sides. The bishops must not listen only to themselves; let them consult, examine together with others, before deciding. And let the faithful speak "with that freedom and trust that befits the children of God and brothers in Christ . . . always with truth, strength, and prudence, with reverence and charity."

But not even dialogue will work like a magic wand that heals everything, resolving and putting in order. Dialogue is useful insofar as those who participate in it have faith in it and observe its just rules.

* * *

Dear Don Gonzalo! These people, who say they are interpreting the Gospel, are seeking freedom. Unfortunately, it is not the freedom that Christ meant, when He taught us to say: "Father . . . deliver us from evil!"

Nor is it that other freedom, of which Saint Augustine spoke: "You will be free if you will enslave yourself; free from sin, slave of justice!"

August 1972

To Saint Bernardino of Siena

"Seven Rules" That Still Hold

Dear smiling saint,

Pope John admired your written sermons so much that he wanted to proclaim you a Doctor of the Church. He died, and so far nothing has been done about it. A great pity!

The ones the good pope admired, however, were not your sermons in Latin, carefully studied, polished, neatly subdivided, but rather your Italian sermons, copied down from your spontaneous preaching, sermons full of life, religious fervor, humor, and practical wisdom. He thought of you perhaps as the "Smiling Doctor" beside the "Mellifluous" Bernard, the "Angelic" Thomas, the "Seraphic" Bonaventure, the "Consoling" Francis de Sales.

He thought that in times when difficult words, bristling with vague *isms,* are used to express even the simplest things in this world, it would be opportune to remind people of the little monk who taught: "Speak clearly, so that the hearer may go away happy and illuminated, and not made dizzy!"

And on hearing your sermon in June of 1427, the pro-

BERNARDINO OF SIENA, saint of the Catholic Church (1380–1444). Franciscan, preacher of exceptional eloquence, he left many works in Latin and in Italian. In 1427, to the students of the University of Siena, Saint Bernardino proposed "seven rules" for becoming worthy men. Pope John Paul I proposes them again for the young people of today.

fessors and students of the University of Siena were anything but "dizzy." You spoke to them about the "way of studying," you proposed "seven rules" and you concluded: "If you observe these seven rules, in a short time you will become a worthwhile man or a worthwhile woman."

With your permission, abbreviating and adapting those seven rules a bit, I will now try to recall them for the students of today.

They are good, likable young people, who don't run the slightest risk of being made "dizzy," for the simple reason that they want to experience things for themselves. They don't welcome "models of behavior" from you or me, because such models smell of moralism from a mile off. And probably the students won't read these lines, but I will write them anyhow; I am writing them to you.

Luigi Einaudi also wrote his "Useless Sermons," which, all the same, proved useful to some people.

*   *   *

First rule: *esteem.* No one manages to study seriously if first he does not respect study. He will not succeed in acquiring culture if first he does not respect culture.

This student's back is bent over his books. You write: "Good!" In this way "your brain will not be full of wild notions, like the brains of other young people, who expect nothing from study beyond dusting their benches!" Love books, you will be in contact with the great men of the past: "You will speak to them and they will speak to you: they will hear you, you will hear them, and you will derive great joy from this."

But what becomes of the idle student? He becomes "like a pig in the sty who swills and eats and sleeps." He becomes "Master Zero," who will never achieve anything great and beautiful in life.

Mind you: for true culture not only books must be appreciated but also discussion, group work, the exchange of experiences. All these things stimulate us to be active as well as receptive; they help us fulfill ourselves in learning, in expressing our thoughts to others in an original fashion; they encourage polite attention toward our neighbors.

But respect for the great "masters" should never flag; to be the confidant of great ideas is worth far more than to be the inventor of mediocre ideas. Pascal said: "He who has climbed on another's shoulders will see farther, even if he is shorter!"

* * *

Second rule: *separation.* Keep yourself apart, at least a little bit! Otherwise you cannot study seriously. Athletes must, after all, abstain from many things; students are athletes to some extent, and you, dear Fra Bernardino, supplied them with a whole list of "forbidden" things.

I will mention only two of them here: bad company and bad reading. "A libertine spoils everyone. A rotten apple, placed among good ones, corrupts all the others." Be on guard, you write, also against the books of Ovid and "other books about loving." Not bothering with Ovid, today you would speak explicitly of indecent books and magazines, bad movies, drugs. But you would not make any change in the following paragraph: "When you, father, have a son off studying, in Bologna or wherever he may be, and you hear that he has fallen in love, send him no more money. Make him come home, for he will learn nothing, except cheap songs and sonnets . . . and he will then be *Master Coram-vobis.*"

This remedy used to be effective: "cutting off supplies." But it no longer works today: the government, in fact, takes the father's place, if needed, passing out the "pre-salary" to students.

One hope remains: that the student will apply to himself, on his own, the "mountebank remedy."

You know it: on market day, climbing on a chair, the mountebank gathered the gaping peasants around him, showed them a little closed box, and said: "Inside this there is the most effective remedy for mules' kicks: it costs little, practically nothing; you're lucky to be able to buy it." And, in fact, many bought it. But one of the buyers chose to open the box. In it he found nothing but six feet of fine string. He raised his voice in protest: "It's a fraud!"

"No fraud at all," the mountebank replied. "Measure a distance the length of that string, keep that distance from the mule, and no kick will ever be able to reach you!"

This is the classic and radical remedy suggested by you preachers; it works for all, it works especially for students, exposed today to a thousand snares. Separation! From all the "mules" that give kicks at morality!

* * *

Third rule: *calm.* "Our soul is made like water. When it remains calm, the mind is like clear water; but when it is stirred, it becomes murky." So this mind must be made to rest, to be calm, if one wants to learn, to investigate, to retain. How is it possible to fill one's head with all the characters in the magazines, in the movies, on TV, in the sports world, all so vital, so aggressive, yet at times so humiliating and polluting, and then insist that the mind must also retain information from schoolbooks, which, in comparison, seems insipid and colorless?

An area of silence is needed around the student's mind so that it will remain calm and clean. You, pious monk, suggest asking this of the Lord; you even suggest the suitable prayer: "Calm our minds, Lord God." Our students, at this point, will smile; they are accustomed to quite different prayers! But so it is: a bit of silence and a pinch of prayer in the midst of all the daily turmoil will do no harm in any way!

* * *

Fourth rule: *ordination,* that is to say, order, balance, the golden mean, both in things of the body and of the spirit. Eating? Yes, you write, but "neither too much nor too little. All extremes are vicious, the middle way is the best. You cannot bear two burdens: study and scant eating, too much eating and study, for the one will make you waste away and the other will thicken the brain." "Sleep? Again, yes, but "neither too much nor too little. . . . It is best to rise early . . . with the mind sober."

The spirit also needs order, and you continue: "Do not send the cart before the horse . . . rather acquire less knowledge but know it well; this is better than learning much badly!" The badly learned, the mere smattering, superficiality, approximation are not serious things. You also advise having personal preferences among the various authors or the various subjects: "Esteem within yourself one doctor more than another, or one book more than another. . . . But do not despise any of them."

* * *

Fifth rule: *continuation*, that is to say, perseverance. The fly barely lights on the flower, then moves, fickle and agitated, to another flower; the bumblebee lingers a bit longer, but he is concerned with making noise; the honeybee, however, silent and industrious, stops, drains the nectar, takes it home, and gives us very sweet honey. Thus wrote Saint Francis de Sales, and I believe you agree completely: no fly-student, no bumblebee-student, you like tenacious and constructive firmness of purpose, and you are abundantly right.

In school and in life, deciding a course is not enough; one must also have willpower. It is not enough to begin to want something: you must keep on wanting it. And even that constant wish is not enough: you must know how to begin again at the beginning, every time you stop out of laziness or because of a failure or a lapse. The misfortune of a young student is not so much scant memory as scant willpower. His good fortune, more than in great talent, lies in a strong and tenacious will. But this is tempered only in the sun of God's grace; it is warmed at the fire of great ideas and great examples!

* * *

Sixth rule: *discretion*. This means keeping your reach within your grasp, not getting a twisted neck from looking at goals that are too high; not having too many irons in the fire; not expecting results overnight.

To be the first in the class is commendable, but if I have only a limited supply of talent, it is not for me; so I will work with all my power and will be satisfied if I even rank fourth or fifth. I would like to take violin lessons, but I give up the idea if they harm my studies and cause people to say of me: "He who hunts two hares catches one but loses the other!"

*   *   *

Seventh rule: *enjoyment*, that is to say, studying with pleasure. No one can study for any length of time if he doesn't enjoy studying a bit. And that pleasure does not come at once, but gradually. In the early days there is always some obstacle: laziness to be overcome, pleasant occupations that are more attractive, difficult subject matter. The pleasure comes later, a reward for the effort made.

You write: "Without having gone to Paris to study, learn from the animal that has the cloven foot [i.e., the ox], which first eats and stores, then ruminates, little by little." The word you use, *ruguma*, means "to ruminate," but for you, dear and wise saint, it means something more, namely: the ox savors the hay slowly, when it is tasty and enjoyable, and to the full extent. And so it should be with the books you study, the nourishment of our minds.

*   *   *

Dear Saint Bernardino! Enea Silvio dei Piccolomini, your fellow-Sienese, pope under the name Pius II, wrote that, at your death, the most powerful lords in Italy divided up your relics. To the poor Sienese, who so loved you, nothing of you was left. There remained only the little donkey on whose back you had climbed sometimes, in the last years of your life when you felt weary of your journeying. The women of Siena saw the poor animal going by one day; they stopped it, ripped off all its hide, and kept those hairs as relics.

Instead of the donkey, I have shorn and "plucked clean," ruining it, one of your very beautiful sermons. Will these "feathers" all be scattered in the wind, or will at least a few of them be picked up by somebody?

September 1972

To Saint Francis de Sales

On the Ship of God

Gentlest of saints,

I have reread a book which concerns you: *Saint Francis de Sales, Theologian of Love.** It was written, some time ago, by Henry Bordeaux of the Academy of France.

Before that, however, you yourself wrote that you had a "heart of flesh," which was moved, which understood, which kept reality in mind and knew that men are not pure spirits, but feeling creatures. With this human heart you loved reading and the arts, you wrote with the most refined sensitivity, even encouraging your friend Bishop Camus to write novels. You leaned toward all, to give all something.

Already as a university student in Padua, you made a rule for yourself never to avoid or curtail a conversation with anyone, no matter how unlikable and boring; to be modest and without insolence, free and without austerity, gentle and without affectation, pliant and without dissent.

FRANCIS DE SALES, *Doctor and saint of the Catholic Church (1567–1622). He studied with the Jesuits in Paris and then at the University of Padua, where he became a doctor of civil law. After entering the Church, he was made bishop of Geneva, where he devoted himself to the conversion of Calvinists. He spent the great part of his time in the service of the young, the poor, the ill. He wrote various works of a spiritual nature, including his* Introduction to the Devout Life *and* Treatise on Divine Love.

Translator's note: The English translation (1927) was published with this title. A more faithful translation of the original would have been *Saint Francis de Sales and Our Heart of Flesh.*

You kept your word. To your father, who had chosen a rich and pretty heiress as your wife, you amiably replied: "Papa, I have seen *mademoiselle*, but she deserves better than me!"

Priest, missionary, bishop, you gave your time to others: the young, the poor, the sick, sinners, heretics, bourgeois, noble ladies, prelates, princes.

Like everyone, you were sometimes misunderstood, contradicted. The "heart of flesh" suffered, but went on loving the contradictors. "If an enemy were to put out my right eye," you once said, "I would want to smile at him with my left; if he put out both my eyes, I would still have a heart to love him."

Many would consider this a peak. For you, the peak is something else. You wrote, in fact: "Man is the perfection of the universe; the spirit is the perfection of man; love is the perfection of the spirit; the love of God is the perfection of love." Therefore the peak, the perfection, the excellence of the universe is, for you, loving God.

* * *

So you are for the primacy of divine love. Must people be made good? Let these people then begin by loving God; once this love is kindled and established in the heart, the rest will come of itself.

Modern therapy says that you cannot cure a local disease unless you take care to restore the health of the whole body through general hygiene and powerful tonics such as blood transfusion or intravenous feeding. On this score you wrote: "The lion is a powerful animal, full of resources; this is why he can sleep without fear either in a secret den or beside a path traveled by other animals." And you concluded: So then, become spiritual lions! Fill yourselves with strength, with love of God, and thus you will not fear those "animals" which are human failings.

And this — in your opinion — was the system of Saint Elizabeth of Hungary. This princess, out of duty, went to balls and court entertainments, but she derived spiritual gain rather than harm from them. Why? Because "in the wind [of temptations] the great fires [of divine love] grow stronger, while smaller flames are blown out!"

The fiancés of this world say: "All I want is your heart and a humble cottage!" Later they find that the cottage, alas, is not enough, and they no longer want to live in it, because their hearts have grown cold.

You wrote: "As soon as the queen bee comes out into the fields, all her little people surround her; thus the love of God does not enter a heart without the whole retinue of other virtues being lodged there too." For you, to prescribe virtues for a heart lacking the love of God is like suddenly prescribing strenuous sport for a weakened organism. To strengthen the organism with the love of God, on the other hand, is to prepare the champion and start him confidently toward the peaks of health.

*   *   *

But what love of God? There is one made up of sighs, of pious groans, of sweet looks toward heaven. There is another, virile, straightforward, the twin brother of the love that Christ possessed when, in the garden, he said: "Not my will, but thine, be done." This is the only love of God that you urge on us.

According to you, the man who loves God must board the ship of God, determined to accept the course set by His commandments, by the guidance of those who represent Him, and by the situations and circumstances of life that He permits.

You imagined an interview with Marguerite, when she was about to embark for the Orient with her husband, Saint Louis IX, king of France:

"Where are you going, Madame?"

"Where the king goes."

"But do you know exactly where the king is going?"

"He has told me in a general way. I am not concerned to know where he is going, however: I care only about going with him."

"Then, Madame, you have no idea of this voyage?"

"None save the idea of being in the company of my dear lord and husband."

"Your husband will go to Egypt, he will stop at Damietta, at Acre, and in several other places; do you not wish, Madame, to go there also?"

"No, in truth. I think only of being near my king; the places where he goes have no importance at all for me, except for the fact that he will be there. I am not so much traveling with him as following him. I do not care about the voyage, but am content with the presence of the king."

That king is God, and we are all Marguerites if we love God really. And how many times, in how many ways, did you return to dwell on this concept! "To feel, with God, like a child in its mother's arms; whether He carries us in His right arm or in His left arm is the same: we leave it up to Him." What if the Madonna were to entrust the infant Jesus to a nun? You asked yourself this and you answered: "The nun would insist on not letting Him go again, but she would be wrong; old Simeon received the Child in his arms with joy, but also with joy he handed Him back quickly. So we must not weep too much in giving up rank, job, office, when its term ends or when it is asked back."

In the castle of God we seek to accept any position: cook or scullion, waiter, groom, baker. If it please the king to call us to his privy council, we will go, without being too moved, knowing that the recompense does not depend on the position but on the loyalty with which we serve.

This is your way of thinking. Some consider it a kind of fatalism, Oriental. But it isn't that. "The human will," you wrote, "is mistress of his loves, as a young lady commands her suitors, who ask her hand in marriage. This, before she chooses; but when her choice is made and she has become a married woman, the situation is reversed: mistress that she was, she now becomes subject and remains under the authority of the one who was formerly her victim.

"The will, too, can choose love as it pleases, but, once it has declared its preference, it remains subjected to its choice. It is true, however, that within the will there exists a freedom which the married woman does not have, for the will can reject its love when it wishes, even the love of God, thus confuting any notion of fatalism."

*   *   *

If politicians were to hear you! They measure an action by its success. "Does it succeed? Then it's worthwhile!" You say: "The action is valid even when it does not succeed, if performed out of love of God; the merit of the cross borne is not its weight, but the way in which it is borne; there can be more merit in bearing a little cross of straw than a great cross of iron; eating, drinking, strolling, done for the love of God, can be more worthy than fasting or taking the blows of discipline."

But you have gone yet a step further, saying that the love of God can — in a certain sense — even change things, making actions that are in themselves indifferent or even dangerous become good. This is the case with gambling and with dancing (the dancing of your day, naturally), if it is done "as a pastime and not a habit; for a short while and not until one is wearied and jaded; and done rarely, so that it does not become occupation instead of recreation."

So it is the quality of our actions that counts, more than their size or their number! Have you read what Rabelais, your almost-contemporary, wrote about the devotions taught the young Gargantua? "Twenty-six or thirty Masses to be heard each day, a series of *Kyrie Eleisons* which would have sufficed for sixteen hermits!" If you did read this, you also gave your reply, when you taught the nuns: "It is good to progress, but not in the multitude of pious practices, but rather in perfecting them. Last year you fasted three times a week; this year you wish to double that number, and the week will just suffice. But next year? Will you fast — increasing again — nine days a week or twice a day? Be careful! It is folly to wish to die as martyrs in the Indies while one meanwhile neglects one's own daily duties!"

In other words: It is not so much a matter of practicing *devotions* as it is of being devout. The soul is not so much a cistern to be filled as a fountain to make burst forth!

And not only the souls of nuns. With these principles sanctity stops being a privilege of convents and becomes a capacity and a duty of everyone! It doesn't become an easy enterprise (it is the Way of the Cross!), but an ordinary one: some achieve it with heroic actions or vows, in the manner of eagles, who soar high in the heavens; many achieve it by performing the common duties of every day, but in an uncommon way, like doves, who fly from one roof to another.

Why wish for the soaring flights of the eagle, for deserts or stern cloisters, if you are not called to them? Let us not be like neurotic patients who want cherries in autumn and grapes in spring! Let us apply ourselves to what God asks of us according to our condition. "Madame," you wrote, "you must abbreviate your prayers a bit, so as not to compromise your household duties. You are married; be a complete wife, without excessive bashfulness; do not bore your family, spending too much time in church; have such devotion as to make your husband love it, but this will happen only if he feels that you are his."

* * *

In conclusion, here is the ideal of the love of God lived in the midst of the world: these men and these women should have wings to fly toward God with loving prayer; let them also have feet to walk graciously among other men and women; and let them not have "grim faces," but smiling ones, knowing that they are heading for the happy house of the Lord!

November 1972

To the Bear of Saint Romedio

Dirty Mouths

Dear bear of Saint Romedio,

"Every good thief has his devotion." This is the reason why, a month ago, as I was passing Sanzeno in the Val di Non, I said to myself: "Just over a mile from here, in a little valley, set between very high cliffs that suggest the canyons of Colorado, there is the shrine of Saint Romedio. Your grandparents, traveling dozens of miles on foot, used to go there; so you go there, too, in your automobile!" And I went.

The shrine is impressive, with its six superimposed churches and the terrace that overlooks the awesome sheer drop. The figure and the memories of the hermit saint are interesting. But you, too, are likable, dear bear!

Perathoner's statue shows you on a leash, all meek, tamed by the saint who is holding you.

The story was explained to me: according to legend, Romedio, returning from a pilgrimage to Rome, stops to rest with his two faithful companions, Abraham and David. At a certain moment he says to David: "It is time to resume our way, go fetch our horses, which are grazing in the meadow nearby." His companion comes back, terrified: a bear is just then devouring Romedio's horse.

The legendary bear which devoured the horse of Saint Romedio was then, bridled and tamed, the hermit's inseparable companion. Formerly count of Thaur, Innsbruck, Romedio became an anchorite in the Val di Non, near Sanzeno, around the fourth century.

Romedio runs over, sees, and, without growing upset, says to you, bear: "You were hungry, obviously. You're eating my horse, and that's all right; but I must tell you: I can't go home on foot, so you shall be my horse!" No sooner said than done: he fits the saddle on you, the bridle, and the other trappings of the animal you devoured, he climbs on as if you were the most peaceful mule in the world, and off you go, toward Trent! As I returned from the shrine, my prayer — can you believe this? — was: "O Lord, tame me too, make me more obliging and less of a bear!"

Don't take offense at this last expression: for us humans, you bears, brown and black, with your long bodies, short thick paws, heavy coats, are clumsy and inelegant creatures. We, in comparison, consider ourselves infinitely slender, trim, genteel. If you start dancing, you do nothing but cause havoc, whereas our dances are miracles of grace, music, and the sylphs of our ballet are so light and agile that they can dance on the flowers of the fields without crushing them.

*   *   *

And yet? And yet, yesterday, I was tempted to reverse my prayer of a month ago, transforming it into this: "Lord, make us all become bears!" I had happened to hear, in fact, some ugly curses. "In this case," I said to myself, "what does it matter to dress so elegantly, to wear ties in the latest fashion, have hair styled so tastefully, if such vulgar words come from our mouths? Better to be as clumsy as bears, but not to have such dirty mouths!"

Especially as the phenomenon is very widespread in our country, a real epidemic, fifteen million habitual blasphemers in Italy, with about a billion blasphemies a day.

Some of these people bear a psychological resemblance to the "spiteful and grim" Capaneo of Dante, who hurls at God fierce words of defiance and bitterness. Others water down their blasphemous expressions a bit. "Does a

God still exist?" they ask. "Stop speaking to me about a good and just God!" "Religion is nothing but a big shop!" "The devil knows more than God!"

It is fortunate that, at times, the speaker's heart is not in agreement with his mouth, and various circumstances exclude a real, profound intention of offending God.

At times the gravity of the expression is attenuated by lack of forethought, by concern, by ignorance, as in the case of Irene Papovna, who presented herself at a teacher's certificate examination in Moscow. The subject of the paper to be written was: "Analyze the inscription carved on Lenin's tomb." The little schoolteacher doesn't remember the inscription very well; she thinks — but is not sure — that it goes "Religion is the opiate of the people." What to do? She takes a chance, writes as much of an analysis as she can, and, after she has turned in her paper, rushes to the Lenin Mausoleum in Red Square to check. When she has made sure she was right, she cries out enthusiastically: "Dear, sweet God! And you, Holy Virgin of Kazan! Thanks for making me remember the inscription!"

* * *

Dear bear! You don't know it, but for blasphemy and cursing, there is now an accepted, established vocabulary, realistic and figurative, even if not always well chosen.

For example, they call blasphemies *moccoli,* candle stubs. But candle stubs cast a bit of light; a blasphemous word is black, "dead water," a stagnant marsh, asphyxiating gas.

"Fishwives' language" is what female cursing is called. But the expression is true only if the word "fishwife" is considered a part meant to signify the whole; in other words, if, thanks to the figure of speech known as "synecdoche," the term also includes women professors, students, workers, employees, stenographers, and so on. Of all these people it used to be said: "They blush because they are ashamed"; of some of them, today, it must be said: "They are ashamed because they blush."

It is also said, "He curses like a Turk," but this is slander: the Turks do not curse. In France, Switzerland, Germany, on the other hand, they say, unfortunately with good reason: "He curses like an Italian."

The disease, then, is widespread. What is the diagnosis?

First symptom: great superficiality. The thinking person does not blaspheme, and the blasphemer does not think. Either there is, in fact, this God whose name is taken in vain, or else God doesn't exist. If He doesn't exist, then blasphemy is silly. If He does exist, then blasphemy is insane, because "donkey's braying does not reach heaven!" We can understand (not excuse) other sins: the thief, after all, grabs a wallet full of money; the drunk, a bottle of good wine; but what does the blasphemer gain?

Second symptom: scant sense of responsibility. Besides God, in fact, there is our neighbor. You, dear bear, famous for tenderness toward your cubs, should say to the heads of families: "In blaspheming, you grieve your wife and daughter, you scandalize your son, who is driven to follow his father's example. What do you gain?"

"I gain something," I have heard some say to me, "because, by blaspheming, I protest against things that are going wrong, I strengthen what I say, I release my anger."

Protests? They are made when they are useful and rational. But does the car's engine, which refused to start, perhaps now turn over as soon as you start blaming God?

Strengthen what you are saying? All right, on condition that you do it with words that are not disrespectful. Our dialects have thousands of phrases that are at once innocent and dynamic. A good Australian parish priest demonstrated this to certain peasants one fine day, when he turned up in the fields, took the plow in his hand, and, cracking the whip, shouted to the oxen in a stentorian voice: "Come on, you sweet archangels! That's the stuff, you nice cherubim! Keep at it, bright seraphim!" At these mystical, celestial orders, the oxen slowly stood up and, although puzzled, began pulling!

As for anger, it should be repressed, not released, if it is true that we must be not the servants but the masters of our passions.

*   *   *

Every diagnosis should be followed by a therapy. In our case, a small and useful "mustard plaster" or bandage could be the moderate and suitable reaction of the "right-minded."

A monk, very similar to your Saint Romedio, was sitting in a train compartment, hearing, helpless and grieved, the blasphemies uttered in competition by two rude young people, when one of them, joking, said: "Father, I have to give you a piece of bad news: the devil is dead!"

"I'm very sorry, and I extend my sincere condolences to you," the monk replied.

"Condolences! Why?" the two young men said at the same time.

"Because I feel so sorry for you, now that you have been left orphans!"

The monk had allowed himself a bit of irony. What we should feel for blasphemers, especially young ones, is not irony but interest, understanding, a wish to help, and an offer to do so. As we are their companions, friends, superiors, relatives, then with tact, delicacy, and respect for their personality, we owe them, according to the situation, friendly advice, polite reproof, scolding, at times even punishment.

The real remedy, however, is for them to shake off, by themselves, the bad habit, with firm and persevering decision, working in the opposite way from Trilussa's gardener.

This gardener,

> If a hair grew the wrong way,
> Began, in fact, to curse:
> God's this . . . and hell's that . . .
>   and curse the . . . !

But one day, as he was cursing:

> . . . the Devil turned up
> And grabbed him in the place where
> Clerk's trousers are the most worn out.

Feeling himself carried through the air, filled with fear,

> The Gardener said a prayer . . .
> God! Sweet Christ! Virgin Mary!
> Have mercy on me! Dear Madonna!

The Devil, at these names, naturally

> Opened his hand and suddenly let him go;
> The gardener fell, like a bundle,
> On to a haystack without hurting himself.
> I was lucky, he said, as he fell;
> God's this . . . and hell's that . . .
>   and curse the . . . !

*   *   *

Dear bear of Saint Romedio! Trilussa was joking and meant to say that the opposite should be done: promising not to curse and then seriously keeping the promise.

Open your maw and, from the shrine, say it as loud as you can to all Italians!

December 1972

To Pavel Ivanovich Chichikov

The Time of Imposters

Mr. Chichikov,

The visiting card, which, when you arrived at the hotel, you gave the attendant, identifies you as "Collegiate Councillor," a position equivalent to that of a colonel in the Czarist army.

Not handsome — so Gogol describes you — but not ugly either; not too fat and not too thin; not old, but not very young.

But there is one thing about you: you have conceived a masterpiece of a plan and you carry it out. You said to yourself: "The government grants lands to be colonized down in the Kherson region to anyone who shows that he has a good number of serfs, or souls. Not long ago there was an epidemic and, thank God, a number of serfs died, though they still appear as living in the census rolls. I will take advantage of this circumstance: I will buy them from their masters as 'live souls,' even if in reality they are dead souls; I will present a list of them to the government; in this way I will be granted the lands and will become immensely rich."

PAVEL IVANOVICH CHICHIKOV is a grotesque character in Gogol's Dead Souls. He makes a fortune thanks to a colossal lie. Nikolai Vasilevich Gogol (1809–1852) is one of the most popular figures in Russian literature. Pitiless observer, endowed with a subtle and contorted psychological sensitivity, he creates in his stories a host of characters, mean, greedy, and arrogant.

Having left your bags at the hotel, you begin immediately your visits in the city.

To the governor you mention — oh, ever so casually — that entering his territory is like entering an Eden, the streets here are of velvet, and people should raise monuments to governments that send out such intelligent officials.

To the chief of police you find something very flattering to say about the city guards.

Speaking with the vice-governor and the president of the court, you let slip the title of Excellency; it's an error, but the two men are highly pleased.

Conclusion: the governor this same evening invites you to a family party, while the other officials expect you at their homes in the next few days, one for dinner, another for a little game of cards, another for a cup of tea. You are already on the crest of the wave, Chichikov; your huge lie promises well, you are about to do profitable business at the expense — naturally — of others.

This is the sore spot. You are certainly a great character, your invention is original, but . . . you are defrauding! And what is worse, since you are a thief in yellow gloves, with witty lies, society pays you compliments and presents arms to you!

If you were the only one! But there are infinite examples! From Talleyrand, who declares that words are a gift of God for "hiding one's thoughts," to Byron, who calls lies "but the truth in masquerade"; to Ibsen, who in *The Wild Duck* defends "the vital falsehood," asserting that ordinary human beings need falsehood in order to live; to Andreev, who, in "The Lie," sadly asserts that there is no more truth. And from them we arrive at the common opinion of many people, who consider fraud and deceit as a proof of intelligence and skill in business.

* * *

Alas! Today we see even more macroscopic cases, made possible by new techniques of communication that you, Chichikov, could not even imagine, exploited today by few to the harm of many.

Gilbert Cesbron has just brought out a psychological novel. It may interest you, a great imposter, to know that he has entitled it *Voici le temps des imposteurs!* According to Cesbron, the list of imposters includes those members of the press who, spreading scandalous indiscretions and slanderous insinuations, appeal to people's lowest instincts, gradually corrupting their moral sense.

To the press Cesbron could add movies, radio, television. These instruments, useful in themselves, when handled by shrewd operators bombard people with sounds and colors and hidden persuasion, which is all the more effective because of being hidden. Such media are capable, little by little, of making the best fathers hated by their children, of making white seem black, and vice versa.

Your lies, Chichikov, with their accompanying smiles and seductive compliments, could today be amplified a thousand-fold, becoming a choral lie, national, international, cosmic, making ours "the ideal time for imposters." Just as Cesbron has written.

There is more. Through the press, radio, television, people do not come into contact with events themselves, but with a version of events, interpreted by different people in different ways. And thus there is insinuated into the mind the pernicious idea that the truth can never be reached, but only opinion. "Once there were certitudes," it is said, "now we are no longer in the era of belief, but in the era of opinion."

The philosophers fan the fire. "Language," they say, "is not suited to expressing thought. Truth is relative; that is, it changes according to the times, according to people." Hence the lack of confidence on the part of many in the truth, in human reason, in the power of logic; hence people are satisfied with mere alogical and uncritical impressions, which they accept readily.

What is false for one is truth for another; truth and lie

are granted equal rights. A genuine slap in the face for human dignity and the goodness of God, who created man capable of certitudes.

If this situation were limited to natural things it would not be so bad. But it extends also to the religious and divine field.

They say: "We are all lame in the face of the truth. Once upon a time there was an authoritative teaching in the Church; now we are all seeking; this is the era of pluralism in the faith."

But the faith is not pluralist: a healthy pluralism may be allowed in theology, in the Liturgy, in other things, but never in the faith. Once it is established that God has revealed a truth, the answer is *yes*, for everyone, in every age: a *yes* with conviction and courage, without doubts or hesitations.

And the idea that the truths of the faith are only a momentary expression of the conscience and life of the Church must be rejected with every strength. These truths are always valid even if it is always possible to understand them better and to express them with new formulas, clearer and more suited to the new times.

As for authoritative teaching, it existed — within the proper limits — yesterday and it exists today. Otherwise, the Church would cease to be "apostolic" and it would no longer be true that "Jesus Christ is the same yesterday and today, and forever."

Unlike these dubious, skeptical people, you, Chichikov, remain sure in the conduct of your business; without batting an eye, you spout figures, give guarantees, remove obstacles. There are those who resemble you in their unperturbed self-confidence: those who, believing themselves struck by the wind of prophecy, point their finger and constantly denounce men and institutions.

This "prophetic denunciation" is a literary genre some propagandize within the Catholic Church. Undeniably, those who employ this genre often have the best of intentions and love the Church; the scandal caused by the denunciation is often deliberately sought. "Thunder is necessary, cannon-fire, to wake up some people," they say. Saint Paul preferred to say: "Therefore, if food is a cause of my brother's falling, I will never eat meat, lest I cause my brother to fall."

The saints, even those venerated in your Russia, like Saint Nicholas, generally proceeded along another path: they criticized themselves more than others, always afraid of offending against charity.

In the seventeenth century, Madeleine de Lamoignon, a noble, cultivated Sister of Charity, having read the satires of the poet Boileau, found them too venomous and told the author so frankly. "I will try to bear in mind your observation next time," Boileau answered, "but allow me at least to write against the Great Turk, the most bitter enemy of the Church!"

"Oh, no!" the nun replied, "he is a sovereign and must be respected for the authority he holds."

"You will allow me at least to write a satire against the devil!" Boileau smiled. "You cannot deny that he deserves it."

And the pious nun said: "The devil has already been punished enough. Let us try not to speak evil of anyone, otherwise we risk going to join him!"

Is it perhaps to avoid this risk that all have granted you complete trust, Chichikov? Others do not have your luck: they are not believed even when they tell the truth!

This was the case of that soldier who, wounded in the leg, begged the soldier next to him to take him to the first-aid post. It so happened, however, that as they were going, a cannonball shot off the head of the wounded man without his kindly helper's noticing it. So when the man reached the surgeon with his burden, he heard the surgeon say: "What can I do for a man whose head is gone?"

Only then did the second soldier look at the body and exclaim: "Nasty liar! Why, he told me he was wounded in the leg!"

The middle way should be chosen: neither blind and boundless faith in every word or action of people, nor exaggerated distrust, which for no good reason suspects all of telling lies.

Blind faith was avoided by that police inspector who had two men in overalls arrested as they were loading some lead pipe on a truck. "What made you think they were thieves and not workmen?" he was asked.

The reply: "They were working too fast to be workmen!"

But a certain doctor did not avoid exaggerated distrust when he said to a colleague: "I won't lend you the money, because I don't trust anyone. If Saint Peter himself came down from heaven to ask me for ten thousand lire, giving me the signatures of the Holy Trinity as guarantee, I wouldn't give him a cent!"

Mark Twain was also distrustful when, after boring insistence, he wrote in a tiresome young lady's album: *Never tell lies.* Then he added, after a moment's reflection: . . . *unless it's to keep in practice!*

* * *

Councillor Chichikov! Gogol writes that you did not set out to accomplish your immense fraud without first making the Sign of the Cross in the Russian way. So before beginning your lie you called on Him who came "to bear witness to the truth." He who is the truth and who said: "Let what you say be simply 'Yes,' or 'No.' " You put together truth and falsehood with inconceivable incongruence. This is the most painful aspect of your lying.

Seekers after an authentic Christian life, we will seek to do the opposite of what you did. We are for a life without pretense and deceit. Nothing personal, you understand!

January 1973

To Lemuel, King of Massa

King Lemuel and the Ideal Woman

Dear Lemuel,

The Bible mentions you as the author of the celebrated poem in praise of the ideal woman. Nothing else is known about you.

I can say, however, that you make a pair with Cornelia, the mother of the Gracchi. She, in fact, showed her children to her women friends and said: "These are my jewels!" You reverse the position and show your mother, declaring: "Her children rise up and call her blessed; her husband also, and he praises her."

Another thing is certain: that your magnificent compendiary poem is opportune and timely these days, when the improvement of woman's position represents a profoundly felt problem.

You want to hear something? The other day a little girl in the fifth grade put me in an awkward spot by stating: "Is it fair that Jesus created seven sacraments and only six of them are available to women?" She was referring, obviously, to Holy Orders to which — according to eternal tradition — only males are admitted.

LEMUEL, *king of Massa, is mentioned in the Bible, in the Book of Proverbs, chapter 31, as author of the famous poem in praise of the ideal woman. Nothing more precise is known about him; some critics, without much justification, say it is Solomon himself.*

What could I answer? After looking around, I said: "In this classroom I see boys and girls. You boys can ask: 'Is anyone among the males of the world the father of Jesus?' The boys' answer: 'No, because Saint Joseph was only the putative father.' But you girls" — I went on — "can ask: 'Was one of us women the mother of Jesus?' And the answer is: 'Yes.' " Then I said: "You are right, but think this over. If no woman can be pope or bishop or priest, this is compensated for a thousand times over by the divine maternity, which honors exceptionally both woman and motherhood."

My little protester seemed convinced.

* * *

To the magnificent praises in your poem some oppose the "crudeness" of Saint Paul, who ordered that "the women should keep silence in the churches."

I believe Saint Paul intended that prohibition to speak only for the women of Corinth and only for that given moment. It so happened, in fact, that in Corinth there was an extraordinary burgeoning of charismata and charismatics. Many, men and women, during the meetings, rose to speak or to pray, filled with the Spirit of the Lord; some women perhaps rose without true charisma, creating confusion and uneasiness. To avoid repetition of this problem, Paul decided — for that group — to stop all women from speaking.

A little earlier, in the same Epistle to the Corinthians, he had recognized that women can "prophesy," provided they do so with their heads covered.

Once, when he was in Caesarea, he went for several days with Saint Luke to the house of Philip, deacon and missionary, and made no objection to the fact that Philip's four daughters "prophesied." In his last years, finally, he urged Titus to educate elderly women, so that they would "teach what is good, and so train the young women."

For that matter, hadn't the prophet Joel solemnly announced that in the time of the Messiah both the sons and the daughters of Israel would prophesy? And hadn't Saint Peter, on the day of Pentecost, declared that the prophecy of Joel was coming true and that the Lord poured out His spirit on His servants and on His handmaidens?

Even before the coming of Christ women had not lacked the gift of prophesying: the priests had always and exclusively been male, but the mantle of prophecy had sometimes rested on women's shoulders.

Miriam, sister of Moses and Aaron, timbrel in hand, during a religious ceremony, directs, with the title of prophetess, the singing of the women and, later, she calls the people to witness that God has spoken through her. Deborah, judge at the time of Barak, is a kind of Joan of Arc, or rather a Peter the Hermit in skirts, who predicts the holy war and predicts the unfailing victory; she holds audience on Mount Ephraim, under "the palm of Deborah," and to her come "the people of Israel for judgment." The high priest Hilkiah, 621 years before Christ, by order of King Josiah, goes with other distinguished figures to consult "Huldah the prophetess . . . who dwelt in Jerusalem in the Second Quarter." And the prophetess begins speaking just as prophets do: "Thus says the Lord!" And the eighty-four-year-old widow, who encounters Jesus being taken to the Temple, then goes speaking of Him everywhere, is also called prophetess.

*   *   *

Your ideal woman is industrious, a tireless bee, a real Martha: "She girds her loins with strength and makes her arms strong"; "She rises while it is yet night"; "Her lamp does not go out at night."

And her work fills her with joy: "She seeks wool and flax, and works with willing hands"; "She perceives that her merchandise is profitable"; "She laughs at the time to come." Thus she reveals another quality: gaiety, given as a sister to goodness, to tenderness, industriousness, and love.

Her husband needs that smiling serenity when he comes home tired from work; her children need it also, for joy is the atmosphere necessary for every effective system of education. Maintaining that gaiety at all costs, even during critical times, displaying it also when uninterrupted, monotonous physical labor seems to break the back, prompting regrets and bringing tears to the eyes, is a great virtue; it is Christian fortitude; it is penance that — under certain conditions — is the equivalent of the renunciations and the prolonged prayer of sisters and nuns.

It does not, however, prevent her from seeing sharply and far: "She considers a field and buys it; with the fruit of her hand she plants a vineyard. . . . She makes linen garments and sells them; she delivers girdles to the merchant." Truly it cannot be said of her house: "house without management, ship without rudder!" And it is obvious why her husband has confidently handed her the keys of the cellar, of the closets, sure that all will go well! A husband like King Malcolm of Scotland, who, illiterate, kissed the prayer book of his wife, Saint Margaret: that book, he said, made Margaret so wise and so good!

*   *   *

Your ideal woman is also socially open-minded: "She opens her hand to the poor, and reaches out her hands to the needy"; she makes servants and maids work, but she leads them in working and never lets them want for anything; even in the case of a severe winter, she takes warm clothing from her chests so that "all of her household are clothed in scarlet."

Today, illustrious King Lemuel, justice and social charity are cultivated in another manner: our women are more often employees, dependent workers rather than mistresses. For them, now aiming at all sorts of positions in politics, administration, and labor, the words *"domi mansit, lanam fecit"* are no longer a formula of praise.

In your time a woman defended her children and family at the door of the house; today they are defended also far from the house: in the electoral booth, in unions, in other organizations. Even nuns must know how to exploit fully the new civil liberties, and women who occupy public positions must be able to do their jobs as well as men, but with that greater diligence, tact, finesse, accomplishment which are woman's qualities.

If little General Bonaparte were to say again today — as he said once, in the midst of the Reign of Terror — that he didn't like to hear women talk politics, he would find not one, but a thousand women ready to answer him with the words of Madame de Stäel: "General! The public beheads also women these days, so it is fair for women at least to ask the reason for this beheading!"

* * *

Your poem — it has been remarked — includes barely one reference to conjugal love. Certain Catholic writers today, speaking of the ideal woman, would give far more space to this subject! Your method, however, is preferable, for it is the method of Christian prudence, of which Manzoni gave a fine example.

The love of Renzo and Lucia, his engaged couple in *The Betrothed*, is pure, legitimate, virtuous, but woven with such delicacy! Lucia, in the house of Donna Prassede, avoids speaking of her own troubles, because in them "there was everywhere mingled a feeling, a word, which it seemed impossible for her to utter in speaking of herself; and for which she would never have found a paraphrase, a substitute, which would not seem immodest to her: the word love!" Lucia herself "is amazed and blushes" and feels a "confused fear" at the investigating questions of the nun Gertrude; she blushes in other situations, and her betrothed, in the hut of the *lazzaretto*, seeks her eyes in vain.

Renzo himself, the night of his escape, as he comes ashore from the boat, does give his hand to Agnese, but, out of modesty, he does not give it to Lucia. A little earlier, walking off the main road, he had offered, in the uncomfortable places, to help his fiancée, but she had avoided his help "gently and adroitly . . . feeling ashamed, even in this trouble, to have been so long alone with him, and on such familiar terms, when she had expected to become his wife a few moments afterwards."

A similar delicate prudence is found also in the novels of the Protestant Walter Scott. The fiancé of Catharine of Perth, for example, complains to his future father-in-law of his beloved's extreme reserve. "She thinks," he says, "the whole world is one great minister-church and that all who live in it should behave as if they were at an eternal mass."

The "Fair Maid of Perth" perhaps went a bit too far. But our "permissive society" exaggerates in the other direction. And greatly!

*   *   *

Your ideal woman is entirely devoted to the family; she breathes and spreads goodness. "She opens her mouth with wisdom, and the teaching of kindness is on her tongue"; "The heart of her husband trusts in her"; thanks to her, "her husband is known in the gates, when he sits among the elders of the land."

But one is reminded of Pope Sixtus V, who is supposed to have said: "Give me a woman whose husband has never complained of anything, and I will canonize her at once!" Such a woman is not only sanctified within the family, but also together with the family, as she elevates her husband and children with herself.

When I heard that a process of beatification had been proposed for the parents of Saint Thérèse de Lisieux, the Little Flower of Jesus, I said: "Finally a double sanctification! Saint Louis IX is sainted without his Marguerite, Saint Monica without her Patrick, but Zelie Guérin, on the contrary, will be a saint along with her husband, Louis Martin, and her daughter Thérèse!"

*   *   *

The ideal woman — you say this — prizes elegance, grace, comfort: "She makes herself coverings; her clothing is fine linen and purple. . . . Strength and dignity are her clothing." But you add at once: ". . . beauty is vain, but a woman who fears the Lord is to be praised."

Beauty is also a gift of God; the art of dressing with good taste and elegance is admirable, especially in women; even cosmetics in many cases are innocent. But these are passing things; to find oneself friends with God, bound to Him by a good life and sincere piety — this is a more sure and lasting thing, to be cultivated therefore along with, and more than, the other things already mentioned.

Maria Cristina of Savoy, the young, pretty, and cultivated queen of Naples, said this in a little poem of hers:

Although I am healthy, rich, beautiful . . .
    What then?
And I possess gold and silver . . . What then?
And am fortunately in a high place . . . What then?
Almost unique in wit and learning . . . What then?
Even if I were to enjoy the world for a thousand
    years . . . What then?
Soon we die and nothing remains:
Serve your God and you will have everything then!

The young queen's thought may seem somewhat melancholy. But it is invincibly true, King Lemuel!

February 1973

To Sir Walter Scott

Nostalgia for Cleanliness

Sir Walter,

How many novels did you write? In your day they had an enormous success; they are not much read today, but they delighted me when I was a boy.

Your simple, free way of writing, your gift for creating characters, your skill in setting these characters against the historical background, in the Middle Ages or in the seventeenth and eighteenth centuries, in England or on the Continent: these things thrilled me.

How many tournaments and besieged cities and castles have you described? How many knights did you send riding through heaths and forests? How many ladies did you have defended, liberated, protected by generous hearts? To how many brave artisans and poor people did you give prominent positions beside the nobles? How many wondrous and extravagant things did you describe in addition to the usual and the commonplace, with your dwarfs and astrologers, soothsaying witches, fortune-tellers and gypsies? And how many spells, mysterious messages, and horoscopes, how many complicated intrigues and how many unexpected solutions?

SIR WALTER SCOTT, Scottish writer (1771–1832). Passionate collector of the folk traditions of his country, he was the pioneer of the historical novel (e.g., Ivanhoe, The Bride of Lammermoor, Anne of Geierstein), conceived as an emotional literature of national events, but still based on serious research. He was widely imitated and, as the initiator of a new genre, had an influence on the literature of all Europe.

And all is clean: books that always extol valor and loyalty, books that can also be put into the hands of the young! This, in the face of today's flood of bad printed matter, is the thing that most amazes me and makes me say: "All honor to the Scotsman, to the father of the historical, and clean, novel!"

*   *   *

I felt a wish to reread your *Anne of Geierstein,* and here are the pages I encountered.

One of the protagonists, the brave young Arthur, is riding toward the Court of Provence in the company of Thiebault. The latter, grandson of troubadors and a lover of ballads, sings one with great grace and skill to his traveling companion.

Its gist is as follows: the troubadour William Cabestaing loves Margaret, wife of the Baron Raymond de Roussillon. The husband discovers the tryst, kills Cabestaing, rips out his heart, and has it cooked like an animal's. He serves it to his wife at the table, and when she has eaten the horrible dish, he reveals its nature to her. She, stoically tragic, says to him that the food was so precious to her that her lips "should never touch coarser nourishment." She persists in this decision and allows herself to die of starvation.

With this as the kernel of his ballad, the teller interweaves a pitying commentary, pathetically bemoaning the fate of the two lovers, hurling terrible thunderbolts only against the cruel husband, and concluding: "Every bold knight and true lover in the south of France assembled to besiege the baron's castle, stormed it by main force, left not one stone upon another, and put the tyrant himself to an ignominious death."

Your hero Arthur, having heard the story, speaks out sharply:

"Thiebault, sing me no more such lays. I have heard my father say that the readiest mode to corrupt a Christian man is to bestow upon vice the pity and the praise which are due only to virtue. Your Baron of Roussillon is a monster of cruelty; but your unfortunate lovers were not the less guilty. It is giving fair names to foul actions that those who would start at real vice are led to practice its lessons, under the disguise of virtue."

But the ballad is "a masterpiece of the joyous science," Thiebault insists. "Fie, sir, you are too young to be so strict a censor of morals. What will you do when your head is grey, if you are thus severe when it is scarcely brown?"

"A head that listens to folly in youth," Arthur replies, "will hardly be honourable in old age."

Thus a saint and Father of the Church might have spoken, but you have been, in a certain sense, more effective than the sainted Fathers!

First, because the Fathers were preachers, and preachers as a rule, perhaps wrongly, give the impression of being *against* their hearers. You, on the contrary, offering your readers entertainment and escape with your novels, appear to be in their favor; you are on their side.

Secondly, because you were clever enough to put the moral teaching on the lips of the hero, for whom the readers feel affection and unconditioned enthusiasm.

It is the age-old tactic of Horace: mix the useful with the enjoyable.

* * *

Alas, it seems today that Horace's tactic and yours have less success. In the comic books our young people read, and in the weekly picture magazines, a hero who perhaps distributes punches, slaps, and blows when he cannot avoid it, but who flies to help the weak and oppressed — on the order of your heroes — is rarely seen. More often it is the hero of evil who cuts a fine figure and is given the final victory.

In today's press gentle maidens, merry or sentimental, but chaste and reserved, at whose feet gallant knights with palpitating hearts deposit their all, can be found only with great effort. Your heroines have delicate feelings and blush often; today's female protagonists never blush; they smoke, drink, jeer: they are portrayed as a biological phenomenon, a plaything; there is no marriage, which is normally the outcome of the novel; very often these women are not only corrupt, but also cynical and bloodthirsty.

In a thriller the lover of a girl has beaten up her father, knocking him to the ground with a bleeding face. And she urges her lover on, against her father: "Again; hit him again!"

In a comic book another girl declares: "We have to steal, but from the poor. It's no fun stealing from the rich!"

You will ask me: "Why do they write these things?" I ask myself the same question and cannot find an answer. Are they perhaps trying with these paradoxically immoral remarks to protest against a society that they think is — and, in part, it really is — lying in its moralism? The trouble is that younger people, in this case, do not understand irony and caricature, and instead they gradually absorb the evil, poisoning themselves morally.

Do they perhaps, in reading, want to find an exciting escape, as a counterweight to monotonous and gray everyday life? It would be a mistaken remedy, a kind of drug, which drives them to demand ever stronger thrills, ever easier pleasures and money, instead of studying and working.

Do the publishers perhaps want to make a fortune, speculating on the fragility of the young and on our worst instincts? I fear, unfortunately, that this is chiefly the case. How foolish, then, to allow oneself to be manipulated by such venal people! The preacher said: "You are more stupid than mice. They fall into the trap, but at least they don't pay for it!" You, in your reading, fall into another trap and, what's more, you pay those who set the lure for you!

Sir Walter! In *Waverley*, the first novel you wrote, there is the following description: "A weekly post brought, in those days, to Waverley-Honour, a Weekly Intelligencer, which, after it had gratified Sir Everard's curiosity, his

sister's, and that of his aged butler, was regularly trans-
ferred from the Hall to the Rectory, from the Rectory to
Squire Stubbs's at the Grange, from the Squire to the
Baronet's steward in his neat white house on the heath,
from the steward to the bailiff, and from him through a
huge circle of honest dames and gaffers, by whose hard
and horny hands it was generally worn to pieces in about
a month after its arrival."

If you could see things now! The papers pour from the
presses every day by the ton; every morning they are un-
loaded by trains and trucks, immediately taken to kiosks
and vendors.

On the tram, going to work or to school, many
— seated or standing — have the paper unfolded in
front of them and are reading it eagerly, sometimes
unaware of what is happening beside them.

In the office, employees pass an interesting article
around, comment on it, repeat the jokes they have just
read. At the restaurant many have the plate to their right
and the newspaper to their left. At school the young ones
read it and circulate it secretly during lessons, and these
newspapers are not the cleanest.

The other day, getting off the train in Rome, I noticed
that workers got on, employees, who grabbed all the papers left on the seats of the compartments: they carried
them away, enjoying the idea of reading them later, in
comfort, at home. There is a greed for printed papers;
and tomorrow it will be worse, because the newspaper
will come into our homes, projected on a kind of tele-
screen and, self-copied, detached, it will be read then and
there.

Add to all this the radio and television today! And then
you will understand what an enormous problem has fallen on parents, educators, shepherds of souls, and public
authorities!

The problem is all the greater since people are attached
to their personal freedom and it is hardly possible today
to resort to censorship and prohibitions. Will the State

find a way to limit freedom, when it is in obvious conflict with the public weal?

Will the young accept at least indications and guides? Motorists do not take offense at road signs. None of them protests, saying that he is an intelligent and mature man, who knows everything and understands everything on his own! Why, then, not accept humbly also some moral road signs?

You were slightly upset one day. You and your lady were walking through a field in which, among a great number of sheep, some pretty little lambs were gamboling. "How beautiful they are!" you cried. And your lady said: "Yes, they are really delicious, especially when served with mint sauce!" At that moment there was a lack of understanding between you.

* * *

Honor to the Scotsman! I repeat this sincerely; but I have one little reservation, concerning some sniping here and there at the Catholic Church. This attitude is easily explained in you, a Presbyterian, obviously in good faith. That did not prevent me, as a young boy in love with my Church, from suffering some discomfort at those potshots. The good you did, however, remains; your exemplary life remains; so let the praise and the honor remain, too!

Sir Walter! I wish that all Christians, and especially the young, would listen to you in the serene regions of the spirit and the imagination, where you loved to live and let your readers live.

March 1973

To the Unknown Painter of the Castle

Four Paintings in the Old Castle

Dear unknown painter,

I have not been able to discover your name; but your four pictures, hung in that corner room of that old castle, illuminated by little Gothic windows, caught my fancy. Their artistic quality seemed scant to me; but their moral significance was persuasive and made me stop and think.

The first painting represents *childhood*. A sailboat has just left the harbor. In the middle of it a boy is sitting, looking idly at the play of the waves. He can sit there, he can be idle, because facing him, firmly at the tiller, there is an angel. Behind, at the poop, there is a dark figure, true; but he is asleep and shows no signs of waking up.

The second painting represents *adolescence*. The boy in the first painting is now a young man; standing, he casts a curious gaze from the boat toward unknown distances, where he imagines there are endless beauties. The tiller is still in the angel's hand, but the waves have grown rougher, and the dark figure is no longer asleep: his grim eyes promise no good; they are yearning for the tiller, and they herald attacks.

The third painting represents *maturity*. In the boat,

now, there is a man, struggling with all his strength against the hurricane raging in a kind of witches' sabbath; the sky is dark; the man is dark; the tiller is in the hands of the dark figure; the angel has been relegated to the background.

In the fourth painting a *old man* is seated in the boat. The storm has calmed down, the harbor is in sight, the sun gilds the waves. The angel is steering, and the dark figure is firmly in chains.

* * *

I agree with you, dear painter, that our life is a voyage, with a point of departure and one of arrival: our twentieth, fiftieth, sixtieth years are only intermediary stations between these two extremes.

But there is also this: whereas we know our precise distance from the point of departure, our distance from our destination is completely unknown. How many years still? We are acquainted with many fine people; they know all about design and mechanics, English and trigonometry; but nobody knows this little matter, this insignificant detail of the years that remain to us. The spirit feels a shudder run through it and makes a declaration: "The years may be very few, it may be only a matter of months or of days. Lord, I will not waste a minute!"

There is an even more worrying problem. Two harbors exist: Heaven and Hell. Only the first is desirable, the greatest of good fortunes. Will we arrive there? Here is the problem. All others, compared to this, are nothing. "I was rich, I was famous, I had a splendid career. All this is nothing but disaster if I do not arrive there. I mean at that first, blessed harbor!"

I agree with you that to be good one must struggle, especially in certain, more difficult moments. It is true that two opposing forces fight for the tiller, that is to say for the guidance of our life. It is true that holiness is the fruit of conquest and of victories won day by day at sword's point.

It is all true. Paul VI wrote: "We are not in conflict with weak and fragile human beings, but against . . . the cosmic dominators of this murky world, against the spirits of evil roaming through space." The Pope, just recently, reminded us of this truth.

I agree with you that a tactic must be used: the tactic of human passions. Dante describes it when, at the beginning of his journey, he finds the way barred by three wild beasts: the leopard, the lion, and the she-wolf.

The leopard, which, swift and light, shows no quarter, is sensuality: it takes advantage of everything to extinguish in us the tastes and joys of the spirit and to kindle desires that are not good. We sense it everywhere, at our heels, and it would be capable of discouraging and humiliating us, if we did not have the help and the protection of God on our side.

The lion, "its head high," represents pride, which aims, in fact, at heads, seen going off high and erect, while, below, the body swaggers, the belly, as one walks, is thrust forward. But there is no reason to be so proud.

In the time of Giuseppe Giusti there was the president of a court; he preened himself when he presided; he wore a top hat and set it on a chair during sessions. But one day somebody sat on it by mistake and the poet fired his shaft:

> They have broken a president's top hat;
> Luckily, inside it, there was nothing!

Oh, certain characters march along, top hats on their heads, even in front of God, people who know everything, nonconformists, self-sufficient folk, protesters! But what then? Underneath? What does all their knowledge amount to?

The wolf, lean and filled with desires, could be worldliness, which devours us with endless engagements: visits, examinations, competitions, business affairs, sports events, performances. We allow ourselves to be engulfed by these things as if by an abyss.

And God? And our soul? They become two minor, secondary matters, which we glimpse now and then like distant dots, to which we grant a few instants, rarely and rapidly, with a sudden and absurd reversal of values.

I agree with you that the forces of good unleash the counteroffensive with a tactic opposed to that of the wild beasts. Fortunately!

For *sensuality* the tactic of the void is valid. Yes, there are moments when God creates the void in us. We realize that certain things are unworthy of us, insufficient, they do not sate us.

This year, 1973, is the centenary of the birth of Trilussa. He once wrote:

> There is a bee which lights
> On a rosebud:
> It sucks it and flies away . . .
> All in all, happiness
> Is a small thing.

Very often, besides, it is not a question of happiness, but only of fleeting pleasure. Often, of unhappiness. One feels a kind of toothache, as a voice shouts: "Go to the dentist!"

Saint Augustine, referring to the time when he was seventeen, leading a debauched life, confesses *"rodebar, crucibar"* — I was gnawed, I was tortured in those years; that was not life, Lord! *"Talis vita, nunquid vita erat?"* Saint Camillus warned himself and others in this way: "Doing evil one feels pleasure, but the pleasure passes quickly and the evil remains; doing good costs an effort, but the effort passes quickly and the good remains!"

For *pride* one wants the Gospel, which is very clear on this point: "Put yourself in the last place"; the Lord lived among His Apostles as "one who serves"; and taught: "You ought to wash one another's feet. . . . If you know these things, blessed are you if you do them."

* * *

Friend painter, you have managed, with your paintings, to strike some response in my spirit. It was a pleasure for me.

Too bad that now a sorrow begins. What? you will ask. I will tell you in confidence: it is the suspicion that I may have irked my readers. Some will have found me romantic, ingenuous, and out of date, thinking about castles; others will have broken off their reading as soon as they caught a whiff of "moralism."

One of the many risks of my job.

April 1973

To Hippocrates

The Four Temperaments

Dear Hippocrates:

You were a contemporary of Socrates and were a philosopher yourself, as well as a physician. But you won far more merit in the field of medicine than in that of philosophy.

First merit: After having traveled halfway around the world, observing and making highly accurate notes, you wrote a whole pile of books, which stimulated medical science for many centuries.

Second merit: You are the author of the famous oath of Hippocrates, a moral code of immortal value. Physicians must swear by it to prescribe for their patients the proper diet, defending them from anything wrong or harmful; they must swear not to interrupt any pregnancy; to have the sole aim — coming into a home — of treating the sick person, abstaining from all corruption of men or women, even slaves; and to preserve professional secrecy as a sacred trust.

Third merit: You were the first to classify the four basic temperaments of human beings: *impulsive*, *phlegmatic*, *choleric*, and *melancholic*. I know that, after you, Nicola

HIPPOCRATES, *famous Greek physician (460?–377 B.C.), contemporary of Socrates. He supported the independence of medical studies from the interference of philosophy. He declared that all diseases have a natural cause. He was author of the famous classification of the four basic temperaments of man: impulsive, phlegmatic, choleric, and melancholic.*

Pende and others have suggested and attempted new, more scientific classifications, but also more complicated ones. Your classification, adapted and corrected, still stands, however, after twenty-five centuries.

* * *

But let us see the four temperaments when put to the test. And let the test be a sheer cliff face proposed for a climb.

First comes the *impulsive* climber.

He takes a glance at the cliff and says: "It's a mere nothing! I'll start at once!" And, in fact, he immediately attacks the cliff with ardor and enthusiasm. But he has foreseen virtually nothing, has not provided himself with the most elementary equipment. Soon considerable difficulties begin, in the face of which our impetuous climber realizes that enthusiasm and muscular strength are not enough.

Then he goes from great enthusiasm to the opposite extreme: "I'm giving it all up. Climbing's not for me!" Like Tartarin de Tarascon, who passes from Don Quixote-like, chivalric fury to the flat, bourgeois reasoning of Sancho Panza's style: "I am leaving," he would say, "for the Africa of lions and panthers!" But then, half an hour later: "Ah no, I'm staying, give me one good reason for going to Africa." "Cover yourself with glory, Tartarin!" But later: "Glory, my foot! Cover yourself with good flannel!" "Hurrah for African hunting! Give me those double-barreled carbines, give me daggers and *lazos* and moccasins!" A moment later: "No, give me a flannel stomach-protector, warm knee pads, and a soft cap with earmuffs! And have Jeannine come in with some chocolate!" He would ring the bell, and Jeannine would appear with the hot, dark, steaming chocolate, with cakes, which made the Tartarin-Panza laugh, stifling the tears of the Tartarin-Quixote!

This is the impulsive man: easily roused to enthusiasm, but unsteady; an optimist, when it is a matter of himself and his own capacities, but unthinking, too in-

fluenced by feeling and imagination. He has good qualities, but if he wants to achieve more in life, he must accustom himself to reflecting, to making detailed, carefully
thought-out plans, to following the advice of that bishop
who said to the new pastor: "Go, first see! Then foresee!
Then oversee!"

*   *   *

Now the *phlegmatic* man arrives at the cliff.

He looks up once, twice, many times; he makes his
calculations: "Here there must be a straight climb, then a
descent with double rope, then a climb over ice."

He consults maps, makes notes, prepares the list of objects he will need, then procures them: rope and cord,
pick and ice-hammer, pitons for rock and for ice, wooden
wedge and hammer, sleeping bag, and spiked shoes. All
this is done without wasting time, but also unhurriedly.
And as he works and prepares, he chews gum and says
to himself: "Maybe I'll make it!" Well, he really does
make it, despite all the obstacles.

This was the style of General de Gaulle, so cold and icy
from his childhood that his brothers said of him:
"Charles must have fallen into an icebox!"

During a battle, a young lieutenant, bearing a message,
looked for General de Gaulle but couldn't find him. "Go
into the fields," a driver told him. "If you don't see him
at once, look on the ground; you'll find him by following
the trail of his cigarette butts." The lieutenant did this
and reached the general, who was calmly seated under a
tree, smoking like a locomotive.   Having read the message, de Gaulle gave some orders to the officers near him
and, maintaining his calm, went on smoking, saying
only: "Things will go better now. You'll see." And so
they did.

A happy temperament, on the one hand. On the other,
however, it risks making its possessors apathetic, insen-
sitive, antisocial, uncommunicative. A bit more enthusiasm, a greater, more open interest in the problems of
others would make them more agreeable, more likable.

*   *   *

But here comes the *choleric,* or *irascible,* man.

He huffs. "Obstacles on this cliff? But obstacles are made for the express purpose of being overcome!" And he tackles the cliff with vehemence, as if facing an enemy. He doesn't spare himself, he engages all his fighting energies; often he achieves brilliant, partial results, but he does not always arrive at the summit.

The choleric man has a vivid, deep sensitivity; he is quick to decide, tenacious in executing; but he needs greater reflection and calm, he should defend himself both against enthusiasm and against excessive pessimism. To him the Abyssinian Ras Tafari would say: "It is true that you have two legs, but you can only climb one tree at a time!" If we were to heed the choleric person, however, we would try to climb an entire forest at once!

So in him, too, along with the good there is also some ballast of which he should rid himself. Among other things, the choleric man, while with his vigor he eliminates obstacles, risks creating others, gaining one enemy after another. Unless, like the choleric Xantippe, he has the good fortune to encounter only people supplied with the patience of Socrates.

The philosopher, husband of the above-mentioned Xantippe, used to say: "I married her deliberately, shrew that she is, because having become able to tolerate her, I know I am able to tolerate anyone else!" But one day, to keep from hearing her scold any longer, he left the house and sat on the doorstep. Irritated, the woman poured a bucket of water on him from a window. "I should have anticipated this," Socrates said serenely. "After so much thunder, the rain has come!"

*   *   *

The *melancholy* character, unlike the choleric, becomes depressed and underestimates himself. "Can't you see it's impossible to scale a cliff like this? You want me to break my neck?" He allows himself to be frightened by the difficulties from the very beginning, a born pessimist.

He is one of those men who, seeing a half-bottle of wine, laments: "For once in my life I feel like drinking, and I find the bottle half empty. I really am unlucky!" He should say, instead: "What! There is still half a bottle left to drink! Who would ever have imagined such plenty? I'm in luck!"

The Christian should be characterized by an effort to see things in the best light; if it is true that the word *Evangelos* means good news, then Christian means happy man, spreader of happiness. "Grim faces," Saint Philip Neri used to say, "are not made for the merry house of Paradise!"

*   *   *

As you see, illustrious Hippocrates, from biotypology I have jumped to Paradise. The fact is that we must seek to arrive there, accepting the temperament handed down to us by our parents, though improving it and trying, through our efforts, to mold it into a good character.

Up there is Saint Thomas Aquinas, a saint so phlegmatic that if an ox had entered his room, he would have gone on studying; and there is also Saint John Eudes, who felt himself boil with rage at the mere sight of a heretic. There is Francis de Sales, the well-mannered saint, an artist in speaking and in writing; and there is the Curé of Ars, a champion in administering disciplinary blows on his own back and in eating moldy potatoes cooked a week before.

And Saint Peter, the great doorkeeper, in weighing our merits, will surely bear in mind the good works we have done, but he will also have to put on the scales the difficulties, the delays, the obstacles, which derived from our more or less happy temperament! If he then adopts your classification or Pende's; if he follows the scientific characterology of Spranger or Kretschmer or Jung or Künkel; or if, instead, he follows the test of Don Cojazzi, I cannot say. This last test, not scientific but completely empirical, is perhaps unknown to you. I'll explain it at once, as I heard it told by Don Cojazzi himself.

Cojazzi said that an excellent milieu for discovering temperaments is a humble eating place. More precisely, an eating place where a thirsty gentleman, having ordered a mug of beer, sees it brought to him with a large fly struggling inside.

Is this gentleman English? Phlegmatic, he sets the mug down on the table. He calmly rings the bell and calmly orders: "Another mug of cold, and clean, beer, if you please!" Having drunk this, he pays and leaves, not at all moved or upset. If anyone is upset it is the waiter: not because of the fly but because of the tip that didn't materialize.

Is the mug of beer brought to a Frenchman? He sees the fly and blanches. He immediately sets down the mug, curses, shouting against all innkeepers and waiters, then leaves, slamming the door, still yelling about the tavern, the beer, and flies in general.

An Italian comes in, looks at the fly, flicks it away, smiling, with a little tap of his middle finger, and jokes with the waiter: "I asked for a drink, after all, and you've brought me something to eat." He downs the beer all the same, then leaves, forgetting to pay the bill!

It is the German's turn. Seeing the fly, he holds the mug up to his nose, frowns, closes his eyes, throws his head back slightly and, with great discipline, drains both beer and fly in one draught!

Now the Dane steps forward. He is highly amused by the struggling of the fly in the beer's foam; he takes out his magnifying glass and is completely absorbed by what he sees; he would even forget to drink, if the waiter, noticing the insect, did not give him a second mug of beer, with a thousand apologies, to replace the first.

The last to come is the Eskimo. He has never seen a fly; he thinks that this one, set before him, is a great delicacy, a local speciality; he eats the fly and pours away the beer.

And now, forgive me, illustrious Hippocrates. It may seem a profanation to place these trifles alongside the lofty science you represent. But what if it is useful? What if this proves that even popular common sense catches and castigates the ridiculous, which remains in a temperament not controlled and not improved?

May 1973

To Saint Thérèse de Lisieux

Joy, Exquisite Charity

Dear little Thérèse,

I was seventeen years old when I read your autobiography.

For me it was like a bolt from the blue. "Story of a little flower" you had called it. To me it seemed the story of a "steel bar" because of the willpower, the courage, and the decision that shone from it. Once you had chosen the path of complete devotion to God, nothing then could stand in your way: no illness, no external contradictions, no inner shadows or uncertainty.

I remembered this when they took me, ill, to the sanatorium, at a time when penicillin and antibiotics had not yet been invented, and so the patient had to expect death, more or less immediate.

I was ashamed at feeling a bit of fear. "Thérèse, at twenty-three, until then healthy and full of vitality," I said to myself, "was filled with joy and hope, when she felt the first access of blood rise to her mouth. And what's more, as the illness receded, she asked and was given permission to conclude her fast, on a diet of dry bread

SAINT THÉRÈSE, *the Little Flower of Jesus (1873–1897) lived a life without remarkable external events, but filled in inner riches, devotion, and love. Having entered the Carmelite convent of her native Lisieux, she died very young of consumption, offering herself up as victim to the merciful love of God. She is the author of an enchanting autobiography,* The History of a Soul, *translated into about thirty languages.*

and water. And now you tremble? You're a priest; wake up! Don't be so foolish!"

*   *   *

Rereading you, on the centenary of your birth (1973), I am impressed now by the way in which you loved God and your neighbor. Saint Augustine had written: "We go to God, not with walking but with loving." You also call your path the "way of love." Christ had said: "No one can come to me unless the Father who sent me draws him." Perfectly in line with these words, you felt yourself like "a little bird without strength and without wings"; in God, on the contrary, you saw the eagle, who came down to carry you to the heights on His own wings. You called divine grace the "elevator," which raised you to God quickly and without toil, since you were "too small to climb the harsh stairway of perfection."

I wrote above "without toil." Let there be no misunderstanding: that is true in one aspect, but in another . . . We are at the last months; your soul advances in a kind of dark tunnel, it sees nothing of what it formerly saw clearly. "Faith," you write, "is no longer a veil, but a wall!" The physical sufferings are so great that they make you say: "If I had not had faith, I would have given myself death." Nevertheless, you continue saying, with the will of the Lord whom you love: "I sing the happiness of Paradise, but without feeling joy; I sing simply that I *want to believe*." Your last words were: "My God, I love you!"

To God's compassionate love you had offered yourself as victim. All this did not prevent you from enjoying beautiful and good things: before your final illness, you painted joyously, wrote poems and little sacred plays, interpreting roles in some of them with the taste of a sensitive actress. In your last illness, during a moment of remission, you asked for some chocolate pastries. You were not afraid of your own imperfections, nor even of having sometimes dozed off in weariness during meditation

("Mothers love their children also when they are asleep!").

Loving your neighbor, you drove yourself to render little services, useful but unobserved, and to prefer, when possible, the people who irked you and had least in common with you. Behind their not very likable faces, you sought the lovable face of Christ. And this effort, this seeking, was not noticed. "Mystical as she is in chapel and at work," the mother superior wrote of you, "she is equally comical and full of fun during recreation, when she makes us split our sides laughing."

These few lines I have written are very far from containing your complete message to Christians. They suffice, all the same, to indicate some lines for us to follow.

The true love of God is espoused with decision firmly made and, when necessary, renewed.

The hesitant Aeneas of Metastasio, who says, "Meanwhile bewildered, in dire doubt, I do not leave, I do not stay," was not the stuff of which true love of God is made.

If anything, your compatriot Marshal Foch was more suited; it was he who, during the battle of the Marne, telegraphed: "Our center is giving way, left flank is withdrawing, I attack nevertheless!" A bit of combativeness and love of risk does no harm in the love of the Lord. You had it: it was no accident that you considered Joan of Arc a "sister in arms."

In *The Elixir of Love* by Donizetti, the "furtive tear" which starts in Adina's eye is enough to reassure the enamored Nemorino and make him blissful. God is not satisfied merely with furtive tears. A visible tear pleases Him insofar as it corresponds to an inner desire, an inner decision. So it is also with visible, external works: they are pleasing to the Lord only if they correspond to an inner love. Religious fasting had actually wrought havoc in the faces of the Pharisees, but Christ did not like those haggard faces, because He found that the Pharisees' hearts were far from God. You wrote: "Love must not consist of feelings but of deeds." You added, however, "God does not need our works, but only our love." Perfect!

Along with God you can love plenty of other beautiful things. On one condition: that nothing be loved against or above or to the same degree as God. In other words: the love of God must not be exclusive, but prevalent, at least in esteem.

Jacob one day fell in love with Rachel: to have her, he passed a full seven years in servitude, and the Bible says the time "seemed to him but a few days because of the love he had for her." God found nothing to reproach; on the contrary, He approved and blessed this love.

To sprinkle with holy water and bless all kinds of love in this world is another matter. Unfortunately, today some theologians try to do this, under the influence of the ideas of Freud, Kinsey, and Marcuse, as they extol the "new sexual morality." If they don't want confusion and general decay, Christians should not look to these theologians but instead to the authority of the Church, which enjoys special assistance both in preserving intact the doctrine of Christ and in adapting it suitably to modern times.

To seek the face of Christ in the face of our neighbor is the only criterion that guarantees we will really love all, overcoming dislikes, ideologies, and superficial philanthropies.

A young man — the old Archbishop Perini wrote — knocks one evening at the door of a house: he is wearing his best suit, a flower in his buttonhole, but inside him, his heart is pounding: how will his girl and her family receive the marriage proposal that he is shyly coming to make?

The girl comes to open the door in person. One glance, and the young lady's blush, her obvious pleasure (only the "furtive tear" is missing) reassures him; his heart swells. He enters, and the girl's mother is there. She seems to him a likable lady; he actually feels like giving her a hug. The father is there, too; the boy has met him a hundred times, but tonight the man seems transfigured by a special light. Later the girl's two brothers arrive: embraces, warm greetings.

Perini asks himself: What is happening in this young man? What are all these loves that have suddenly sprouted like mushrooms? The answer: These are not several loves, but a single love: he loves the girl and the love he feels for her is extended to all her relatives. Anyone who truly loves Christ cannot refuse to love mankind, for all are Christ's brothers. Even if they are ugly, bad, or boring, love must transfigure them a little.

Commonplace love. Often it is the only kind possible. I have never had an opportunity to throw myself into the waters of a rushing stream to save someone whose life was in danger; very often I have been asked to lend something, to write letters, to give simple little directions. I have never run into a mad dog in the street; on the other hand, I have encountered any number of tiresome flies and mosquitoes; I have never had persecutors who beat me, but many people disturb me by speaking loudly in the street, by turning up the volume of their television sets, or even by making certain noises while eating soup.

To help others as best you can, to avoid losing your temper, to be understanding, to keep calm and smiling on these occasions (as much as possible!) is loving your neighbor, without fancy talk, but in a practical way. Christ practiced this charity constantly. How much patience He had in putting up with the quarrels among the Apostles! How much attention in encouraging and praising: "Not even in Israel have I found such faith," He says of the centurion, and of the woman of Canaan. You have stayed with me even in the difficult moments, He says to the Apostles. And once He asks Peter please to lend Him his boat.

"Lord of every courtesy," Dante calls Him. Christ

knew how to put Himself into others' shoes; He suffered with them. He did not only forgive sinners, but also protected and defended them: He did this with Zaccheus, with the woman taken in adultery, with the Magdalene.

You, in Lisieux, followed His examples; we should do the same in the world.

Carnegie tells about a lady who one day prepared for her menfolk — husband and sons — a nicely laid table, but with a handful of hay on each plate. "What's this? You're giving us hay for dinner today?" they asked her.

"Oh, no," she answered, "I'll serve the dinner at once. But let me tell you something. For years I have cooked for you, I've tried to vary the meals: rice one day, broth another, roast, stew, etc. And you never say: 'We like it,' 'Good for you!' Please say something. I'm not made of stone. Nobody can work without recognition, without encouragement."

Public or social charity can also be ordinary. A justified strike is in progress: it may cause me some discomfort, as I am not directly concerned with the dispute. To accept this discomfort, not grumbling, to feel solidarity with brothers fighting to defend their rights, is also Christian charity. Not much noticed, but no less precious for that.

Joy is mingled with Christian love. It appears already in the song of the angels in Bethlehem. It is a part of the essence of the Gospel, which is "good news." It is characteristic of the great saints: "A sad saint," Saint Teresa of Avila said, "is a poor saint." "Here in our midst," Saint Dominic Savio said, "saints are made joyfully."

Joy can become exquisite charity, if communicated to others, as you used to do at Mt. Carmel during recreation.

There's a story about an Irishman who, having died suddenly, approached the divine tribunal and was considerably worried: the balance sheet of his life looked fairly poor to him. There was a line waiting in front of him, so he watched and listened. After having consulted the great ledger, Christ said to the first in line: "I see that I was hungry, and you gave me something to eat. Good for you! Step into Paradise!" To the second: "I was thirsty and you gave me something to drink." To the third: "I was in prison and you visited me." And so on.

As each one was sent into Paradise, the Irishman made an examination of his conscience and found cause to fear: he had never given anything to eat or to drink, he had never visited the sick or the imprisoned. His turn came, and he was trembling as he looked at Christ examining the ledger. But now Christ raises His eyes and says to him: "There's not much written here. However, you also did something: I was sad, dejected, humiliated: you came, you told me some jokes, made me laugh, and restored my courage. Paradise!"

This is a joke, I agree, but it underlines the fact that no form of charity should be neglected or underestimated.

* * *

Thérèse, the love you bore God (and your neighbor, out of love of God) was truly worthy of Him. So our love must be: a flame that is fed on everything great and beautiful in us, that renounces everything rebellious in us; a victory that takes us on its own wings and carries us, as a gift, to the feet of God.

June 1973

To Alessandro Manzoni

The Only Aristocracy

Dear Don Lisander,

When you died, a century ago, your friends, who had quickly gathered in the room of your death, said in chorus: "Today a new saint has gone up to Heaven."

Later, when the cause of your sainthood was officially opened by the Church, the ingenuous, greathearted Antonio Cojazzi wrote and fought for it. There was some exaggeration.

In the opposite direction, Maria Luisa Astaldi and others, in novelized and desecrating pages, have also exaggerated, presenting you with great superficiality as a man suffering from a hereditary disease, an incurable neurotic, torn by racking, haunting doubts about the faith.

The truth is something else. Though conditioned by some complexes, by your temperament and by painful family events, you were a sincere, convinced, and great Catholic. Even as an old man, you went every day to the altar to receive the Eucharist.

The nature of your life can be glimpsed through the wholly evangelical thoughts that fill your writings. These,

ALESSANDRO MANZONI (1785–1873), great writer and convinced Catholic. He wrote the most important novel in Italian literature, I promessi sposi (The Betrothed), as well as numerous collections of poems: the Inni Sacri (Sacred Hymns), the odes Marzo 1821 (March 1821) and Cinque Maggio (The fifth of May), the tragedy Adelchi. Born an aristocrat, he recognized a sole aristocracy: the service of the poor.

for example: "Life is not meant to be a burden for many and a holiday for some, but a job for all, of which each will render an account"; "Misfortune is not suffering and poverty; misfortune is doing evil"; "The mere idea of causing dispute saddens me"; "God never disturbs the joy of His children unless it is to prepare for them a greater and more certain joy."

Wherever your pen lighted, it struck sparks of religious faith, and this could not have happened if the mind and heart that guided your hand in writing had not been filled with religion. *The Betrothed* is evidence of this from beginning to end; it is, in fact, symptomatic that of it, a novel, a love story, Ludovico da Casoria, a saintly monk, could say: "It is a book which could be read in a choir of virgins presided over by the Madonna."

* * *

A "story of poor people," your novel. The chief setting is poor: the mountains, the countryside, the lake. And the protagonists are poor: Renzo and Lucia, two good young people, who ask only to love each other. Renzo has prepared a nest for the girl he loves; and she, in her turn, passing that nest, often steals a glance at it, not without blushing, enjoying the anticipation of a happy, perpetual home as a wife. Over that nest then the storm comes, which separates and scatters the engaged couple. "But the Lord knows I exist!" Lucia says at the most difficult moment. "Whatever God wills!" says Renzo, though without renouncing a bold and just reaction.

Around this couple there are other people, equally simple and honest. The illiterate but experienced Agnese, who firmly advises: "This is the best way to act." "But isn't it wrong to force the pastor into performing a surprise marriage?" Lucia objects. "It's like giving a Christian a slap," Agnese answers. "It isn't a good thing, but once you've given it to him, not even the Pope can take it away from him."

And, along with Agnese, there are many, many others: a pusillanimous pastor, egoistic and timid, who is concerned only for his own skin; Perpetua, the housekeeper and boss, who gives good "opinions" to the pastor; the sacristan Ambrogio; a very practical taverner; "Paolin dei morti," the grave-digger; "a certain Tonio" with his simple-minded brother Gervasio and Gervasio's wife; the thin girl who fights the thin cow for some grass; Bettina, the little child who cries happily, "The bridegroom, the bridegroom!"; Menico, a boy very good at playing ducks and drakes; and the consul of the village.

But who knocks at the door and says: *"Deo gratias"*? It is Fra Galdino, who, with his sack hanging from his left shoulder, comes looking for walnuts, and as he chats, tells of a great miracle that has taken place down in Romagna, in a convent.

And who is this other Capuchin, who looks in at Agnese's door and stands erect on the threshold? "A monk," Renzo says, "a hair of whose beard — no offense — is worth more than all of yours," an open enemy of tyrants in word and, where possible, in deed. This is Fra Cristoforo, Lucia's spiritual father, who has tempered her conscience, turning a poor peasant girl, alone in the world except for her mother, into a pure and strong woman, full of faith and of hope.

* * *

All these characters move about in the village. But within and beyond the village you created a total of two hundred and fifty-five characters, all drawn from life, perhaps with only a few words, like the woman who was "a pot with two handles," like the fat man standing at the door of his shop and looking as if he wanted to ask questions more than give answers, like the trumpeter of Don Gonzalo. Like Don Pedro, Ferrer's coachman, who in the midst of the rioting crowd smiles at the multitude with ineffable grace, praying mellifluously: "If you please . . . a bit of room"; once the people have thinned out, however, he regains his former heart, puts aside all ceremony, gaily lashes the horses, and shouts: "Hey, hey!"

But what about the great of this world? In your novel

you also admit them, but in the service of the humble or else opposed to the humble in such a way as to make the latter come off best.

An aristocrat by birth, you allow a sole aristocracy: the service of the poor. For you "there is no superiority of one man over other men except in their service."

Cardinal Federigo, Fra Cristoforo, the converted Unnamed, the marquess heir of Don Rodrigo, the well-to-do merchant's wife all belong to the aristocracy of souls, because they concern themselves with the sufferings of the poor. The other characters of high degree, especially the violent and the bullies, do not please you, and how clear you make it! "They are those who are always right." "They are of Adam's rib." They send their younger sons to the monastery in order to leave their wealth intact to the firstborn, "destined to procreate sons to torment him and for him to torment." Don Rodrigo is a bully; he doesn't fear God, but fears the world and the contempt of the countryfolk among whom he lives; he is capable of insulting a poor monk and driving him from his house, but he is filled with fear in the face of the Order ("Did you want me to turn all the Capuchins of Italy against me?").

Of the prince, who forces his daughter to become a nun, you say: "Our heart cannot bear to give him the title of father." Branded, without indulgence, is the Uncle Count of the secret council, vainglorious and hypocritical ("an ambiguous way of speaking, a meaningful silence, a habit of saying things halfway, a narrowing of the eyes, holding out hope without promising"). Branded also is Count Attilio, great supporter of the methodology of beatings to be inflicted both on the bearers of challenges ("a club doesn't dirty anyone's hands") and on Capuchin monks ("you must learn how to redouble your politeness in a timely way to a whole body, and then you can freely give a good beating to one member of it"). Branded also is Doctor Hairsplitter ("that doctor of lost causes"), a calculating opportunist, "player of the shell game," that is to say charlatan, a puppet in the hand of the mighty and an ally in the outrages they plot against the poor.

* * *

To tell the whole truth, you like no violence, not even that attempted by the poor when they are unjustly downtrodden. Renzo, determined to take justice into his own hands, exclaims: "In this world there is justice at last," a sentence which you roughly destroy with this comment: "The fact is that a man overcome with grief no longer knows what he is saying."

And instead of violence what do you advise against violence? Forgiveness. Forgiveness is what Fra Cristoforo asks of the brother of the man he has killed, and for all the rest of his life he preaches forgiveness. He keeps in his purse the famous "bread of forgiveness," which, before dying, he gives, as a bequest, to Renzo and Lucia with these words: "Show it to your children . . . tell them to forgive always, always! everything, everything!"

A year before, to a distraught and angry Renzo, he had said: "I, too, have hated . . . the man, whom I hated cordially, whom I hated for a long time . . . I killed. Do you believe that if there had been a good reason I wouldn't have found it, in thirty years? Ah, if I could now put into your heart the feeling that, since then, I have had always . . . for the man I hated!"

The lesson is not in vain. Renzo grants forgiveness to Don Rodrigo: a forgiveness marked by recurrences of anger and upsurges of vengefulness in the flight from Monza to Milan, in which "he had killed Don Rodrigo in his heart, and resuscitated him, at least twenty times"; a forgiveness "really from the heart" after the renewed reproaches of Fra Cristoforo in the *lazzaretto;* a forgiveness repeated in Lucia's hut and again at the announcement of Don Rodrigo's death, always with this modifier: "from the heart, from the heart."

* * *

Another nonviolent feeling pervades your whole novel: trust in Providence.

Lucia, bidding farewell to her mountains, weeps in the bottom of the boat, but the last thought that dwells in her spirit is this: "God, who already gave so much joyfulness, is everywhere." Opposed to a surprise marriage, she had said: ". . . let us go on with faith, and God will help us . . . let us leave things to Him above. Do you think He won't know how to find the way to help us, better than we can do ourselves, with all these sly tricks?"

Renzo, in the woods, "before lying down on that bed that Providence had prepared for him, knelt to say thanks for that gift and for all the help he had received during that terrible day." Then, when he has closed his eyes, his thoughts teem tumultuously in his mind, but this last thought finally predominates: "God knows what He is doing: He exists also for us. Let everything be considered penance for my sins. Lucia is so good! He would not want her to suffer for a long, long, long time!"

Still half-overcome and distraught after the chase and the leap, with which he saved himself, from the wagon of the *monatti,* the dread burial squad, he "meanwhile thanked Providence in his heart as best he could for having escaped such a situation, without receiving evil or doing any."

And he always remains in this atmosphere of faith. "There Providence is seen!" he says, before stripping himself of his last coins, to give to the poor at the gates of Bergamo. "I said myself there was Providence!" he exclaims when his cousin Bortolo assures him help. "I must thank the Madonna as long as I live!" he says to his friend, returning from the *lazzaretto.*

And in the end, seeking with Lucia, he finds the kernel of the whole story and sums it up in this way: troubles, "when they come, whether through our fault or not, can be lightened by faith in God, which turns them to our own improvement."

In this, he agrees with Cardinal Federigo: "Do what you can: work, help one another, and then be content."

He also agrees, dear Don Lisander, with all true followers of the Gospel.

July 1973

To Casella, Musician

The Music of Reconciliation

Dear musician and friend of Dante,

What you told Dante on the slopes of the mountain of Purgatory is about to be renewed. Seeing you land on the shore of the vestibule of Purgatory, at Easter of 1300, Dante was greatly amazed: "My friend Casella, you've been dead for some time; how is it that you are still here, not yet admitted to that Purgatory to which you too have been assigned?"

And you said: "It's a long story. I must tell you that the souls to be purged, as soon as they leave the body, all gather in a kind of station, a 'Pre-Purgatory,' at Ostia, at the mouth of the Tiber. There, a boatman-angel lands with his boat and loads aboard those he likes, when he likes, in accord with the decrees of God. I presented myself to him a number of times, but in vain. Luckily, for the past three months — that is, since Pope Boniface VIII proclaimed the Jubilee — the angel takes on board all those who want to come; it is a stroke of luck, a period of generosity and great compassion; I also took advantage of it, and here I am."

CASELLA, a dear friend of Dante. Born perhaps in Pistoia, he was a gifted composer and performer of music. He set to music some sonnets and songs by Dante, including "Amor che nella mente mi ragiona" (Love, which reasons in my mind). Little is known about his life and his death. Dante encounters him outside Purgatory, as he is about to be ferried there: it was the spring of 1300 and Pope Boniface had announced the Jubilee a short time earlier.

* * *

In the place of Pope Boniface today there is Pope Paul.

He too, dear Casella, has proclaimed a Jubilee, though in conditions somewhat different from those of 1300. Your Pope Boniface had a fairly uncertain tradition behind him; he had, true, heard other Jubilees in the past spoken of, but the investigations that he prompted on this subject had not turned up much.

An old Savoyard, aged one hundred and seven, recounted that, as a seven-year-old boy, he had come to Rome in 1200 with his father, and that his father made the son promise to return to the eternal city, to benefit by the exceptional indulgences, if he were still alive in a hundred years' time(!). Two other old men of Beauvais said that, a century earlier, a plenary indulgence had been granted.

Tradition or no, Pope Boniface, responding to the desire of many, signed his famous Bull and there was a sensational Jubilee: all Europe, in the year 1300, seemed to gather in Rome.

They came there in crowds, on foot, on horseback, dragging the old and the ill in wagons. The basilicas of Saint Peter and Saint Paul remained open night and day. The cardinals themselves, early in the morning, made the thirty visits prescribed for the regular inhabitants of Rome; young girls — who in those days remained always shut up in the house — made the visits at night, under secure escort.

Among the illustrious pilgrims, dear Casella, there were your fellow-Tuscans Dante, Giotto, and Giovanni Villani. This last-named was inspired by the pilgrimage — as he himself tells us — to write the history of his Florence, and he went home with his imagination filled with the spectacles he had witnessed in Rome. "It was," he writes, "the most wondrous thing ever seen, as continuously, throughout the whole year, there were seen in Rome, besides the city's population, two hundred thousand pilgrims, not to mention those who were on the roads, coming and going; and all horses and persons were supplied and rightly content with victuals, and with great patience and without uproar or quarrel; and I can testify as I was present and saw it. And from the offerings made by the pilgrims the Church acquired great treasure, and the Romans, through their provisions, became rich."

Unlike Boniface VIII, Paul VI now has behind him a long "Jubilee tradition." The term set by Boniface and fixed in the motto *"Annus centenus — Romae semper est jubilenus"* (in Rome the hundredth year is always a Jubilee) was soon changed: a Jubilee every fifty years, then every twenty-five, so that anyone who chose could, at least once in his lifetime, take advantage of this great grace.

And gradually, as the centuries progressed, the means of transport also progressed and so did the number of pilgrims: trains, automobiles, airplanes brought to Rome far more than the thousands of pilgrims of 1300.

Still — can you believe it? — even in the Jubilee of 1950 there were a good ten thousand individual pilgrims who came to Rome on foot, by bicycle, on horseback, in canoe, in wheelchairs, in dogcarts, or on stretchers fitted with wheels.

Silvio Negro mentions the young Kurt Herming Drake, a Finnish student, who left Helsinki in July and reached Rome in November. Baron Fritz von Gumpenberg, aged twenty-nine, almost blind, came alone, on foot, from his castle at Poltmes, near Munich, and he also returned there on foot, going by way of Padua, out of his devotion to Saint Anthony.

For this Jubilee Pius XII had set a theme: *"Gran perdono — gran ritorno"* (great pardon — great return). Paul VI, for his part, launches the Jubilee with the motto: "Reconciliation!" Reconciliation between us and God, between us and our brothers, on the personal level and on the social level.

A theme, a motto, which is like music and which you, Casella, if you were here, would sing sweetly, as you sang to Dante, who preserved of your singing a nostalgic memory that made him say: "The sweetness still sounds within me."

*   *   *

True music is reconciliation with God, as we abandon the twisted, broad, and spacious road that leads to perdition. On this road all the human passions gallop by, riding those horses of the Apocalypse that are called desire and greed, never sated with pleasures, money, honors. He who walks on this road cannot be well.

The great Tolstoy wrote of a horse which, halfway down a slope, rebelled and reared up, saying: "I'm tired of pulling the carriage and of obeying the driver. I'm stopping!" He was quite free to do so, but it was to cost him dearly. From that moment on, in fact, all turned against him: the driver whipped him, the coach slammed into his legs, the passengers in the coach yelled and cursed.

So it goes. When we take the wrong road and rebel against God, we overturn order; we break the pact of alliance with the Lord; we renounce His love; we become irritated with ourselves, discontent with what we have done, gnawed by remorse.

Dear Casella, it's true that some say music is sung and played quite well also on the wrong road, and they indignantly reject Tolstoy's anecdote, declaring that in sin they feel freer than ever. I must take the liberty of contradicting, with only two words: "master" and "illness."

Yes, sin becomes, willy-nilly, the master of the sinner. Perhaps at first it pays him compliments and caresses him, but the sinner remains its slave and sooner or later will get a taste of the whip.

As for "illness," there are two kinds: latent and evident. A living, aching wound hurts, but at least we know it exists and we try to heal it. But imagine, on the other hand, a hidden tumor; it grows large, spreads; you don't know this, you deceive yourself and assure your friends you are fine. Suddenly: metastasis, the irreparable. This is the situation of one laden with sins who insists he doesn't have them and doesn't feel them. Instead, to have one's own burden of sins, but to feel its weight, to decide seriously to change one's road, really to turn over a new leaf, really to fling oneself into God's arms: what music that is, Casella!

* * *

Music is also our reconciliation with our brothers.

In your time there were the struggles between Guelphs and Ghibellines, between Whites and Blacks, between Montagues and Capulets, Monaldis and Filippeschis, and I don't know how many other factions. Your friend Dante, dejected and embittered, wrote:

> Come and see Montagues and Capulets,
> Monaldis and Filippeschis . . .
> Come and see how much people love one another!
> For the cities of Italy are all full
> Of tyrants, and every peasant who takes sides
> Becomes a Marcellus.

Today, my dear Casella, the same thing happens: tyrants apart, we see blocs opposing other blocs, nations against nations, parties against parties, currents against currents, individuals against individuals.

Often we read of assassinations, of hijacked airplanes, of banks attacked, bombs deliberately thrown to slaughter the helpless and the innocent. Hotbeds of disorder spring up more or less everywhere; the revolution is proclaimed as the only remedy to the evils of society and the young are educated in violence.

In the midst of all this anarchic and senseless confusion, reconciliation truly established among men would be the most desired and necessary music. The Jubilee wants to bring a strong contribution to it with this dynamic: "Reconcile yourselves first with God, renewing your hearts, putting love where there is hate, serenity where there is wrath, moderate and honest desires where there is unrestrained greed.

"Once renewed and changed within, look outside with a new eye and you will find a different world."

*   *   *

It is curious, in fact, dear Casella, how the same world, with the very same things, with the same places and with the same inhabitants, can become completely different only if, with reconciliation, we introduce into it love and peace, which formerly were missing.

We are told this by the story of that Korean general who you, an expert in harmonies, will understand very well. Dead and judged, he had been assigned to Paradise, but turning up in front of Saint Peter, he felt a wish and he expressed it: to take a peep first, for a few minutes, into Hell, just an instant, to have an idea of that sad place.

"Granted!" replied Saint Peter.

He peered in then at the gate of Hell and saw an immense room with many long tables. On these were so many bowls of cooked rice, properly spiced, aromatic, inviting. The diners were all seated there, filled with hunger, two at each bowl, one facing the other. But then what? To carry the rice to their mouth they had — in Oriental fashion — a pair of chopsticks, but so long that, no matter how great their efforts, not a grain of rice could reach the mouth. This was their punishment, this was Hell. "I've seen enough!" the general said, and went back to the gate of Paradise and entered.

The same room, the same tables, same rice, same long chopsticks, but here the people were happy, smiling and eating. Why? Because each, having picked up the food with the chopsticks, raised it to the mouth of the companion facing him, and all managed splendidly.

Thinking of others instead of oneself resolved the problem, transformed Hell into Heaven.

A true fairy tale, dear Casella. Rather than thinking of *being well*, Manzoni used to say, we should think of *doing well*, for then everybody would be better!

September 1973

To Luigi Cornaro

We're Old;
Are We Falling Apart?

Dear supernonagenerian of Venice,

Why am I writing you? Because you are a likable Venetian of four hundred years ago. Because, with a little book — widely read thanks to its delightful ingenuousness — you made propaganda for the sober life. And, above all, because you were a model of serene old age.

Until you were forty you suffered from "very cold and very damp" stomach, a "pain in the side," "incipient gout," and a hundred other ailments. One fine day you threw away all your medicines. You discovered that "he who wishes to eat much should eat little," and you devoted yourself to sobriety.

Having regained your health, you could thus devote yourself to study, to "holy agriculture," to hydraulics, to land reclamation, to patronage of the arts, to architecture. Always filled with good humor, you looked well, kept writing, and, between the ages of eighty and ninety,

LUIGI (ALVISE) CORNARO (1475–1566), a singular figure in the Venetian world of the sixteenth century. He died at the advanced age of ninety-one, his long life presumably due to the methods of treatment that he invented and described in a work: Discourses on the Sober and Temperate Life. *These discourses still persuade the elderly that their life can be serene and usefully employed. Cornaro was also a good architect.*

completed your *Discourses on the Sober and Temperate Life,* meant to instill courage and to convince others that even for us elderly folk life can be serene and usefully employed.

In your time not many people could reach old age. Very few norms of hygiene were known; there was not the comfort and the ease of today; certain diseases had not been virtually extirpated, as they have been now; our surgery, with its powerful means and prodigious results, did not exist; people did not reach an average of seventy years of life, as they now do in some countries.

Today we old people are advancing in number all along the line.

In Italy those of us who are sixty or over represent almost a fifth of the whole population. They call us those of the "third age." Just counting our numbers should give us courage.

And instead? Instead we allow ourselves at times to be seized with dismay. It seems to us that we have been set aside, like wheels now worn out, like bicycle racers left behind by the group. If we retire, if our children marry and go to live elsewhere, we feel the affective emptiness beneath our feet and don't know where to cling. When the ailments come, and the signs of physical decline, we are alarmed. Instead of thinking especially of the happy things that God still grants us, we give way to the melancholy of the Venetian saying, which you never took for your motto: *"We are old; we are falling apart . . . this is our disease!"*

The phenomenon becomes worse if, after the age of sixty, we have to leave the home that was ours, with which we had identified ourselves, to become the residents of a "rest home." Many adapt themselves and get on well there; but some feel like a fish out of water. "They don't let me want for anything," a man said to me. "It could be the vestibule of Heaven, but for me it's Purgatory in advance!"

* * *

The problems of the old are more complicated today than in your time and, perhaps, more profoundly human; but the chief remedy, dear Cornaro, still remains yours: to react against all pessimism or egoism. "Perhaps I have whole decades of life still left: I shall use them to make up for lost time, to help others; I want to make the life that remains to me a great fire of love for God and my neighbor.

"Is my strength scant? I can still pray at least. I am a Christian, I believe in the effectiveness of the prayers that cloistered nuns raise to God in their convents, I also believe with Donoso Cortés that the world has a greater need for prayers than for battles. Well, even we old people, offering God our sufferings and bearing them serenely, can have a great effect on the problems of the men who are struggling in the world."

This is one thing. If then we still have energy and time available, there is something else that can be said. Namely: Why not devote ourselves to good works? In certain parishes retired schoolteachers and elderly employees represent a very precious help.

In France, to avoid being excluded from life, the elderly have actually organized themselves. "On all sides," they said to one another, "spontaneous groups of the young are springing up. Let's make some spontaneous groups of us elderly!" A really considerable movement then developed, which has a bishop as its adviser, which promotes the friendship and the spirituality of its members, assistance and apostolate among other old people, which rescues many of them from isolation and discouragement, and which sometimes causes unsuspected, dormant energies to burst out.

You, in fact, are not the only one to have written books after the age of eighty, dear Cornaro. Goethe completed his *Faust* at eighty-one. Titian painted a self-portrait after ninety. For that matter, we are always old for those who come after us; for those, on the contrary, who age along with us, we are always young! And moreover, with a hint of maliciousness, we might say that the calculation of our years is done in rather an accordion style. When Gounod — at forty — composed his *Faust*, they asked him: "Just exactly what age should your Faust have in the first act?" "Why," Gounod answered, "the normal age of an old man: sixty." Twenty years later, when Gounod himself was sixty, he was asked the same question and he innocently replied: "Why, Faust should have the normal age of an old man: eighty!"

* * *

At this point it is easy for me to make a prophecy. And here it is: this letter written to you, but meant to be read by others, will not interest my young readers, who will say in irritation: "It's stuff for the old!"

But won't they also become old? And if there really exists an art, a methodology for being "good old folks," wouldn't it be best for them to learn it in time? When I was a young student it so happened that the instructor in canon law, reaching the canons of the Codex which explain the duties of cardinals, patriarchs, and bishops, said: "These are rather exceptional things, we'll skip them; if one of you by any chance should reach such an office, you can study this on your own!" And so it was that, becoming bishop and patriarch, I had to start from zero.

Now, if few young theologians become cardinals, almost all the young people of today, on the other hand, will eventually reach old age, with the duty of learning on their way the secrets of life and preserving them. Is one man, at the springlike age of twenty, twenty percent a grumbler? At sixty it is sure that he will grumble to a degree of seventy percent, if he doesn't correct himself. It is best for him to sweeten his character in time.

Further, it is not a bad idea for the young to know that, besides their own problems, there are the delicate problems suffered by others, with whom they live side by side. To Timothy, a young bishop, Saint Paul urged: "Do not rebuke an older man but exhort him as you would a father."

It is nevertheless true that, in writing, I have thought chiefly of us elderly people, for we need understanding and encouragement. In line — dear nobleman Cornaro — with what you wrote. And in line with what the editor of a daily newspaper used to recommend to his contributors: "Write often something for the elderly! If you come across some case of longevity (for example, a man who is approaching the age of a hundred with a fully lucid mind and youthful vigor), don't let this good news escape you; print it, give it space in your column. There is an audience of old people who will enjoy it and who will cry: Here's a well-informed paper!"

How pleased I will also be if people say: "How well-informed *The Messenger of Saint Anthony* is!"*

October 1973

Translator's note: This letter, like the others, first appeared in *Il Messaggero di Sant'Antonio,* a magazine published in Padua.

To Aldus Manutius

From the Times of the "Rialto Hunchback"

Illustrious humanist and printer,

I have just come back from a visit to the exhibition "Venice, city of books." I was shown some very interesting things, but I lingered with special pleasure at the case containing books from your very celebrated printing shop at the beginning of the sixteenth century.

I admired once again your typefaces, neat, clear, slanting to the right. I saw again your coat of arms with the anchor, the dolphin, and the motto *"festina lente"* (make haste slowly).

In sixteenth-century Venice, between the Rialto and St. Mark's there were five hundred printers' establishments and bookshops, but yours surpassed them all. Working out of love of culture and art, you died almost in poverty, while your colleagues enjoyed success. I think, for example, of Nicholas Jenson, of whom Marin Sanudo wrote that he "earned much money with printing."

I was sorry to see, side by side, a book of yours and a book "pirated" by the Florentine printer Giunta, who, in

ALDUS MANUTIUS, printer and publisher (1450–1515), born at Bassiano, in the province of Velletri. In 1494 he founded in Venice a press that then became famous for the elegance of the typefaces he invented, called "italic" or "Aldine," and the philological care that marked his editions of the classics.

Lyons, copied your work crudely, causing you harm with his plagiarism and dishonest competition. Even when one is examining books of four hundred years ago, shifty dealings and a deplorable hunger for gold spring immediately to one's notice.

We note also the tendencies of readers of the past. In fact, as I went on to visit the eighteenth-century books of another celebrated printer, Remondini, the guide explained to me: this printer issued a translation of *Gil Blas*, the novel by Lesage, which sold out in a flash; he printed the *New Flower of Virtue* and the *Day of the Christian*, and the booksellers wrote him, "Nobody wants them."

It's like being in the twentieth century! It is really true that humans, Christians, have a hard time changing!

*   *   *

Dear Manutius, I would pay ready money to see you in a modern printer's shop.

Your press used to print three hundred sheets in a day; now our rotary presses turn out tens of thousand of newspapers in an hour. In your time books were so precious that they were chained to the shelves; only a few people could purchase them; popes threatened with excommunication those who dared steal them.

Today, newspapers, once read, are disposed of by the ton. In America some young readers don't bother to keep books: they buy them and, as they read, they tear out the pages and throw them away; when they come to the end, all that is left of the book is the cover, until that, too, is discarded.

You will say: "Those must then be books of scant worth!" My answer is: There are some with worthwhile contents, others that are empty; some are dreadful, and beside them the *Polifili* which you printed — the most beautifully produced book in the world — seems a book of prayers for nuns.

Humanist that you are, you will surely recall the third chapter of Book VIII of Plato's *Republic*. In it are listed the signs of democratic decadence: rulers are tolerated by their subjects only on condition that the worst excesses be authorized; those who obey the law are called stupid; fathers are afraid to correct their children; children insult their parents ("in order to be free," Plato writes ironically); the teacher is afraid of the pupil and the pupil despises the teacher; the young act as if they were old, and the old tell jokes to imitate the young. Women dress like men, and so on — you know the chapter.

Well, in certain books of ours, the things Plato wrote, as an ironic reproach, are written in earnest, at times actually as theological theses.

Are the young impatient to develop their sexual life? It is affirmed that chastity is a repression, favorable to capitalism, an out-of-date medieval practice, and it is time to bring about the "sexual revolution."

In a woman's body is a new life burgeoning, "thanks to bad luck"? After a fine theological distinction between "human life" and "humanized life," it is stated that human, but not yet humanized, life can be cut off without any scruple.

Are children disobedient? Well then, let parents stop giving orders and tormenting the little creatures! Do pupils no longer learn their lessons at school? The answer is simple: do away with lessons; the schooling that society imparts is enough, without the intervention of teachers, because it is not so much a matter of learning subjects as of having young people debate social problems.

Are the students annoyed at their grades and their standing in class? Abolish grades: they represent discrimination, and are unworthy of an egalitarian society. Does somebody want to practice medicine? Who will prevent him, if he has been enrolled — with or without exams, with or without studying—for six years at the university?

I will omit some other splendid declarations that would make a humanist's hair stand on end.

But I wish you could see the newspapers, the magazines, things that in your time existed only in a rudimentary state. There existed, and, in fact, there still exists, in Campiello San Giacometo, the "Rialto Hunchback," the statue of a dwarf, to which fugitive sheets of paper were attached, full of quips and bits of news, which people went to read with curiosity. A miniature newspaper with minicirculation!

If you could see, today, the processions that line up at the newsstands. If you could read some of the illustrated weeklies, at times filled with indecencies. And if you were to become accustomed to reading the daily papers, you would see how far we have come since the days of the "Rialto Hunchback!" No fugitive sheets now: the news pours out in avalanches on people every day, never keeping them waiting.

The Republic of Venice used to boast that, in the space of three months, it could know all the events of the Mediterranean. We see the astronauts, from the distance of a few feet, at the very moment they land on the moon.

Unfortunately the news almost swamps us with its frequency and abundance. It doesn't give us time to reflect: we are so constantly amazed that gradually we lose our capacity for being surprised at anything, and we don't enjoy even beautiful things.

We also have to consider the pressures. Try to form an idea of them. In America there are university courses in advertising; they teach how to exploit the psychology of consumers, acting directly on the nervous system of the individual and on his inferiority complexes, until he is faced by the following dilemma: either I purchase such-and-such product, or I am doomed irrevocably to unhappiness.

In a magazine, for example, they show you the likable young Rachel. She is beautiful and attractive, but at parties nobody invites her to dance. Why not? She finds this out for herself, accidentally overhearing a conversation: "Rachel should see a dentist about her breath!" And the dentist, immediately consulted, decrees: "Your problem isn't serious, young lady. Just switch to such-and-such toothpaste." Rachel uses it, and here she is happy again, sought after, admired! The case is typical of the consumer society: it concerns advertising, but I could cite other examples taken from politics, from trade unions, where ideological propaganda and hidden persuasion also operate.

*   *   *

And so, my dear Manutius, today we pay less attention to printers and more to those responsible for periodicals. If only they had your professional delicacy! The "cult of news" should not make them forget the duties of charity and justice toward society and toward private individuals normally helpless against the press. Not all are in a position to react to the paper, when it attacks them, as the statesman Thiers did when he said: "Let them write! I am an old umbrella, on which insults have been raining down for more than forty years. Another drop, more or less, makes no difference!"

You, in Venice, had censorship, which supervised your books. Today censorship is gone, practically speaking. If only a bit of self-censorship were functioning! It is true, however, that a great deal depends also on the readers: if they showed more serious tastes, self-censorship would function at once, and the newspapers would also become more serious, because, as everyone knows, people have the newspapers they deserve, the ones they wish.

Will this happen? Let's hope so.

For the moment, if you were here, your heart would ache to see an enormous mountain of bad printed material, compared to a little molehill of good printing. It is a problem that Catholics, if they are such, should make sincere efforts to solve.

The Germans say: "The cow is thin and you expect her to produce abundant milk? Give her more hay!"

In the days when he was editing a newspaper, Mark Twain did not merely write and have others write, he also advertised his paper by every possible means. One day, on the front page there was a cartoon, showing a donkey at the bottom of a well. The legend asked: *Who can say why this poor donkey died at the bottom of the well?* A few days later the cartoon was printed again, and the legend said: *The poor donkey died because he didn't call for help!*

Dear Manutius! I am that donkey. And I am calling for help, for good reading matter!

November 1973

To Saint Bonaventure

Was He Also a "Big Gun"?

Most learned saint,

Your monks are preparing a great celebration for the seventh centenary of your death (1274–1974).

Which aspects of your personality will they underline?

You were first a student, then a professor at the University of Paris, general of the Franciscan Order, bishop and cardinal, a very important orator at the Ecumenical Council of Lyons, a writer on theological and mystical matters with great influence also in the centuries after your own.

Where will the monks place the accent, what will they underline? I don't know. If I were to decide, from all your books I would choose the *Life of Saint Francis*, and I would try to spread knowledge of it as widely as possible. It is a literary masterpiece. You wrote it with a spirit profoundly moved, with a style both lofty and rich in picturesque imagery. As you were writing the book, your friend Saint Thomas could foretell its beauty, and he said: "We have a Saint writing about another Saint!" He foresaw, as I like to think, also its great spiritual fruits.

But I would bet that neither you nor he could in any

SAINT BONAVENTURE of Bagnorea (1221–1274) was a teacher of theology, general of the Franciscan Order, bishop and cardinal, a much-appreciated orator at the Council of Lyons, a fertile writer on theological and mystical subjects. His thinking, focused on the figure of Christ the Redeemer, culminates in the doctrine of his Itinerarium mentis in Deum.

way foresee the interpretation of it offered the other day by a university student speaking with me. "We young people of today," he said, "are with Saint Francis."

"Splendid," I replied.

"Yes," he went on, "as Saint Francis contested the authority of his father, flinging his clothes in the older man's face, we fling in the face of this dirty consumer society everything it has given us, or rather, has forced on us!"

In the days when you, a simple layman, were studying, there were ten thousand university students in Paris. They disputed, they made noise, they brawled, and they also protested often, but with another style.

The style and the problems of our young protesters are different. May I tell you something about them?

*   *   *

In your day, too, the young wanted to renew the world, to break with the past. But today they — or rather, a number of them — preach a complete break with the past, rejecting, with one swoop, society, family, marriage, school, morality, and religion.

"You want to throw everything out," I said to the interlocutor I mentioned above, "but then what? What will you put in the place of the institutions you have eliminated?"

He answered me: "That's a bourgeois question!"

So our young people insist on *disposal,* but they make no *proposal.*

You will say: "Perhaps these are poor young people, outcasts. That's why they have it in for the bourgeoisie!" Oh, no, they are actually children of the middle class, often young people who lack for absolutely nothing. They have the means to live, but they have no ideals for living.

And now you will say: "There must at least be some reasons, some excuses, to explain this situation." Of course. And I will try to indicate some of them to you.

Today the doors of the upper schools and the universities are open wide: the young enter, in Italy, by the hundreds of thousands every year. Not everything that should be there, however, is to be found there; and, moreover, a gap exists between the doors opened to study and the doors opened to jobs.

Young people armed with a degree or a diploma cannot find suitable employment, and the number of unemployed intellectuals is destined to increase considerably in the next few years. Society has been unable to foresee this very serious imbalance, and the young take it out on society.

There is more. In this same society there is a terrible moral and religious void. Today all seem frantically directed toward material conquests: make money, invest, surround oneself with new comforts, live the "good life." Few think also of "doing good."

God — who should fill our life — has, on the contrary, become a very distant star, to which people look only at certain moments. People believe they are religious because they go to church; but outside of church they want to lead the same life as many others, marked by small or big deceits, acts of injustice, sins against charity; and thus they totally lack coherence.

The young, who want consistency, on the other hand, do not accept the situation. They then find inconsistencies, real or apparent, in the Church itself, so they reject the Church as well. And since one has somehow to profess something, they follow the worst fashionable ideologies and the frantic cult of sex, which is a religion in reverse, under the slogan of "sexual or erotic freedom."

And that is not all. There is the cult of freedom. But it is not the classic freedom to do what must be done, without interference, or to choose between one thing and another. No, this is absolute independence. "I'm the only one to decide what is good and what is bad. I want to fulfill myself without dependence on any law imposed from the outside. Anyone who opposes my wishes is trying to destroy my personality. All authority is repression. All structure is imprisonment. All superiors are policemen."

You, most sweet and most learned saint, taught for several years, and teaching to you meant being in the service of truth, of students, of families. But if you were to come back today! Precisely because you are a teacher, they would look on you as a university "mandarin" or a "big gun," one who wants to impose his culture in order to chain his pupils to the "system."

You would hear talk of "de-scholarization." "If there has to be schooling, the pupils should not learns *subjects*, but should become accustomed to discussing present-day political problems." You would have to accept "social administration" of the school: you would have to deal not only with the pupils and their parents, but also with the political parties and the trade unions; the time set aside for preparing lessons would be partly consumed by long meetings and debates.

Not that this is entirely bad: dialogue with the young is necessary; it is right that the various components of society should take an interest in the school and that it should be something live, avoiding exaggerated and tiresome abstractions and parroted information. But the excess simply distorts everything.

* * *

Are they then pitiless, these young people, toward their teachers? I would say yes. But — and this is the good thing — they show pity for the poor, the outcast, the underprivileged. They declare themselves opposed to all social barriers, against all discrimination by class or race. This is beautiful and generous. Unfortunately, here again, they encounter very grave injustices, and they rebel against them.

They hear talk of nations that call themselves Christian and still tolerate cases of torture, used to combat ideas. They see workers' families forced to live on a hundred thousand lire a month, while a few people grow incredibly rich, by mysterious means.

In a single evening a singer makes two million lire and soon becomes a billionairess through the sale of the records of her songs. The young read about aid granted the Third World, then they realize it is a drop in the bucket: the amount of money squandered for arms is immensely greater, and meanwhile, in the Third World, people continue to suffer and die.

There is, truly, something to be indignant about; but then this righteous indignation of the young is deliberately exacerbated: certain of our societies are depicted in even more dark and sinister colors, while the monstrous enormities of other societies go unmentioned, and those societies, instead, are presented as models, actually as "ideal, paradisiacal countries."

*   *   *

But I would not wish, myself, to paint things in too-harsh colors. Not all our young people are like this. Many think about working hard, they are respectful, they prepare themselves seriously for their future life; unfortunately, while the others speak and write, these remain silent. Even the ones who protest often expect a great deal from the adults they are contesting, and they remain disappointed when they are given vague answers and are told that "solutions are being sought."

They should be offered concrete proposals. *Freedom?* Of course, but, without God, what freedom? Progress, science tell you more and more about *how* this world is made; only the doctrine of Christ tells you *why* you are in the world.

A model? Christ is the valid choice, always, for all. He took a certain road and He said: Follow me! The road is a bit narrow, but it is the road of loyalty, of love for all, with special love for the humble and the poor; and the road leads to the "glory of the Father." On the Cross, He offered Himself to the Father; in resurrecting Him, the

Father declared acceptance of the offer, glorifying His humanity and the humanity of all those who are His, joyously announcing that the whole world will one day be transformed into "a new heaven and a new earth."

A world to improve, fighting for justice, to eliminate the causes of wrongs? Of course, but let each begin by improving himself. And let us make sure we are not falling into ingenuous utopias; there will always be imperfections, in whatever system. Let us not judge men without appeal; let us not make radical divisions: all good on this side, all bad on that; only loyalty here, only tyranny there; this one is progressive, that one is conservative. Life is always very complex: even the good have failings, even the bad have virtues.

Faithless Church? The Holy Fathers called it that, too, long ago. But they specified: the *holy* Faithless Church. Made up of sinners, in fact, the Church is perforce also a sinner, but it continues to give valid help and examples of holiness to all those who have faith in it. We must also see whether all the failings attributed to the Church are true. The Church that a certain writer (perhaps also in good faith) has in his mind is one thing, the true Church, as it really exists outside that writer's mind, is something else.

* * *

Most gentle Saint Bonaventure! Your contemporaries, who had the good fortune to hear you, were intoxicated by your words. They wrote: "He spoke with angelic tongue." I wish you would still speak like an angel: especially to parents, to educators, to politicians, to all those who, today, are responsible for the young. And I wish you would say: "Do not fear any effort, any just reform, any expense, any dialogue, if it will help these sons of ours. It is for their good, but also for your own good. In fact, those who fear effort and expense today may have to pay dearly tomorrow."

Tolstoy would be prepared to underline these last words of yours with a parable of his.

In the little Principality of Monaco, many years ago, the judges sentenced a rogue to the guillotine, but then they realized that, to carry out the sentence, they had neither a guillotine nor an executioner. The Principality of Monaco was so tiny! They asked to borrow both things from their neighbor France, but when they heard what the charge would be, they took fright: "Too expensive!" They made a similar inquiry at the court of the king of Sardinia. Again the price was too high.

So they left the rogue in prison: but the jailer, the cook, the prisoner's food also cost money. "We'll open the jail door," the judges decided, "and let him go off on his way!"

Seeing the door open, the prisoner went out for a stroll along the seafront. But at noon he went to the prince's kitchen to claim his meal. He did this the first day, the second, the third, and for many days thereafter. . . . The matter was becoming a serious threat to the budget of the principality. The authorities decided to send for the man. "Haven't you realized yet that you must go away?"

And he answered: "All right, I'll go, I'll go, but first you must pay me."

They had to pay him. And thus, with the excuse that it was "too expensive," and with constant postponements, another criminal was set loose in the world to continue his misdeeds.

So you must not keep saying, "It costs too much!" if you want to stop the criminal, furious, revolutionary protest from traveling about the world. Solutions of problems, expenditures, dialogue must not be put off. Let us speak with these young people, and let us try to help them with new assistance and new methods, suited to the times, but with the same impassioned love with which you, dear saint, helped them, in your own times.

December 1973

To Christopher Marlowe

The Devil's
Most Successful Trick

Illustrious poet,

I encountered you for the first time as I was reading the poet Carducci.

He imagines himself in a carriage, traveling along the
Chiarone, a little river in the Maremma area of Tuscany:
the "wan horses" gallop, the darkness increases, a light
rain is falling, and the poet is reading, in fact, a book of
yours. His reading must give him haunting visions, for
he writes:

> From the wicked, grim verse,
> Like the dream of a man
> On whom much beer is weighing . . .
> There rises a harsh fog
> Of horrid sadness.

At a certain point he can actually stand no more and he
throws your book away:

> Away with you, Marlowe! Into the water!

*CHRISTOPHER MARLOWE, English writer (1564–1593). A reckless ad-
venturer, member of the group known as the University Wits, he was the author of inspired and vigorous poems and plays, peopled with characters of a
preromantic titanism. His best-known work is* The Tragical History of Doctor Faustus, *the famous story of the doctor of Wittenberg who sells his soul
to the devil.*

I was a boy then. Naturally, I asked myself: "What can the horrid thing in that book be? I can't fish it out of the waters of the Chiarone; I wonder if I can fish it out of the library?"

I did: *The Tragical History of Doctor Faustus.*

Tragical, indeed, and grim. In the first pages I found the terms of the contract between Faustus and the devil: "First, that Doctor Faustus can be a spirit in form and substance. Secondly, that Mephistophilis shall be his servant, and at his command. Thirdly, that Mephistophilis shall do for him, and bring him whatsoever he desires. Fourthly, that he shall be in his chamber or house invisible. Lastly, that he shall appear to the said John Faustus, at all times, in what form or shape soever he please. I, John Faustus of Wittenberg, Doctor, by these presents, do give both body and soul to Lucifer prince of the east, and his minister Mephistophilis: and furthermore grant unto them, that, twenty-four years being expired, . . . full power to fetch or carry the said John Faustus, body and soul, flesh, blood, or goods, into their habitation whatsoever. By me, John Faustus."

On reaching the end of the drama, I also asked myself: "Marlowe is a splended poet of the horrible, but isn't the devil stupid and isn't the doctor mad, to fulfill a contract of this sort?"

Today I am able to answer: "Yes, the devil is stupid, the doctor is mad, and it's a lucky thing that contract never existed!" But then I hear others speak up, saying: "The lucky thing, on the contrary, is that the devil doesn't exist!"

To you, Marlowe, this modern denial of the devil is no surprise, I should think; you tended toward it, if I have not misunderstood you, already four hundred and fifty years ago. But, for my part, it makes me very unhappy.

With Charles Baudelaire, a poet like you and, like you, hardly a pillar of the Church, I believe that "the devil's most successful trick is this: making people believe he doesn't exist." He, one of the protagonists of history, tries to move through this world completely incognito; he leads men to deny his existence so that he can bring them to foment the revolution against God which he himself began; and now, to some extent, he has succeeded.

There was evidence of his success a few months ago, when Pope Paul VI made a stern reference to the devil, saying that he exists not only as impersonal evil but also as a real person, invisible, yes, but industriously active in harming mankind.

There were big reactions. Some writers, from their newspapers and magazines, becoming makeshift theologians, declared pompously that it was not a serious speech on the pope's part, that he was reviving medieval myths, interrupting the "progress" of a theology that, by now, was relegating the devil to a tiny corner established by "culture."

A book even appeared: *The Pope and the Devil.* You, Marlowe, would have defined it *"malignantis naturae."* That book, in fact, uses the devil only as a pretext: the service of Paul VI to the Church and to the world is the real subject, handled apparently with a stern apparatus of objective data and research; underneath, however, there is sometimes a congenital inability to understand the things of the Church, sometimes an amateur's naïveté, sometimes an unfortunate tendentiousness.

The reaction of some "broad-minded" theologians was more positive. Called upon for a statement, they answered — perhaps gritting their teeth — that a Catholic cannot decently deny the existence of the devil, as the Bible speaks of him so openly.

This is the crux: the Bible and the proper reading of it. One thing is surprising: while the religions of the ancient Orient had an elaborate and picturesque demonology, the Old Testament confines the devil within narrow limits. Fear of confusing monotheism, of wronging the official Hebrew worship, of falsifying the problem of evil can perhaps explain this reserve on the part of the writers of Scripture.

In the New Testament the devil is more abundantly

present. You often encounter these names: "demons," "spirits," "malign spirits," "impure spirits," "the malign one," "the tempter." These "spirits" — according to the Gospel — try to oppose the coming of the Kingdom; they can tempt man, as they tempted Jesus in the desert.

For Saint John, the Passion of Jesus is a struggle against the devil; in the Acts it is said that the preaching of the Apostles will be the continuation of the struggle between the Kingdom of God and the realm of the devil.

At various times both Jesus and His listeners blame the devil for diseases: blindness, dumbness, deafness, convulsions, mental disorders. Jesus heals those diseases, but never through magical formulas or exorcisms, always by giving an order, making a simple gesture.

Saint Paul speaks often of the power of the devil and of temptation, which he declares is frequent, various, harmful: the devil transforms himself even into an angel of light, the better to deceive Christians. Paul himself feels the slap of an "angel of Satan," with attacks that are left unspecified. But they do not frighten him: the power of darkness will not be able to separate him from the charity of Christ. Jesus — he says — has freed us from the power of the devil and it is the Christians who, in the end, will judge the angels.

The Book of the Apocalypse is more colorful. To tell the truth, its demonology, based on struggles and victories of angels over devils, is not easy to interpret. The demonology of the first centuries of Christianity is influenced by the Apocalypse. The theme of "slyness" is frequent in it. God is said to have concealed the divinity behind the human nature of Christ. The devil presumably attacked it unknowingly. Caught like a stupid fish on the hook, Saint Gregory the Pope says. Imprisoned like a greedy mouse by the trap of the Cross, says Saint Augustine. Saint Cyril of Jerusalem speaks instead of poison, which, swallowed, forces the devil to spit out souls, which he keeps prisoner.

This theme of the tricky devil tricked, abandoned by theologians for centuries, was taken up again by artists.

You, Marlowe, didn't like it, and you made your poor Faustus finish forever in the clutches of Mephistophilis; but Dante liked the idea, and so did Goethe.

In Dante we have Buonconte di Montefeltro, excommunicated, and certain victim of the devil, who is already awaiting Buonconte as his prey. But Buonconte, before dying, has the good idea of invoking the Madonna. The angel of God carries his soul away promptly and the devil, foiled and disappointed, can only take it out on the angel, shouting after him:

Oh you, from heaven, why do you deprive me of him?

In Goethe, poor Mephistopheles, after having toiled for years and years to satisfy all the whims of Faust, as an old man and as a youth, is also left empty-handed. At the last moment, in fact, whole choirs of angels descend from Heaven to defeat the diabolical hosts and to save Faust. The spiteful Mephistopheles shouts:

The promised soul . . .
I have been cheated of, with fraud!

But God does not cheat anyone, whatever Mephistopheles may say.

And this is the dominant theme of the demonology of the early Fathers, who took refuge in the desert during the first ten centuries of the Church. They do not think of this desert as a refuge opposed to the corruption of the world, a place where God speaks, in the solitude and in a special way, to man's heart. On the contrary, it is the battlefield where the solitary fighters go to pit their strength against the devil's, to defeat him as Jesus had done before them. The devils — according to those Fathers — consider the desert their own domain. "Out of our house!" they shout to Saint Anthony; and they set a hundred snares in his path, to keep him from proceeding, from coming to disturb their last refuge, filling it with monks.

The nasty tricks they played are famous, and they become the daily plague of all anchorites: devout pilgrims,

who come to visit the Fathers in the desert, hear them tell
of these deceits with wonder. Saint Pachomius bends his
knees to pray, and the devil digs a hole before him; the
saint is working, the devil suddenly pops up in front of
him in the form of a rooster, crowing under his nose; he
is praying, and a wolf or a fox leaps on him, screaming.
Saint Macarius, traveling to a temple of idolatry, has
stuck some little reeds in the sand along his route, so
that he can find his way home; he falls asleep, and meanwhile the devil pulls up all the reeds. The saint finds
them in a bundle, like a pillow, under his head.

In other words, there are tempting, spiteful devils, envious, troublesome; but still the monk, if he keeps vigil
and prays, will be victorious over them. We are not dealing with real stories, obviously, so much as didactic or
moralistic writings.

And yet they were read and believed as historical fact,
and the simple faithful were deeply impressed, and these
writings gave rise to other books and other beliefs.

In the Middle Ages people still believed that the devil
comes to torment the good especially, in guises sometimes frightening, sometimes sexually tempting. Does
some poor nun go out to fill a basket with greens? In that
basket there is Satan. Does a monk enjoy the singing of a
little bird in his solitary cell? Satan is in that song. Even
in the illumination of prayer books Satan can be nesting,
even in the painted image over the altar, even in the very
rope that binds the friar's habit.

And worse still: it is Satan, the incubus, who rapes
virgins and procreates accursed children in their wombs!
Alas! Medieval religion often crosses the boundary of
superstition in this field.

Robert, duke of Normandy, was nicknamed *le diable*,
because people believed the devil had sired him.

Despite the efforts of the Church, demonology was
joined and often strengthened by magic. The soothsayer,
the malevolent woman, the woman who uses poison is
believed in, even as late as the sixteenth and seventeenth
centuries. People believe that she can use infernal powers

against an enemy. People insist that possessed women steal off in the night to take part in witches' sabbaths.

How can all this be explained? Not merely by wickedness, because often there was only ignorance: people believed honestly. Let us say then: the ingenuousness of writers, who accepted events without the proper checking; facile credulity, which imprudently mixed the word of God with superstitious manifestations; psychological and pathological phenomena, which were regarded with a superficially religious eye instead of with a scientific eye.

Rejecting these exaggerations and these errors, however, does not mean rejecting everything.

The existence of the devil, a pure invisible spirit, cannot be more of a problem than the existence of God and of the angels. To admit his power over mankind cannot be frightening, if we believe in the victory won by Christ. He, on the Cross, seemed defeated. But instead He was the victor, and we see this in the Resurrection.

We find ourselves in the same situation: Subject to many temptations, tests, and sufferings, we seem defeated; with the Lord's grace we will be victors!

January 1974

To Saint Luke the Evangelist

Forbidden to Forbid

Dear Saint Luke,

I have always been fond of you, because you were a man of great sweetness, filled with the spirit of conciliation.

In your Gospel you stressed that Christ is infinitely good, that sinners are the objects of a special love on God's part, that Jesus, almost ostentatiously, made the acquaintance of those who did not enjoy any consideration in the world.

You are the only one who gives us the story of Christ's Nativity and childhood, which we hear read at Christmas always with renewed emotion. One little phrase of yours in particular captures my attention: "Wrapped in swaddling clothes, and lying in a manger." It is the phrase that inspired all the Christmas crèches in the world and thousands of stupendous paintings. I set beside this phrase a stanza of the Breviary:

> He was willing to lie on straw,
> He was not afraid of the manger,

SAINT LUKE *is the author of the third canonic Gospel and of the Acts of the Apostles. He lived in the first century* A.D. *A doctor, bound by close friendship to Saint Paul, and the saint's faithful collaborator, he followed Paul also on his third missionary journey. Though not an eyewitness of the life of Christ, he made a vast contribution to the New Testament, especially in his attention to Christ's childhood.*

> He was nourished with a little milk,
> He, who feeds even the least of the birds.

Having done this, I asked myself: "Christ took that very humble place. What place do we take?" Now let me repeat the answers I have found for this question.

In God's presence is our place that of Abraham, who said: "Behold, I have taken upon myself to speak to the Lord, I who am but dust and ashes"? Or is it that of the publican, who, at the threshold of the temple, far from the altar, did not even dare raise his eyes to Heaven, thinking of all the sins he had committed?

In the presence of an infinite and omnipotent God, we must accept being very small and repress in ourselves any tendency opposed to proper submission. It so happens that God wants us to imitate Him in certain things, whereas in others He wants to be unique, inimitable. He says: ". . . Learn from me; for I am gentle and lowly in heart"; "Be merciful, even as your Father is merciful." But he also says: "To the only wise God be glory, forevermore"; "the Lord . . . alone has immortality and dwells in unapproachable light."

We try to reverse these positions; we would like autonomy, honors, independence for ourselves, and we don't want to be dependent, meek, patient. We sustain our views, if necessary, with the "new philosophies" (which soon will be old) and with Kulture with a capital K. Progress too has gone to our heads: we are very aware of having reached the moon, of having created a civilization with every kind of consumers' goods and every kind of comfort.

We were, however, about to forget Him from whom every gift of talent and energy came, but there some Oriental sheikhs came to give us the harsh and brusque reminder: "You people of consumer civilization and opulence," they said to us, "the party's over: there's oil now for only about another thirty years; if you want it, you have to pay plenty; rethink your way of life: go look for other sources of energy."

The reminder and the hard moments ahead of us can be useful: on the one hand they stimulate new research and new avenues of progress; on the other, they recall the limits of all earthly things and the duty to place our supreme hopes only above.

I heard a "Christian critic" say: "Enough of this petty bourgeois religion, which speaks of Paradise and of individual souls saved. It all smells of capitalist individualism and distracts the attention of the poor from the great social problems. He who preaches the Gospel should speak of the people, the masses, of general salvation. Christ, in fact, came to free the people from the exile of capitalist civilization and to guide them to the homeland of the new society, which is about to arise."

The only truth in these words is that the Christian must concern himself, and effectively, with the great social problems. In fact, the more one is passionately devoted to Heaven, the more one must lend a hand in establishing justice on earth. As for the rest, capitalist or socialist, civilization is temporary for each of us; we live here only in passing.

Our true homeland, toward which Christ is leading us — together, but each with his own destiny — is Paradise. He who does not believe in Paradise is unfortunate: he is "without hope," as Saint Paul would say, and he has not yet discovered the profound meaning of his own existence.

With regard to our neighbor, our place has three different natures, depending on whether we are dealing with superiors, equals, or inferiors.

But can we speak of superiors these days? Can we still say that children must love, respect, and obey their parents; pupils, their teachers; citizens, the established authorities?

In the seventeenth century, here in Venice, there was

the famous Carnival: on those days people seemed to go crazy, they did more or less what they pleased, and — with the complicity of their masks — they released their resentment against proprieties and laws, as if to get their own back for the months spent in obedience and proper behavior. I have the impression that something similar is happening now.

Personally I am not so frightened to hear that there are assassinations in the world, thefts, robberies, kidnappings, and murders. They have always existed. What is frightening is the new attitude many people have toward these phenomena. The law, the norm, is considered something to mock or simply a source of repression and alienation. People take real pleasure in speaking ill of any law whatsoever. The only thing prohibited today — it is said — is prohibition, and anyone who tries to forbid something reveals that he belongs to the old, out-of-date, "oppressive society." Some magistrates, in pronouncing sentence, give the impression of opening arbitrary gaps in the fence of the law; very often the press derides the forces whose duty it is to make order respected.

In the clerical world itself, in "knocking down," one after the other, ecclesiastical laws, the *quantum potes tantum aude* of the "Lauda Sion" is applied in a reckless, unexpected fashion. Inquiries, scientific or not, are multiplied, and all seem to end with this refrain: "Dear public, you are unhappy in the present situation; if you want to be happy, you must change everything and turn the structures upside down!"

Psychology, the science that explains human events, also intervenes. Then what? Adulterers, sadists, homosexuals are virtually excused almost all the time by "psychologists of the profound." The fault lies with parents, who didn't love their tender, angelic offspring as they should have. A whole literature seems to have as its watchword "blame it on the father!" and it makes fathers responsible for almost everything. Another literature, propagandizing a complete liberalization of every law, asks for unrestrained contraception, abortion at the mother's wish, all the divorce you like, premarital relations, homosexuality, use of drugs.

It is a tidal wave, a kind of cyclone, which advances, dear Saint Luke; in the face of it what can a poor bishop do? He can admit that in the past the law was often an absolute, a kind of altar on which the individual was too often sacrificed. He can concede that at times it is the parents themselves who loosen all restraint on their children ("I don't want my son to undergo the severity I had to suffer!"). He can confess that the same parents have sometimes forgotten the admonition "Do not provoke your children, lest they become discouraged." He knows very well that all exercise of authority is a service and must be performed in the spirit of service. He bears in mind the words of Saint Peter: "Live as free men, yet without using your freedom as a pretext for evil; but live as servants of God." These words exclude so-called power and demand authority that promotes freedom; they do not want a servile obedience, but rather an adult obedience, active and responsible.

But then what? Then, the bishop must trust in God, recalling firmly the divine word: "He who fears God, honors his parents. . . . My son, honor your father in work and word." "Children, obey your parents in everything, for this pleases the Lord." "Let every person be subject to the governing authorities. For there is no authority except from God. . . . Therefore he who resists the authorities resists what God has appointed." "I urge that supplications, prayers, intercessions, and thanksgivings be made for all men, for kings and all who are in high positions." "Obey your leaders and submit to them; for they are keeping watch over your souls, as men who will have to give account. Let them do this joyfully, and not sadly. . . ."

Then there are our equals. Toward them our duty is to be simple, to avoid singularity, the exaggerated desire to distinguish ourselves. There could be a tendency, at times, not to do what the others do, but to do what the others don't do; to contradict their statements, to despise what they admire, to admire what they despise.

Some want to stand out by their elegance, luxury, bright colors, showy clothes; others by their original, fastidious language. A ring on the finger, a curl that peeps from beneath the hat's brim, a feather on a Tyrolese hat make some people incredibly proud. These things, mind you, are not grave in themselves, but often they become a cheap way of showing off, of shocking others, of hiding one's own mediocrity.

The simple and straightforward man, on the other hand, does not try to appear richer, more cultivated, more devout, nobler, more powerful than he actually is. To be what one should be, to seem what one is, to dress according to one's own position, to shun deliberate ostentation, to avoid putting others in shadow: these are his aims. Jesus approved them and recommended them in advance; and you, dear Saint Luke, have kept them for us: "Sit in the lowest place"; "Woe to you . . . for you love the best seat in the synagogues and salutations in the market place."

There are finally our inferiors, or rather those who are less fortunate than we, because they are ill or poor or in trouble or sinners. Toward them we have the duty of effective Christian love, which must be directed to each person and also to the group or class that they form.

Here I see two mistaken positions today. One man says: I love and help the individual poor person and that's enough: I'm not interested in the "class" of the poor. Another says: I fight only for the whole class of the poor, for all outsiders, for the Third World; to help the poor individual with small-scale charity is no help; in fact, it delays the definitive revolution.

To the first man I reply: You must also effectively love the poor who, joined together and organized, are fighting to improve their situation. You must do as Christ did, who loved all, but who showed the poor a special and intense love.

To the second I say: It is well to chose the cause of the poor, the outsiders, the Third World. But be careful that, with the excuse of the distant, general poor, you do not neglect your poor neighbors. One poor neighbor is your mother: why do you disobey her and maltreat her? Another poor neighbor is your teacher: why are you so disrespectful and inconsiderate with him? And why did you use violence and picketing to prevent your classmate from entering the classroom with you, on the pretext that his political ideas are opposed to yours? You are for the great cause of peace. Fine. But take care that the words of the prophet Jeremiah do not come true: "They have healed the wound of my people lightly, saying 'Peace, peace,' when there is no peace." Peace, in fact, has a price: it is not made with words, but with sacrifices and loving renunciations by all. Nor is it possible to obtain it with only human efforts: God's intervention is required.

It is the Christmas message of the angels, one of the most beautiful things that you, dear Saint Luke, ever "recorded": "And on earth peace among men with whom He is pleased!"

March 1974

To Quintilian

Other Times,
Another School...

Illustrious Quintilian,

You were a great lawyer, a great master of eloquence, but, especially, a great and impassioned educator of the young!

The younger Pliny was one of your pupils. The Emperor Domitian entrusted to you the education of his
nephews, the sons of his sister Flavia Domitilla.

The first of the twelve books of your chief work, the *Institutio*, served as a text from the Middle Ages until a few
years ago.

I glanced through it recently; I reread some of your
maxims.

1) The master must not expect from a child that which
only an adolescent can give, nor from an adolescent that
which is expected of an adult. Say to him, when he has
learned well: You are already someone! And add: Your
best is still to come! In this way you encourage him, you
stimulate him, and you open to him the paths of hope.

2) It is not good for there to be a single master for a

*MARCUS FABIUS QUINTILIANUS, Latin writer of Spanish origin (circa
35–96), lived in Rome under the emperors Vespasian and Domitian. A
lawyer, a dedicated teacher, he directed a prestigious school of oratory in
Rome. He was also the first orator paid a salary by the State. His chief work
is the* Institutio oratoria, *an admirable treatise on the education of the
young.*

single child. If he does not compare himself to others, the student risks becoming too proud; with only a single scholar before him, the teacher does not give his best. If there are several in the class, there is competition, and this is often more stimulating to study than the exhortation of teachers and the pleas of parents.

3) The critical spirit is not suited to the young; it should not be allowed to prevail in them over their imagination and their creativity.

4) The teacher should not be too stern in correcting; otherwise, the timid will lose heart, fear everything, and attempt nothing; the livelier ones will become angry and put up tacit resistance. Be paternal, do not have bad habits and do not tolerate them. Austere, but not rigid; benevolent, but not without energy. The teacher should not allow himself to be hated for his severity or despised for his lack of vigor. Let him speak very often of what is good and honest . . .

* * *

These maxims, as I looked over them again, filled me both with tenderness and with sadness, since they are so far from the maxims I read today in certain treatises of pedagogy, which I see, here and there, approved.

1) What if I were to say to you, illustrious Quintilian, that there are some teachers who, already in the fourth grade, discuss — and constantly dwell on — Vietnam, Chile, the Palestinians? What matters — they say — is not so much handing on to the children notions that have been acquired from others in the past, but making chil- dren learn to discuss the great problems of the present.

2) Emulation? Competition? Today these are forbidden words; they would foster individualism, class spirit, meritocracy, capitalism. Grades should not be given to the individual student, but only to the group.

3) As for the critical spirit, this is one of the things that causes most concern. Society is shown to the pupils in its worst aspects, at times deliberately exaggerated, then the pupils are told: "Kids, here is your target: shoot at it!"

You were afraid of *tacit* resistance. Today we have active scholastic protest, which is anything but tacit!

4) A *paternal* teacher? Don't let anyone hear you say that! Today *"paternalism"* is a beast to be hunted down; it is sought in every cranny, feared; it is the synonym of oppression, repression, and authoritarianism. The words that today, on the other hand, are extremely fashionable are: group work, "open classroom" school, socially and democratically directed, enriched with assemblies and demonstrations. If you were to return to teaching after nineteen centuries, dear Quintilian, you would have to do a lot of homework, to bring yourself up to date!

Not that it is all bad. The four points I have set in opposition, along with the other slogans, to your four maxims contain extremist views and solutions. There are, however, intermediary positions, which perhaps you, too, would not dislike, and to which, adapting them a bit, your maxims could very well be applied.

*   *   *

One good thing, for example, is *group work*, something you do not know.

In a group, assuming it works well, there is not only the phenomenon of three, four, or five minds added together quantitatively, but there is also a new stimulus acting and operating on the mind of each. I, in fact, try to understand what the other has already understood: his light strikes another light in me, and this, in turns, helps him or a third or a fourth.

Further, the "group project" stimulates me to be "active," as well as "receptive," to be myself as I learn, to express my thoughts to others and to illustrate them in an original way.

And, more, there is an exchange of experiences, which enriches the others and me; reciprocal loyalty is fostered by this exchange and by consideration toward the others.

This, however, does not exclude, but rather assumes, instruction from the teacher. And in fact — dependence is natural for the mind, which does not create truth but must simply bow before it, from whatever direction it comes — if one does not benefit from others' teaching, one loses a great deal of time in seeking truths that are already known. It is not possible always to make original discoveries; often it suffices to be critically certain of discoveries already made; and finally, docility is also a useful virtue.

A certain university professor realized this, when his maid asked if she could take some glowing coals from the stove for her iron. "Go ahead," he answered, "but where are you going to put the coals?"

"Here," the maid answered, showing the palm of her hand. She put a layer of cold ash in it, set the coals over the ash, and went off, thanking her employer.

"Well!" the professor said, "with all my knowledge, I didn't know that!"

It should not be believed that, in listening to a professor, the student remains purely passive or receptive. Students, if they are real disciples of the truth, are not like pots open to receive the beans that the professor pours into them, stirring at top speed with the spoon of his erudition. Dante, Leonardo, Galileo, placed before the desk, are not left "sitting there," and Saint Thomas indicates that he wants students "on their feet," when he says: The teacher confines himself to moving, to stimulating the pupil, and the pupil arrives at true learning only if he responds to this stimulus, both during and after the teacher's explanation.

Besides, is it better to be the confidants of great ideas or the original authors of mediocre ideas?

*   *   *

Attention to the weaker members of the class is a fine and positive thing. But it can be achieved still without losing a certain amount of competitiveness. School is a preparation for life, which is made up of inequalities. Sports, too, which have such an appeal to the young, would be nothing if there were not rivalry and emulation! A school without a leading pupil or one at the bottom of the class is neither realistic nor pleasant; it resembles too much a flock of sheep.

Don Bosco saw love of the young in a different light. "I believe," he wrote, "that it is every professor's duty to bear in mind the worst in the class, to question them more often than the others, to spend more time on explanations for them; to repeat and repeat until they have understood; to adapt the assignments and the lessons to their capacity. To keep the students with livelier minds suitably occupied, let extra assignments and lessons be made, rewarding the students with points for diligence. Rather than neglect the slower ones, let accessory things be dispensed with, but the chief subjects should be entirely adapted to them."

Perhaps you, too, agree that in the past the schools exaggerated on the side of rote learning. Some names come back to me: Zenoni (Latin and Greek grammar), Campanini-Carboni (Latin vocabulary), Sanesi (Greek vocabulary). Connected with them I see declinations, paradigms, rules, exceptions, exercises, translated pages in endless number.

History, as recorded in textbooks, seemed to me a distillation of noise, as Carlyle said, all made up of dates, wars, armistices, treaties. In studying a bit of science, I committed to memory series of names, of neuroptera, lepidoptera, coleoptera, diptera, and so on, but I was never sure whether the housefly and the mosquito belong to the order of the diptera, and I was never able to see hymenoptera in the red ants that painfully stung my legs when I sat down in a meadow.

A living school is much better. It offers children ideas on which to form their interests, and beside dictionaries, uses spoken recordings and cassettes for studying languages; it underlines, in history, the progress of culture and social conditions; in physics and natural sciences, it proceeds on the basis of laboratory experiments; it moderately encourages the pupils to take an interest and an active part in the life and events of their own country and of the world.

I say "moderately." I am, in fact, convinced that pupils can usefully debate in class; but I can't bear the idea of their showing disrespect to their teacher, giving way to filthy language and obscene gestures in his presence. I know that both the Italian constitution and Vatican Council II recognize the right to strike; I am unable to see this right in certain school strikes, which perhaps end with stones thrown at the school windows or with worse destruction.

*   *   *

For a social administration of day schools, elementary, secondary, and artistic schools of the Italian State, Law 477 will be applied, starting with the next scholastic year.

In it (article 6) parents are considered an integral and fundamental part of the world of the school. A Council of Institution or a club will be set up. It will comprise representatives of the teaching staff, of the nonteaching staff, of the parents, of the pupils, and the principal or headmaster. It will be presided over by one of the parents elected from among the members of the council itself. The parents, moreover, will be part of the Council of Discipline of the pupils and of the class and interclass councils.

This is a real conquest, illustrious Quintilian: parents are becoming co-responsible inside the school, by official decision. But are all of them prepared to deal with scholastic problems? And will they be capable of letting themselves be guided solely by their children's interests, leaving outside the school any party concerns, today when politics infiltrates everywhere, like fine dust, even into the lungs? And won't the broad deliberative powers granted parents by article 6 be nullified by the freedom of teaching which some professors are already demanding, with an appeal to article 4? If professors and teachers have too broad freedom to teach whatever they like, then that will be an end of the parents' freedom!

The Italian school is at a historic turning point. If the

families don't understand this and don't keep their eyes well open, there could be a real disaster.

* * *

Illustrious Quintilian! Many centuries separate us. After you came many philosophers and many, many pedagogues.

Humanist culture, which was also your culture, today is obscured by the sciences dealing with the world and with man; these prevail in the era of the atom and of technology. And yet a century ago Theodor Mommsen, the Protestant historian of Rome, defined you still as "inspired by good taste and correct judgment, instructive without pedantry." Fifty years ago Concetto Marchesi, a Communist, recognized your culture as a "shaper of the spirit."

I hope that not everything in humanistic culture will be dropped in the school and that your most celebrated maxims will continue to influence educators. The following one would suffice: *Non multa, sed multum.* In other words: *In the school, not many things, but deeply studied.*

Don Bosco repeated this, in his own way, when he wrote: "He who does little does much, if he does what he must do; he who does much does nothing, if he does not do what he must do." Much then, and profoundly, without complicated exaggerations in the style of Anatole France.

This writer suggested the following procedure, to assure that an olive would be savored to perfection: put it in a lark, enclose the lark in a pigeon, the pigeon in a chicken, the chicken in a suckling pig, this in a calf, then cook the whole thing on a spit. Thus the most delicious juices of the calf would flow together with those of the pig, the chicken, the pigeon, and the lark, into the olive, and would make it superlatively exquisite. Thanks a lot! The price of that exquisiteness was slaughter!

You — with your *multum* — did not mean a slaughter of values, nor is that what we wish for our schools.

April 1974

To Guglielmo Marconi

You'd See Some Fine Things

Illustrious Marconi,

We are celebrating the centenary of your birth (1874–1974).

With the talent you possessed, it was fortunate for the world that, from your boyhood, you devoted yourself to the problems of modern physics, which you found fascinating.

At the age of twenty-one — without a university degree, without even a high school diploma — you had already discovered wireless telegraphy, transmitting electric signals over a long distance. In the years that followed, there were further studies and an avalanche of new discoveries.

In 1924 you succeeded in perfecting the radiophone and in carrying the human voice from England to Australia. With the discovery of short waves and microwaves you made possible new developments for television.

I remember with what interest the whole world followed you: I was a poor boy, but I knew that in 1912, thanks to your inventions, it had been possible to save

GUGLIELMO MARCONI, scientist from Bologna (1874–1937). He succeeded in applying practically the electromagnetic phenomena already studied by Hertz and Maxwell, creating the first apparatus for wireless telegraphy, based on a long-wave circuit. After the first experiments in his house at Pontecchio, he eventually established intercontinental communications. He was awarded the Nobel Prize in 1909.

many of the passengers of the *Titanic,* which sank in a very few hours after striking an iceberg; I heard people talk of your *Elettra,* your laboratory-ship, as if it were a kind of ghost vessel; it was impressive to see you in a photograph next to Pius XI, and to hear that at a simple signal from you thousands of bulbs had come alight simultaneously in Sydney, that you had crossed the ocean all of eighty-seven times, for your experiments.

It seemed impossible to go farther than that. But what has happened instead?

Instead, progress has continued rapidly. If you were to come back to the world, you would find some new things since 1937, the year of your death.

Now color television is commonplace, and so are videocassettes, transistors, artificial satellites, radar, penicillin, intensive care units. In factories there are complex machines that turn out finished products after having worked on them from the beginning to the end. The various pieces are not even touched by the human hand. Quality-control machines check the products so that any defects are automatically discovered and corrected. Electronic brains record information and perform the most varied operations in a very short time. Men have gone to the moon several times and are planning journeys to other planets. We are deep into the technological, post-industrial, and interplanetary era!

* * *

So all is going well! you will say, since you were also an economic entrepreneur and producer, as well as a great discoverer.

Let me make a distinction. Many things are going very well, but they are creating some consequences pregnant with problems and dangers. So they should be corrected and better directed.

Paul VI, for example, has spoken of "nations of hunger, which today invoke dramatically the nations of opulence" and of the "rage of the poor, with its unforeseeable consequences." In fact, this is happening: in one-third of the world there is an extraordinary abundance of everything and a shameless squandering; in two-thirds of the world there is a poverty that is increasing all the time. It would suffice to cancel the insane expenditures for arms and reduce certain luxuries: in a short time technology could bring the entire human family to a very high economic, social, and cultural level. This is well known, and this, above all, irritates the poor.

I mentioned the "human family." . . . We have never felt as we do today how small the world is: we hunger and thirst for unity, but we are constantly pulled by opposing forces.

For unity we have at work the prodigious network of communications, which now girdles the earth in a hundred different ways; the universal yearning for peace; the existence of the U.N. and of other supernational organizations; the writings and the work of an elite of thinkers and statesmen.

To promote disunity there are the sudden flareups of exaggerated nationalism, which are kindled from time to time here and there, both in old nations and in new ones; the division of the world into opposing blocs led by superpowers; social tensions, which no longer exist only between one class and another, but now between one region and another as well, between rich countries and poor countries.

*   *   *

You will say: But I was also a believer. Why doesn't the Church exploit the immense impulse of renewal that is in the Gospel, renewing herself and progressing with modern times?

A very just wish. And it has already been incorporated in the *Message of the Council to Men of Thought and of Science.* "Your path" it said, "is ours. . . . We are the friends of your vocation for research, the allies of your labors, the admirers of your conquests, and, if needed, the consolers of your dejection and your failure." Words that, I am sure, you would have appreciated deeply; they have been followed by deeds; the Church is going through a process of internal renovation and of dialogue with external forces.

But some difficulties are encountered. I, who am a bishop, often feel myself in the position of the son of John II, king of France.

In 1356, at the battle of Poitiers, the king was wielding great blows with his sword; beside him, his son was also fighting, but he was keeping watch over his father and shouted to him every now and then: "Papa, look to your right! Papa, look to your left!"

This is the task that I must perform constantly. The Church wishes, for example, to apply Rosmini's invitation to "hear loftily of God" with worthy liturgical celebrations, stripping the concept of God from the guises, at times ingenuous and caricatural, in which an agrarian and prescientific civilization had dressed it.

But it is a hard job. On the right, they shout impiety and sacrilege every time an old ritual is abandoned for a new one. On the left, vice versa, novelty is indiscriminately hailed for the sake of novelty, the whole edifice of the past is merrily dismantled, paintings and statues are sent up to the attic; idolatry and superstition are found everywhere, and it is even said that, to safeguard God's dignity, God must be spoken of in only the most select terms, or there must actually be silence.

*   *   *

Illustrious Marconi! In the field of science, you rightly demanded physical and mathematical certitude. In other fields, however, you were satisfied with the certitude of common sense, which is also a certitude. I know very well that God cannot be spoken of in the way He deserves, but He must still be spoken of somehow.

I do as that mother did when, shut up in a windowless prison, she gave birth to a child, which grew up with her, never seeing the sun. To give him an idea of it, when the child was six, his mother pointed out to him the jailer's lighted lantern. "There," she said, "the sun is like that flame: it gives light, it warms, but the sun is much, much bigger!" It was a scant idea, an analogy, but it was better than nothing.

In the social and economic field, the Church also finds difficulties in making its contribution. As Church, first of all, it declares that it has neither the mission nor the skill nor the means to resolve strictly technical problems. The faithful, who are also citizens, must themselves act in unions, in politics, in commercial enterprise according to the inspiration of their religious faith.

The Hierarchy proposes to them and to everyone a social teaching derived from the principles of the Gospel, which today must make its way amid the opposing ideologies of capitalism and Marxism.

The former has the merit of having fostered industrial development and having defended personal liberty. It is reproached, however, for having caused the very serious sufferings of the poor in the last centuries and today's inequities.

Marxism tramples personal liberty underfoot and sweeps aside all religious values; it cannot, however, be denied credit for having made many people realize the sufferings of workers and the duty of solidarity.

Capitalism, to be in order, according to the teaching of the Church, should be profoundly modified. The wealth produced is good; provided that the heart does not become too attached to it, that it can be shared among as many people as possible, and that it no longer creates the serious inequities of today. Earnings are good only if achieved through the right means, that is, without sacrificing the dignity of any human being. Competition can also be good, provided it does not degenerate into fierce fighting, with no holds barred. The Church, after the example of Christ, must love all, but must surround the poor and the more unfortunate with its preferential love.

As for Marxism, it today is trying to infiltrate the Catholics' ranks through a subtle distinction. "The analysis Marx made of society," people say, "is one thing; the ideology that guided Marx is another. The analysis is so strictly scientific, enlightening, useful for solving problems, that we accept it; we reject the materialist ideology."

The Hierarchy is alarmed by these positions. The French bishops wrote, on 14 November 1973: "We refuse to accept the scientific character of an analysis that actually rests on a certain number of philosophical postulates, some debatable, others unacceptable."

Paul VI had warned (*Octuagesima Adveniens* no. 34): "It would be a dangerous illusion . . . to accept the elements of Marxist analysis without recognizing their relationship with the ideology."

Perhaps, illustrious Marconi, you will say to me: "You are writing me a letter, a very humble literary form, which will prove inadequate for a criticism of the giants, capitalism and Marxism!" You are right, but what can I do? The fly kicks as best it can!

* * *

The Church's contribution to the unity of the world is expressed by Paul VI in these terms: "An expert in humankind . . . without claiming to interfere in politics . . . the Church offers what it possesses of its own: a world view of man and of mankind. This view is rooted in the Bible, which shows all men heading toward the same destiny, redeemed by a Savior, who declared His solidarity with the whole human race, and who had the mission 'to reconcile with Himself all things, whether on earth or in heaven.' "

In the Old Testament Jonah does not believe that he must share with other peoples the privileges of his own people. Sent to preach in Nineveh, to the east, he tries to flee toward the west, because the people of Nineveh are not Jews. God, thanks to His system of unleashed storms and gaping whale's jaws, brings him back to the east. Preaching to the people of Nineveh, Jonah hopes to himself that they will not be converted. The opposite happens, and they are converted, God forgives them, and Jonah, with the spirit of a spoiled child, complains to

God: ". . . I knew that Thou art a gracious God, slow to anger, and abounding in steadfast love, and repentest of evil."

But God gives him a lesson of universalism, with subtle humor and with equal firmness.

Having left the city, Jonah prepares himself a shelter of boughs against the heat, and God lends him a hand, having a gourd plant grow in great haste. Jonah falls asleep happily, but in the morning he finds the plant withered and the sun beating down on his head. He complains again, but God answers him: "You pity the plant, for which you did not labor, nor did you make it grow, which came into being in a night, and perished in a night. And should not I pity Nineveh, a great city, in which there are more than a hundred and twenty thousand persons who do not know their right hand from their left . . . ?"

This universalistic theme — very clear also in the prophecies of Isaiah, of Micah, and in some of the Psalms — is picked up again, in full, by Jesus. To the manger, along with the shepherds, come also the Magi, who are not Jews; Jesus praised and benefited also the woman of Canaan and the Roman centurion; the mission entrusted by Christ to the Apostles is described in these precise terms: "Go therefore and make disciples of all nations," so then Saint Paul can expound the divine plan of salvation in the following words: ". . . reconcile to Himself all things, whether on earth or in heaven."

Following the Bible, recent popes have perorated the cause of unity and peace. Paul VI especially even initiated unusual paths, speaking at the U.N., sending telegrams to the heads of Communist states, offering his services as a mediator.

You will say: With what results? At the very minimum there is the result of the conviction, described and publicized, of a new atmosphere, a change that is taking place. Using a classical reference, I would say that from the mentality of Gian Galeazzo Visconti we are passing to that of Petrarch.

The former, in the style of Renaissance lords, could not even conceive of a government without fighting wars and he even went so far as to forbid priests to repeat the words of the Mass *"dona nobis pacem."*

The latter was of a diametrically opposed opinion, and he used to tell of a dialogue between himself and a madman. The madman, having seen some soldiers on the march, asked the poet: "Where are they going?"

"To war!" Petrarch answered.

"But," the madman remarked, "this war will have to end with peace one of these days, won't it?"

"Of course!" the poet replied.

"Then," the madman continued, "why not make peace at once, before starting the war?"

And Petrarch concluded, in a melancholy tone: "I agree with that madman!"

God willing, it seems that, thanks also to the Church, a bit of this good madness is spreading in all minds.

* * *

Illustrious Marconi! Your intense life, spent in research and achievement to its last day, can be summed up in this phrase: *Few words, many deeds.* From this point of view you teach something also to us, who today seem inclined to the opposite tendency, with many words (spoken or written) and scant practical fruit.

June 1974

To Giuseppe Gioacchino Belli

Words, Words, Words

Dear poet,

In your verses you treated rather badly my fellow-citizen Pope Gregory XVI, who came from Belluno. This doesn't prevent me from recognizing the fact that in the more than two thousand sonnets in Roman dialect which you left us, you have at times portrayed with very lively truth the people of Rome, their language, their personality, their customs, habits, beliefs, prejudices, virtues, and also their defects.

Sometimes, to tell the truth, you slipped, in your writing; your life was that of a gentleman, and you made a point of saying so: *"Scatagnàmo ar parlà, ma aràmo dritto"* (We sin in speaking, but we go straight).

How many happy remarks, however! This one, for example: "I don't mean to brag, but today's a lovely day." Some of your sonnets are real genre paintings, from which, alive and speaking, artisans spring forth, women of the populace, conspirators, merchants, prelates, and simple priests.

In this last category there is the abbot Francesco Cancellieri. You described him in famous verses, which you

GIUSEPPE GIOACCHINO BELLI, Roman dialect poet (1791–1863). An employee of the papal government, he had a tragic childhood and a difficult life. In his happiest period (1830–1836) he composed, in a flow of inspiration, some two thousand sonnets, in which he portrayed with lively accuracy the personality, the customs, the virtues, and the defects of the Romans.

then commented on in prose, writing: Cancellieri "began speaking of radishes, and then from radishes to carrots, and from carrots to eggplants, he ended up with the burning of Troy!"

* * *

It is a shame that, with his rambling and grievous logorrhea, the good abbot made bad propaganda for conversation, which, if carried on in the proper fashion, is, on the contrary, a fine thing in our life as poor human beings.

Conversation, in fact, brings us close to others and gives us a deep sense of ourselves; it rests us from our labors, distracts us from our worries, develops our personality, refreshes our thoughts.

Am I sad? The agreeable nature of the person conversing with me is a consolation. Do I feel alone? Conversation makes loneliness cease: if it is familiar conversation, I am happy to be admitted to the privacy of others; if it is important conversation, I feel honored to be treated as an "intelligence."

Is this the first time I am conversing with such-and-such person? I feel as if I were traveling pleasantly through an unknown land. Is it the second, third, fourth time? I feel as if I were revisiting places already seen, whose beautiful landscape, however, I had not yet fully explored. I also find that, in conversing, I am enriched. To hold firm convictions, in fact, is a beautiful thing; to hold them in such a way that you can communicate them and see them shared and appreciated is even more beautiful.

The clarity of what I say increases the clarity of what I think. If I realize that my feelings strike a chord in another's spirit, I sense that feeling return to me, resonant, increased.

Jesus also found solace in conversation; to ascertain this, you have only to read in Saint John the confidences to His Disciples during the Last Supper. Jesus often made conversation the vehicle of His apostolate: He spoke as

He walked along the roads, as He strolled under the arcades of Solomon; He spoke in houses, with people around Him, like Mary, seated at His feet, like John, who rested his head against the Lord's bosom.

I have often asked myself: Why did the Lord so often expound the loftiest truths at the table? Perhaps because at mealtime people lay aside all hauteur and assume a calm, modest, relaxed attitude. At table, cares and disturbances are few or none; people sit there without a polemical spirit, ready to welcome, friendly.

* * *

And it was, in fact, during a conversation at table, the day before yesterday, that I was almost able to persuade a guest. He declared himself — between morsels, between smiles — a great supporter of pluralism in the faith. "It's clear to me," he said, "that nobody has a monopoly on the entire Christian truth. Each of us has only a little bit, and he must be allowed to enjoy it in peace. Only God creates unity from above, putting the various bits together and making a synthesis of them!"

"Forgive me," I answered, "but your idea of God and of truth seems to me that of the blind men of India."

"What blind men?" he asked.

I said: "Wait!"

I rose, went out, and came back with Lev Tolstoy's *Fables and Fairy Tales for Children* in my hand. "Let me read just one page to you," I said. And then I read him the fable "The King and the Elephants."

An Indian king ordered all the blind to be gathered together, and when this was done, he had them shown his elephants. One blind man touched a leg; another, the tail; a third, the root of the tail; a fourth, the belly; a fifth, the back; a sixth, the ears; a seventh, the tusks; and an eighth, the trunk.

Then the king had the blind men brought into his presence and asked: "What are my elephants like?"

The first blind man answered: "Your elephants are like columns." This was the one who had touched the legs.

The second said: "They are like a broom." This was the one who had touched the tail. The third said: "They are like a branch." This was the one who had touched the root of the tail. The one who had touched the belly said: "Your elephants are like a mound of earth." The one who had touched the back said: "It is like a mountain." The one who had touched the ears said: "They are like a mortar." The one who had touched the tusks said: "They are like horns." The one who had touched the trunk said: "They are like a big rope." And all the blind men began quarreling among themselves.

Putting down the book, I said: "Listen, it revolts me to think that God sent His Son to say to us: 'I am the way, the truth, and the life,' with the fine result then that all of us find ourselves in the situation of those blind men, each with a wretched little fragment of the truth in his hand, each fragment different from the others. We know the truth of the faith only by analogy, yes; but blind to this degree, no! It seems to me unworthy both of God and of our reason!"

This unexpected theology based on elephants' tails and backs did not completely convince my guest, but it shook him, making him say: "Well, nobody had ever said this to me!"

"Don't you know?" I said to him; "at times it is the ducks who lead the geese to drink. When Rahner fails, with all his big volumes of theology, Tolstoy can step in with his little fable!"

* * *

From Rahner and from Tolstoy, illustrious Belli, I return to you, recognizing that — in conversation — there is also the other side of the coin: the tedious rambling of your abbot Cancellieri is only one of the conversation's drawbacks.

There are others, and we know them in Venice, where Goldoni described the troubles caused by conversation in *I pettegolezzi delle donne* (The Women's Gossip), in *La bottega da caffè* (The Coffeehouse) with Don Marzio, so backbiting and troublemaking, in *Il bugiardo* (The Liar) with Lelio, who piles lies upon lies, passing them off as "witty inventions"; in *Le baruffe chiozzotte* (The Chioggia Quarrels) and in *Il campiello* (The Little Square) with those women who seem to ask a friend to keep a secret only in order to spread the news.

But you also know something about this, as is shown by the delightful little picture, which I will transcribe below:

> Now here is how I found it out.
> Nanna confided in Vincenza;
> She told Nina, at the Sapienza;
> Nina told it in confidence to Tuta.
> And so it reached the ear of Clemenza,
> Who ran to tell it to the woman with the
>   mustache:
> And she, who's a friend of mine, came today
> To tell me privately, in secret.
> And if I've told you, I know for sure
> That you're a woman who's listened
> To my secret under the seal of Confession.
> Friend, mind you, for the love of God,
> If you should ever be tempted to tell it,
> Don't say I was the one who told you!

Converse, therefore, but not at the expense of charity, of truth, of work, of study: of sense of proportion, in other words. We must make sure our grave doesn't bear the following epitaph:

> Here is buried the great talker Soemus:
> Now, we, too, will be able to talk a little.

* * *

To converse is one thing; it is another thing to chatter mindlessly, stringing one piece of futile information after another, concealing one's soul rather than revealing it, blocking the chance of other speakers, leaving people in a daze, weak and prostrate!

I read that Thomas More, during a journey in Holland, happened to travel a way with a man whose discourse was very agreeable, since he left room for his interlocutor, and since he said interesting things, with great spirit. At a certain point, delighted at a particularly witty and apt remark of his traveling companion, Thomas cried: "Why, you are either the devil or you are Erasmus of Rotterdam!"

"I am not the devil," the other man said, "but I am Erasmus."

This episode shows that our conversation reveals us as we are and that in it we must try to say something useful, interesting, and pleasant, without sermons, without poses, without highfalutin, arcane words. Such words, dear Belli, used to annoy you too, and you said so clearly, picking on an innocent conjunction which, used today, would only make people laugh, though in your day was very fashionable.

> *Conciossiacosaché,* inasmuchasnotwithstanding:
> This is a word that our fathers heard first,
> At their first entrance to their first school,
> And they felt such great respect for it
> That they kept their throats full of it,
> To spit it out everywhere, in prose and rhyme.

If you were to come back today, you would no longer hear *conciossiacosaché*. You would have to accustom your ear, however, to other phrases: "to confront the word of God," "prophetic speeches and actions," "social instances," "mediation between faith and history," "structuralism," "communion," "liberation," "in-depth investigation," "check out," "read according to this parameter, and understand on this level." These are all words that express exalted concepts, mind you, but it is somewhat comical to see people declare themselves nonconformists, then blithely conform to these words only because they are the ones used by some big shots.

I am surprised by them much as you were surprised by other expressions:

I can't understand what is the reason
Why, when people hear sneezing,
They have to spout out so many salutations,
And not a word for coughs or clearings of the throat.
"Gesundheit, your health, God bless you,
Good luck, happiness, and drink your fill,
Et iterum all hail and lots of sons . . ."

You couldn't understand the reason then. I am unable to understand now. Is it the fault of fashion? It has been defined as "horror of the past tense," "not the mother, but the mother-in-law and tyrant of sound reasoning."

How much better it would be if, at least in conversation, instead of the difficult words in fashion, we were to use simple and easy words, perhaps borrowed from the tales of Tolstoy or from your sonnets, obviously selected with care and expurgated!

July 1974

To Felix Dupanloup

The Text Exists, but What about the Readers?

Dear bishop and Academician of France,

"Glowing coal, on which now nature blows, now grace." This is how they defined you. I feel, however, that far more grace "blew" on you than nature.

Even when you were fighting your great battles in the newspapers or in the French National Assembly or in the Senate or in Vatican Council I, you were always led and animated by a deep religious sense, a heart that was enthusiastic, true, but upright and loyal.

You directed a seminary, and even Renan, your one-time pupil, declared you an "unparalleled educator."

There was a campaign for the free school, and Lacordaire, Montalembert, and Falloux had you at their side in the battle and in the victory.

The *Syllabus* of Pius IX appeared, arousing vast and painful reactions; and you made a commentary on it, so temperate and sound that it partly calmed the storm, winning the applause of all of six hundred bishops and the approval of Pius IX himself.

FELIX DUPANLOUP, bishop of Orléans, born at St. Felix (Savoie) in 1802, died in Lacombe in 1878. He distinguished himself by his zeal, intelligent and tireless in the preparation of the clergy, the education of the young, and the teaching of the catechism. Author of pedagogical works, he fought for the freedom of instruction and took part in French political life.

Talleyrand, that great sinner and apostate, was considered by all a man beyond recovery; God won him back, but He made use of you, your tact, of your understanding and patience.

In short, you were a great bishop, great man of letters, a leading figure in all movements of ideas and opinions in your century.

For me, however, the most interesting aspect of your personality and of your work is your passion for catechism.

You began instructing the young when you were still a cleric in Saint Sulpice; you continued, as a very young priest at the Assumption and the Madeleine; all Paris rushed to hear you. Also as a bishop, you kept catechism prominent in your thoughts, and it invaded the majority of your books. You wrote in your diary, "As soon as I was assigned the class of the little ones, I caught fire at once: for whatever is not catechism, the pure action of grace on souls, is nothing to my eyes; the little man of letters, who was in me, gave way and placed himself completely at the service of the catechist." You wrote further: "The most beautiful of ministries is the pastoral ministry. But catechism is still more beautiful. It is the ideal beauty of the heart of God. Nothing can be compared to it. It is the purest, the most altruistic, the most selfless of ministries."

* * *

I happened to think of you, and of those impassioned convictions of yours, because I have before me the text of the "Catechism of Children" which will be tried out in Italy, starting next October. A good text, it seems to me. But what use is the text, if we do not have the minds and the hearts of catechists?

To me, when I was a young priest, they used to say: "The text is merely an aid, a stimulus, not a comfortable armchair in which the catechist settles for a rest." "The text, no matter how well done, remains something dead: it is the catechist who must bring it to life." "The lesson is worth only as much as its preparation!" "To children you do not teach so much what you know as what you are: fine words from the catechist's mouth are worth little, if other words come from his behavior to contradict them."

I was told of Pedro Ribadeneira, a tempestuous child, a "Peck's Bad Boy" *ante litteram*, whom Saint Ignatius brought with him to Rome from Spain. "Make the Sign of the Cross more properly!" Saint Ignatius said to him one day.

"But Father Ignatius, I make it exactly the way your Jesuits do!"

"What are you talking about? My Jesuits make the Sign of the Cross in the right way."

The boy didn't answer; he kept his own counsel.

The Jesuits got up very early in the morning and went into the chapel along the dark corridors, in black cassocks and white surplices. Pedro filled the holy water stoup with black ink. The Jesuits, passing it, dipped in their fingers, crossed themselves, went to the pews for meditation, after which they left the surplices in the sacristy. Little Pedro quickly gathered up all those surplices and took them to Saint Ignatius: "Come, Father, and take a look at the Signs of the Cross your beloved Jesuits make!" Alas, the ink marks clearly said that also the Jesuits sometimes make the Sign of the Cross hit or miss, and missing more than they hit.

And here, in my imagination, the host of the lay catechists passes by.

Parents, first of all. They are the "first preachers of the word," the Council said. Through the holy pictures in the home, through the prayers said there, through family conversation, through the respect shown priests and sacred things, children can find themselves immersed in a warm and natural environment of religiousness. But something more must be done.

When a lady asked Windhorst, a German statesman, how to pose before a photographer, he answered: "With catechism in hand, Madame, as you instruct your children!"

In reality, the first book of religion that children read is the parents themselves. It is a good thing, if the father says to the boy: "There is a monk confessor at church, don't you think you could take advantage of the opportunity?" Better still if he says: "I'm going to church, to Confession; do you want to come along?"

* * *

Here, however, I find some objectors today: parents who call themselves Christians, but who postpone even the baptism of their children. "No pressure on my child! He will choose when he's twenty!"

You, my colleague Dupanloup, already answered this objection, in the following way: At twenty! The age of all the passions! The age in which your son would have particular need of a faith that has penetrated into the depth of his being, to call on its help! And how will this boy manage to choose among all the existing religions, if he hasn't studied them all first? And how can he study them all, busy as he is with school, sports, amusements, friendships? To become the heir of a great fortune, one has to be born to it. To inherit riches, in fact, is a great piece of luck, and one thinks, one assumes that, even if for the present he is unaware of it, the child will be, in time, very happy and accept very gladly the luck that has befallen him. If a father is really a Christian, he must think that to become, in baptism, son of God and brother of Christ is an immense fortune; why should he deprive his son of that?

"Yes," the objector continued, "but heavy moral commitments are connected with this fortune! These must not be loaded on my son without his consent!"

You, Dupanloup, answered this, too: How many things are imposed on children without their consent! Without asking their permission, to begin with, you brought them into the world! Name, family, environment, and social situation, clothes, the school of their first years: all this happens without asking permission of those concerned. But is it then a misfortune that a child should have good Christian laws to observe? Did God perhaps give mankind His laws out of some triumphalistic whim or with a view to His own advantage? Doesn't man become morally great and happy, if he accepts duties and limitations? Freedom? Yes, of course, but it doesn't consist of doing everything you please, rather of being able to do what must be done!

* * *

After parents come the elementary school teachers as catechists. You wrote some very acute things about your first teachers.

I, in my turn, think tenderly of mine and I agree with the words of Otto Ernst: "For me there is no one greater than an elementary school teacher."

I see myself a boy again on the benches of my school in Canale, with the feelings of schoolboys, of which Goldsmith speaks in *The Deserted Village:* dazed, openmouthed, before the teacher, and all asking themselves how, for such a small head, such great and wonderous things could come forth!

Mind you: I am not so ingenuous as to invent myths about children and teachers. There is also the other side of the story, I know. Innocent as angels, children are; but often as haughty as princes, bold as heroes, unrestrained as colts, stubborn as donkeys, fickle as sunflowers, with a stomach as big as a whale's; but always, still, in a precious age, trusting, susceptible to being shaped.

As for the teachers, there are some who know how to take their pupils in the right way, aware that they need a leader, imposing their leadership with skill and affection; there are others who are tamed or dominated, instead of being the tamers and dominators.

The first-grade schoolmistress recalled by our writer Mosca seems to belong to the "tamed" category. Passing along the corridors, he writes, one could hear her voice ask: "Do horses have fifteen legs?" No, the little pupils could be heard, answering in chorus. "Do they perhaps have twelve?" No again. And, reducing the number of legs progressively, she arrived finally at the correct number. "Do they have four?" No, the students answered enthusiastically. Poor teacher!

The above-mentioned Mosca, instead, was made of different stuff. How did he manage to "conquer" the terrible "Five C"? It was very simple: by winning the affection of its forty children. And how did he do that? He tells us:

"A horsefly was my salvation." A horsefly entered the classroom, and its buzzing attracted the attention of all the students. Another teacher would perhaps have said: "Pay attention to me and not to the horsefly!" Instead, Mosca said to one of the boys: "Do you think you could kill that horsefly with a slingshot in one try?" "That's my regular job," the boy said, immediately coming from his desk, slingshot in hand. He aimed at the insect and fired, but missed the target. "Give me the slingshot!" Mosca said, then took his turn aiming at the horsefly. He fired and the insect fell dead at his feet. A shot of superlative bravura gained him the immediate admiration of the boys, who had previously assumed an attitude of threat and defiance.

"If you at least had a mustache!" the principal had said to Mosca, mistrusting the youth of his new teacher. But, obviously, other gifts count more than a mustache! The good that teachers, with their ascendancy, can do for the young, in teaching religion, is incalculable.

On one condition: that they expound faithfully the genuine word of God and not their own personal opinions. At times it happens: truth is replaced with "progressivism"; there is contempt for what the Magisterium of the Church teaches, because someone wants to replace old things with new ones. But renewal, legitimate, opportune, and even necessary when it is a question of secondary and out-of-date things of the Church, is very dangerous in other cases.

The teachers tell their pupils the fairy tale of Aladdin and his magic lamp stolen from the magician. The latter, at a certain point, wants his revenge. He goes through the streets, crying: "New lamps for old!" It looks like an excellent deal, but instead it is a fraud. Aladdin's credulous wife falls for it. In her husband's absence, she goes to the attic, takes the lamp, whose wondrous powers she knows nothing about, and hands it over to the magician. The rascal carries it off, leaving in exchange all his lamps of tin, shiny but worthless.

The trick is repeated: every now and then a magician comes along, philosopher or politician as he may be, and offers to trade merchandise. Watch out! The ideas offered by certain "magicians," even if they shine, are tin, a human matter, lasting only a day! What they call old and outdated ideas are often ideas of God, of which it is written that not even a comma will pass away!

Alas, dear Dupanloup, I have almost forgotten you, writing about catechists and teachers.

But it is precisely to these catechists and teachers that you have something to say. And that is: to unite, as you did, fidelity to God with trust in the true values of modern civilization and in the perpetual youth of the Church.

August 1974

To Petrarch

Confession Six Hundred Years Afterwards

Illustrious poet,

In Italy and abroad this year the sixth centenary of your death (1374–1974) is being celebrated.

Conferences, studies, publications underline your significance, this or that aspect of your position, this or that aspect of your personality or of your immense literary work.

Dead for such a long time, you prove to be more alive than ever, arousing curiosity and attracting the attention of the men of today to Petrarch the man of letters, the subtle psychologist, the politician, the impassioned tourist, the Christian both sincere and critical as you were, and to a hundred other facets.

Will someone also speak of you as a sinner, penitent, but recidivist, a Christian thirsting often for holiness, but unable to make a really clean break with sin and to renounce the passions, great and small, that were dear to

FRANCESCO PETRARCA (Petrarch), poet from Arezzo (1304–1374). He led a wandering life (Florence, Provence) in search of the tranquility he managed to find only in Vaucluse (France) and Arquà (province of Padua). His fame rests on the Canzoniere, *a collection of verses (three hundred sixty-six sonnets, ballads, songs) inspired by his unrequited love for Laura. The poems are an unsurpassed model of elegance and style.*

you? I don't know. If so, he will have to speak also of your attitude to Confession.

Because you used to go to Confession, illustrious Petrarch!

Writing from Rome to your friend Giovanni Boccaccio, you told him of the mishap that had befallen you: a colossal kick from a horse, striking your precious knee, causing two weeks of very sharp pain: "But I accept all on account of my sins," you wrote, "and as substitution for that penance which my confessor, too good, did not impose on me."

What commitment you showed in examining your soul even to its most secret crannies, as your books reveal.

When you write that you are too self-satisfied with your talent, your eloquence, the culture you have acquired, and even with your bodily attractiveness. When you reproach yourself for thirsting after honors, comforts, riches, and of having too often given in to lust. You bemoan the bonds of passion, which you are unable to break, and the strength of "perverse habit," and the "most bitter taste" of your lapses.

Writing to your brother the monk, you deplore your desire for "most elegant clothes," the "fear that a hair may be out of place and a slight breeze might disturb the very elaborate array of my locks." The iron used to curl your hair causes you broken sleep and pains even more atrocious than those inflicted by a "cruel pirate," but still this does not make you think of giving it up. And you put to Saint Augustine — an imaginary interlocutor — some troubling problems: "The *falling* was mine, but the lying there, the failure to rise again, does not depend on me."

"It depends also on you," Augustine replies.

And you rebut: "But you can clearly see that I weep for my wretchedness!"

And Augustine says: "It is not a matter of tears, but of willpower!"

Luckily, the right principle never failed you. "God can

save me," despite my weakness. The mercy of God dispels fears, solves many problems.

*   *   *

At a distance of six hundred years, are we, today's penitents, better or worse than you? This is a question that stimulates my curiosity.

It seems to me that, in us, there is less willingness to recognize the failings we are guilty of. We say often: "Holy Mary . . . pray for us sinners," "Father . . . forgive us our sins," "Lamb of God . . . have mercy on us," but very superficially. In practice, we excuse ourselves with the oddest pretexts ("We are free, autonomous, mature"); we appeal to the "demands of nature, of instinct, of culture, of fashion."

The Bible, in the Book of Proverbs, thus presents the case of an adulterous woman: "She eats, and wipes her mouth, and says, 'I have done no wrong.' " That woman, my dear Petrarch, is an emblematic figure; she exactly portrays a good part of our permissive Christian civilization.

Just as you never lacked tears, so they are not wanting in us either: it is willpower we need. Or rather: We often manage to stop wanting what we wanted with sin, to disapprove what we have approved, but we never manage to do what is more practical: to avoid occasions of sin. You who, even in the climbing of Mont Ventoux, took along with you a copy of the *Confessions* of Augustine, know the case of Alipius.

A strong man, capable of holding his own against very powerful senators, he had come to Rome from Africa, and had conceived "disgust and hatred" for the combats of the gladiators, who killed one another to offer a spectacle to the populace. Some friends invited him to witness the combat at least once. Alipius first answered no, but then said: "I will be there, but as if I were absent, and I will win a victory over you and over the spectacle."

So he went then, to meet the challenge; and, in fact,

when he took his seat in the amphitheater, he closed his eyes so he wouldn't even see. Unfortunately he did not close his ears: at a certain point an immense shout of the crowd made him start. He opened his eyes out of pure curiosity, but "to see that blood and to become eager for cruelty was all one: he not only did not look away from the spectacle, he stared at it; he breathed in its fury without realizing it; he began to enjoy that struggle, drunk with sanguinary pleasure. He was no longer the man he had been on coming there: he looked, he shouted, he waxed enthusiastic," he came away, bringing a fever with him, which drove him to return, drawing others with him. Subsequently he corrected his error, but only after a long time.

In the line of the extraordinary weakness of Alipius (later bishop and saint) we find ourselves, unfortunately, more or less all of us. This is why, in every Confession, we are urged to pray: "I vow . . . to avoid occasions of sin," but . . .

I fear that we are less complete than you, as far as faith in God is concerned. True, God is the father of the prodigal son; Jesus is the good shepherd, who brings the strayed sheep back to the fold, who forgave the adulteress, and Zaccaeus, and the good thief. All, or almost all of us, can go this far.

But others conclude: "I'll work things out with Him personally," and do not follow you as far as the mention of the confessor, who mediates between God and the sinner thanks to the words of Jesus to the Apostles: "If you forgive the sins of any, they are forgiven."

They do not understand that the confessor must not only *declare* the already accomplished remission of the sins, but must *make* the remission with a sentence.

And this sentence cannot be left to mere whim ("I like you, so I absolve you!"), but must be based on certain well-pondered elements, which only the penitent can supply, precisely through his own Confession.

*   *   *

You found your confessor "too good." In our times, someone making a proper Confession looks for a good, but not "too good," confessor.

Augusto Conti, the illustrious philosopher, dedicated an entire chapter filled with affectionate gratitude to his confessors in his book, *Le sveglie dell'anima* (The Awakeners of the Soul).

Saint Jeanne de Chantal and other penitents declared themselves very happy with Saint Francis de Sales, who in Confession was both father and physician, particularly skilled in instilling courage. "Holiness," he used to say, "consists of fighting our defects, but how can they be fought if they don't exist? How to conquer them if we don't encounter them? To be wounded sometimes in this battle does not mean being defeated. One is defeated only if one loses one's life or one's courage; anyone who decides to keep on fighting is a victor."

He is the type of confessor people want today: firm, but delicate; a lover of God, but a man who knows the problems of human beings.

It is true, however, that today, at the wish of the Church, the accent is placed less on the accusation of sins than on conversion presented biblically as a moving away from sin, and even more, as approach to God and the amorous embrace of Him. "We beseech you, . . . be reconciled with God," Saint Paul said. Today this is repeated and it is hoped that the reconciliation be preceded by the word of God itself, read and meditated. We, in fact, go to God, if He calls us first and speaks to us. Ideally, too, this word, if possible, should not strike us as individuals, singly, but rather gathered together, in a community.

You of the Middle Ages, dear Petrarch, made Confession a very personal and secret affair. Today we think with nostalgia of ancient times when, at the end of Lent, the bishop gave his hand to the first of the penitents, who then gave his to the next, and so through a long chain of all the others, who were thus led into the church for solemn reconciliation.

I didn't know how frequently you went to Confession.

In your Middle Ages it was the custom to go often to Confession and rarely to Communion. Today the opposite seems to happen; even devout souls prove to be a bit allergic to frequent Confession and devotion.

They remind me of Jonathan Swift's manservant. After having spent a night in an inn, Swift asked for his boots in the morning and saw them brought to him still covered with dust. "Why didn't you clean them?" he asked.

"I thought it was useless," the manservant answered. "After a few miles of traveling, they'll become dusty again anyway!"

"True, but now go prepare the horses for our departure." A little later the horses were pawing the ground outside the stable, and Swift was also fully dressed for the journey.

"But we can't leave without breakfast!" the manservant said.

"It's useless," Swift answered; "after a few miles of traveling, you'd be hungry again anyway!"

*   *   *

Dear Petrarch, neither you nor I follow the logic of Swift's valet, I believe. Will the soul become soiled again after Confession? It is quite likely. To keep it clean now, however, can do nothing but good, because Confession not only removes the dust of sins, but instills a special strength to avoid them and reinforces our friendship with God.

September 1974

To Saint Teresa of Avila

Teresa, a Penny, and God

Dear Saint Teresa,

October is the month of your feast day: I assume you will allow me to converse with you, though it must be in writing.

The visitor who looks at the famous marble group in which Bernini portrays you transfixed by the arrow of the Seraph thinks of your visions and ecstasies. And he is right: the mystic Teresa, transported in God, is a real Teresa.

But the *other* Teresa is also real, and I like her more: the one closer to us, as she emerges from the autobiography and the letters. This is the Teresa of practical life, who experiences our same difficulties and knows how to overcome them deftly; who knows how to laugh and make others laugh; who moves through the world and the most various vicissitudes with ease, thanks to her abundant natural talents, but more because of her constant union with God.

The Protestant Reformation breaks out, the situation of

SAINT TERESA OF AVILA, born Teresa de Cepeda y Ahumada (1515–1582). Daughter of a rich and noble family of Avila, in Spain, she became a Carmelite at the age of twenty-one and devoted herself to a vigorous activity of the reform of the Order, which she wished to restore to its original austerity. This work of reformation was accompanied by her ascetic and mystical experience, which inspired admirable writings: El Camino de la Perfección, *an autobiography, and numerous letters.*

the Church in Germany and in France is critical. You grieve over it and you write: "To save even one soul of the many that were being lost there, I would have sacrificed my life many times over. But I was a woman!"

Woman! But one who is worth twenty men, one who never leaves any means untried, who succeeds in carrying out a magnificent internal reformation, and who with her works and her writings influences the whole Church: the first and only woman — except for Saint Catherine — to be proclaimed a Doctor of the Church!

Woman with a frank tongue and a brisk, cutting pen. You had a very lofty concept of the mission of nuns, but you wrote to Father Gratian: "For the love of God, take care what you do! Never believe the nuns, because if they want something, they try every possible means." And to Father Ambrogio, rejecting a postulant, you say: "You make me laugh, telling me you understood that soul merely at seeing her. It is not so easy to know women!"

Yours is the succinct definition of the devil: "That poor wretch who cannot love."

To Don Sancho Davila: "I also have distractions in the recitation of the Divine Office. . . . I confessed them to Father Domingo [Bañez, famous theologian: author's note], who told me not to mind. I say the same to you, because the disease is incurable." This is a piece of spiritual advice, but you scattered advice generously, and of all sorts; to Father Gratian you even gave the advice of riding, on his travels, a gentler donkey, one which did not have the bad habit of throwing monks to the ground, or else of having himself tied to the donkey, to keep from falling!

But it is in the moment of battle that you are incomparable. None other than the Nuncio has you shut up in the convent of Toledo, declaring you "a restless woman, vagabond, disobedient, and rebellious. . . ." But from the convent, your messages to Philip II, to princes and prelates, unravel every knot.

Your conclusion: "Teresa alone is worth nothing;

Teresa and a penny are worth less than nothing; Teresa, a penny, and God can do anything!"

For me, you are a remarkable example of a phenomenon regularly repeated in the life of the Catholic Church.

Women, in themselves that is, do not govern — that function belongs to the Hierarchy — but very often they inspire, they promote, and at times they direct.

On the one hand, in fact, the Spirit "blows where it wills"; on the other, woman is more sensitive to religion and more able to give herself generously to great causes. Hence the vast host of women saints, mystics, and founders of Orders, who have appeared in the Catholic Church.

Alongside them we should list the women who started ascetic-theological movements, with wide-ranging influence.

The noblewoman Marcella, who on the Aventine directed a kind of convent made up of rich and cultivated patrician women; she collaborated with Saint Jerome in the translation of the Bible.

Madame Acarie influenced illustrious people like the Jesuit Coton, the Capuchin de Canfelt, and Francis de Sales himself, as well as many others, thus influencing the entire French spirituality of the early seventeenth century.

Princess Amalia von Gallitzin, from her "Münster Circle," admired even by Goethe, spread through all of northern Germany a current of intensely spiritual life. Sophie Swetchine, a Russian convert, in the early nineteenth century appeared in France as the "spiritual guide" of the most outstanding laymen and priests.

I could mention other instances, but I prefer to come back to you, who were not so much the spiritual daughter as the spiritual mother of Saint John of the Cross and of the first reformed Carmelites. Today everything is limpid and smooth on this score, but in your day there was the conflict mentioned above.

On the one hand there was you, rich in charismata, ardent and luminous strength granted you for the Church of God; on the other, there was the Nuncio, that is to say the Hierarchy, who had to judge the authenticity of your charismata. At first, on the basis of distorted information, the Nuncio expressed a negative opinion. Once the necessary explanations had been given and things had been better examined, all was clarified: the Hierarchy approved everything and your gifts could expand in favor of the Church.

* * *

But today, too, there is much talk of charismata and Hierarchy. You were a specialist on the subject, so I will take the liberty of drawing the following principles from your works.

1) Above everything there is the Holy Spirit. From Him come both charismata and the powers of pastors; it is up to the Spirit to achieve the harmonious accord between Hierarchy and charismata and to promote the unity of the Church.

2) Charismata and Hierarchy are both necessary to the Church, but in different ways. The charismata act as accelerator, fostering progress and renewal. The Hierarchy must rather act as brake, with a view to stability and prudence.

3) At times charismata and Hierarchy meet and overlap. Certain charismata, in fact, are given conspicuously to pastors as the gifts of governing recalled by Saint Paul in the first Epistle to the Corinthians. On the other hand, since the Hierarchy must regulate all the main developments of ecclesiastical life, the charismatics cannot avoid its guide on the pretext that they have charismata.

4) Charismata are not anyone's private preserve: they can be given to all: priests and laity, men and women. To be *able to have* charismata, however, is one thing; actually *having* charismata is another.

In your *Book of the Foundations*, I find written: "A penitent declared to her confessor that the Madonna visited her often and stayed to speak with her for over an hour, revealing the future to her and many other things. And since, among many bizarre things, there were some true ones, everything was then considered true. I understood at once what it was all about . . . but I confined myself to saying to the confessor that he should await the outcome of the prophecies, that he should inform himself about the penitent's way of life, and that he should require other signs of holiness. In the end . . . it was seen that they were all ravings."

Dear Saint Teresa, if you were to come back today! The word "charisma" is squandered; the title of "prophet" is distributed at full tilt, attributing this title even to students who confront the police in the city squares or to the guerrilla fighters of Latin America. There is an attempt to set the charismatics up against the pastors. What would you say, who obeyed confessors even when their advice was the opposite of that given you by God in your prayers?

And you must not believe I am a pessimist. The business of seeing charismata everywhere is, I hope, a passing fad. For that matter, I well know that the authentic gifts of the Spirit have always been accompanied by abuses and false gifts; nevertheless, the Church has gone ahead.

In the young Church of Corinth, for example, there was a great burgeoning of charismata, but Saint Paul became somewhat concerned because of some abuses that were found. The phenomenon was later repeated, in more notable and aberrant forms.

Two women, Priscilla and Maximilla, supporters and backers of Montanism in Asia, began by preaching "charismatically" a moral awakening, based on great austerity, total renunciation of matrimony, absolute readiness for martyrdom. They ended up opposing the bishops with their "new prophets," men and women, who were "invested by the Spirit," preached, administered the sacraments, and awaited Christ, who was to come any moment to inaugurate the millennial kingdom.

At the time of Saint Augustine there was Lucilla of Carthage, a rich lady whom the bishop Caecilian had scolded because, before Communion, she had the habit of pressing to her bosom a little bone that had belonged to some martyr or other. Irritated and offended, Lucilla led a group of bishops to oppose Caecilian's authority. Having lost one suit before the African episcopate, the group protested, without success, to the pope, then to the Council of Arles, then to the emperor himself. Then they founded a new church. In almost all the African cities there were thus seen two bishops, two cathedrals frequented by two opposing categories of faithful, who, on encountering one another, traded blows: on one side, the Catholics; on the other, followers of Donatus and Lucilla.

The Donatists called themselves the "pure"; they would not sit in a place previously occupied by a Catholic until they had cleaned it with their sleeve; they avoided Catholic bishops like the plague; they appealed to the Gospel against the Church, which they said was supported by the imperial authority; they formed assault squads. The very mild Saint Augustine was once driven to address them: "If martydom means so much to you, why don't you take a rope and go hang yourselves?"

In the seventeenth century there were the nuns of Port-Royal. One of their abbesses, Mother Angélique, had started out well: she had "charismatically" reformed herself and the monastery, ejecting even parents from the cloister. Endowed with great gifts, born to govern, she became, however, the soul of the Jansenist resistance, intransigent to the last, in the face of the ecclesiastical authorities. Of her and her nuns it was said: "Pure as angels, proud as devils."

How far all this is from your spirit! What an abyss between these women and you! "Daughter of the Church" was the name you liked most. You murmured it on your deathbed, whereas, during your life, *for* the Church and *with* the Church you had worked so hard, accepting even to suffer something *from* the Church!

What if you were to teach a bit of your method to the "prophetesses" of today?!

October 1974

To Carlo Goldoni

The Feminists and the
Beard of Saint Wilgefortis

Dear Goldoni,

At the end of August this year (1974) I had occasion to see your *Rusteghi* (The Boors) and, a short time afterwards, *The Taming of the Shrew* by Shakespeare. Without thinking, spontaneously I felt the contrast between Shakespeare the "antifeminist" and you, the "feminist."

The shrew is Katharina, daughter of a rich man of Padua. Wrathful, spiteful, intolerant of everyone and everything, she flings furniture about the room, drives away the servants, and even has the pretty habit of biting. Nobody wants to marry her.

But from Verona comes Petruchio, his appetite whetted by Katharina's very sizable dowry. He presents himself as a suitor for her hand; she rejects him, but he, sly and imperturbable, woos her cleverly: the more she maltreats him, the more he insists he finds her sweet and gentle.

The marriage takes place. Petruchio carries his bride to

CARLO GOLDONI, famous Venetian playwright (1707–1793). First a lawyer, he abandoned this profession to devote himself to the theater. His works include one hundred and twenty plays (La locandiera, La famiglia dell'antiquario, I rusteghi, Il campiello, Le baruffe chiozzotte are among the most popular) and his Memoirs, written in French. An innovator in the theater, he achieved a happy balance between moralism and realism, narrative magic and social analysis of the rising mercantile middle class.

Verona, but here the roles are reversed. With the excuse that the food and bed are unworthy of his bride, Petruchio, amid a thousand blandishments and protestations of affection, does not allow her to eat or sleep.

Without food and without rest Katharina is "tamed"; if her husband so desires, she is willing to call the sun the moon and vice versa, to say that it's a fine day when actually it's raining and vice versa; to her father, her sister, brother-in-law, and to the public she declares that a wife's duties are to obey and serve her husband and always to share his opinion.

In *I rusteghi* the procedure is reversed: four husbands start out "tamers" and end up, instead, "tamed."

Their wives? "Let them stay at home, let no one see them, let no one know anything about them!"

What about the daughter of Lunardo, one of the four? On the day of her wedding she neither knows she has a fiancé nor has she ever seen him: everything is arranged with the greatest secrecy by the fathers of the couple. The bride complains to her stepmother: "And I, poor thing, who never go out of the house? He won't even let his daughter go out on the balcony!"

But now the wives decide to have redress, and the enterprising "Sora Felice" is at their head. After having discovered and spread the secret of the imminent wedding and having given the "boors" a great surprise, she overcomes their final resistance with a speech worthy of a lawyer. It amazes them.

The four, defeated more than convinced, have to confess that their wives and daughters should not be "tamed," but be listened to: in any case, if the husbands don't give their wives the floor, the wives take it all the same.

*   *   *

Between the thesis of Shakespeare's and yours, dear Goldoni, I prefer yours: more human, more just, closer to the reality of then and of today, even if your "feminism" now seems bland. Since your times, in fact, women have made some conquests!

Conquests that, for the most part, are positive.

In *Le femmine puntigliose* (The Obstinate Woman), you laughed at salons "where there are women with the *cavalieri serventi*, who sit there, hard, stony, to have themselves adored: some sigh around them on one side, some kneel before them on the other, one hands a saucer, one picks up her handkerchief from the floor, one kisses the hand, another offers his arm, one acts as secretary, another as valet. . . ." Well, today not only has all this disappeared, but the difference between "ladies" and "women of the people" has also disappeared almost entirely.

Time and, especially, the two terrible wars with the consequent, considerable "shuffling of the cards" have changed the mentality and the social position of women. Girls no longer stay shut up in the home: even the better-off study or prepare themselves for a job with which to earn their living. Perhaps they still receive bows, perhaps their hands are kissed, but in a hurry: they know that, in general, they must count only on themselves, suffice to themselves, like men, and bring their own contribution of work and money to the family.

As in your time, they possess treasures of intuition and feeling, but today they must orient them half toward forming a family and half toward achieving a social position and maintaining it.

In your plays the categories of women can be counted with the fingers of one hand: noblewomen, bourgeois housewives, peasants, innkeepers, maids. Today a whole dictionary would not suffice: clerks, students, workers, window-dressers, teachers, hostesses, professors, nurses, employees, doctors, policewomen, social workers, lawyers, and so on, through an endless array that extends to members of parliament and of the cabinet.

"She knows how to do everything," you have Lunardo say with pride of his daughter, Lucietta. And you mean: knitting, mending, embroidery, cooking, playing music.

Today, women's work extends to all forms, even to those that in your day were reserved only for men: today you find women in political contests, in sports competition, and often with a strong and carefree attitude, which despises, or pretends to despise, any external display of feeling. Underneath, perhaps, the heart dreams and weeps like those of your Rosauras, Marinas, Luciettas, and Colombinas, but on the outside, for the most part, there is the mask of indifference.

At this point you will ask: "But do you consider all this a good thing or a bad thing?"

In itself, it is good, dear Goldoni; the evil, if there is any, lies in the worsening atmosphere which surrounds women today and which waits to corrupt their healthy convictions and their religious and moral life. On July 26 — for example — the Italian daily newspapers reported: Yesterday in a press conference, the member of the parliament Signora N., proposing the liberalization of abortion, declared: "The right to live one's own sexuality is today restricted by the sense of sin. . . . There exists the woman's right to live her own sexuality not only within a family or with reference to a future family."

Dear Goldoni, you were not what they call a "bigot," you spoke little of God and you even sprinkled a pinch of irony over some clergymen; lawyer-dramatist, you knew the world and life. And what a life! That of strolling players, of eighteenth-century Venice, of the court of Louis XVI.

But you believed in the family, in conjugal love and fidelity, in woman's dignity, despite your innate amorousness and your confessed attraction toward the "fair sex." Your "respectable girl," your "good mother," your "obedient daughter," even your "clever widow" (clever, yes, but with a respectable second marriage in mind) would have blushed to hear the woman member of parliament mentioned above.

In your time it would have been unthinkable to imagine the exercise of a female sexuality outside the family being claimed as a right in the name of all women, before the eyes of everyone, without euphemism, without reticence. Unthinkable, too, that sin could pass for a pure invention of the "authorities" to make people toe the line and to deprive them of their freedom.

The women of your time, even if they sinned, admitted, almost all of them, that, beyond us, a God — to our advantage and not to His — could set laws upon human actions. Today? I wonder how many women agree with the thesis of the parliamentarian. I hope they are not numerous, but I don't know. If they were numerous, then we would have not so much an advance of "feminism," but a collapse of feminity and of humanity.

*   *   *

You heard the woman parliamentarian: liberalized abortion and new regulation for the advancement of women.

But will it be real advancement? Investigations by Japanese, English, and Hungarian physicians into abortions, even those carried out under the aegis of the law and in specialized hospitals, show that such abortions are always a trauma for the woman's health, for later childbearing, and for later children. Psychologists and psychiatrists, furthermore, indicate other bad consequences: these, they say, perhaps generally lie dormant in the unconscious mind of the woman who has had the abortion, but they surface later, in moments of crisis.

We have said nothing of the moral aspect: abortion not only violates the laws of God, it goes against the deepest aspirations of woman, troubling her greatly.

In many cases, too, the abortion does not free the woman so much as it frees her partner, whether he be her husband or not, from nuisances and irritations, allowing him to give free rein to his sexual desires without assuming the obligations involved: it is a retrocession, rather than an advance, for women with regard to men.

*   *   *

On the subject of abortion, dear Goldoni, the parliamentarian and the feminists today have some powerful allies.

"Regulated abortion," some say, "is a lesser evil; it will prevent illegal abortions and the deaths of numerous young women, formerly the victims of the abortionist."

But the experience of other countries proves that illegal abortions do not diminish at all with the advent of legalization, unless this permits *any* abortion. The number of the young victims of illegal operations is, besides, often exaggerated, for propaganda purposes. "Other civilized nations have legalized abortion: why not Italy?" I reply: If legalizing abortion is an error, why should we also err? A disease imported into Italy from outside does not become health just because it is imported; it becomes infection, epidemic.

In defense of abortion an even more specious line is beginning to be heard. "What is important," they say, "is the twelfth week."

Yes, because that is the moment of the *two lives* of the fetus in the maternal womb.

The first life is *human*, still vegeto-animal; the second is *humanized*, but humanized on one condition. Namely, on the condition that the parents, the moment the presence of the new little being has been perceived, "call it to be born," want it, recognize it, create a bond of love with it, thus conferring on it the "right to be." And they add: as a rule, the parents have to make this call; if, however (a very ugly *however*), there is a motive, the parents can, without sin, reject the child and expel it. At most, to avoid abuses, so that it will not be too easy to expel, they should consult doctors or magistrates before deciding.

Alas, dear Goldoni, those "two lives" exist only in the heads of some theologians. Outside those heads, in the mother's womb, concretely, there is only one life to make its imploring appeal to parents and to society. These theorists suppose that, after the famous twelfth week, it is up to the parents to create rights in the new being. The opposite is true: it is the new being that, from the very beginning of his development, creates duties in the parents.

And, beyond the new creature, there is God, who has commanded: "Thou shalt not kill!" "Life," Vatican Council II wrote, "must be protected with the greatest care from the moment of conception; abortion, like infanticide, is an abominable crime."

* * *

Dear Goldoni, there would be other, not very delicate "feminists" to mention, but we'll leave them alone. My wish, instead, is that women may achieve new conquests, but just and lofty ones, developing everything the Lord has revealed about the true greatness of women.

Some help, my dear Goldoni, could come from your plays, so full of good sense, with girls who shyly await conjugal life, wives who do indeed want a happier life and do also have faults, but who are honest, pay heed to their own duties, and are jealous guardians of their own virtue.

Some feminists, on the other hand, find all this out of date, antiquated, and try to pass off as "slavery, imposed by the male" even some laws of God. This means that they are choosing models of life that are not Christian.

If we were to recommend them to a saint, that saint might be Wilgefortis, with her strange name and her even stranger story.

Born, in fact, in Portugal of pagan parents, she was baptized without their knowledge. According to legend, she made a vow of virginity. Promised by her father in marriage to a king of Sicily, she asked and obtained from the Lord a miracle: namely a thick, horrible beard, which actually sprouted on her maidenly chin. The marriage naturally came to nothing; the maiden was freed from her bridegroom, even if she was then crucified by her father.

This reference is not meant maliciously. Jokingly, however, one could say that a bearded lady saint, liberated from a husband, is just what the feminists need, as they speak with fierce intentions against bearded men.

After *La vedova scaltra* (The Clever Widow), *La donna di garbo* (The woman of Charm), *Le massere* (The House-wives), *Le Morbinose* (The Bluestockings), *La putta onorata* (The Respectable Girl), *Il cavaliere e la dama* (The Knight and the Lady), *Le femmine puntigliose* (The Obstinate Women), *I pettegolezzi delle donne* (Women's Gossip), *La moglie saggia* (The Wise Wife), *La castalda* (The Stew-ardess), *La sposa persiana* (The Persian Bride), *Donne de casa soa* (Women of His Own House), and so many oth-ers, *La donna barbuta* (The Bearded Woman) would add the final character to the vast Goldoni female gallery!

November 1974

To Andreas Hofer

The Call of the Iselberg

Dear Hofer,

A month ago, passing through Innsbruck, I visited the Hofkirche, formerly a Franciscan church, built in the Renaissance on a design by our own Andrea Crivelli. It was there, to the left of the main door, that I came upon your tomb. Near you are buried Joseph Speckbacher and the Capuchin Joachim Haspinger, both companions in your battles.

In reality, you, the innkeeper of San Leonardo in Val Passiria, fought two kinds of battle: first you were a regular soldier in the war against the French in 1796 and in 1805; then, as a partisan, you were the leader and the soul of the uprising of the Tyrolese people against the Bavarians and the French in 1809. Your incredibly able and brave leadership of this guerrilla war wrested admiration even from Napoleon's generals and made you become an undying hero in the hearts of your people.

It all began in 1809, when the count von Montgelas, minister of the king of Bavaria, without reason or warn-

ANDREAS HOFER, Tyrolese patriot, was born at San Leonardo in Passiria in 1767 and died before a firing squad at Mantua in 1810. A gifted captain, he led the national war of the Tyrolese people against the dominion of the Bavarians and the French, whom he defeated respectively on 29 May and 13 August 1809, near Mount Isel. Betrayed, he was taken prisoner by the French, and Napoleon had him shot. In addition to being an unvanquished partisan, he was also a firm Christian.

ing suddenly suppressed all ceremonies of Catholic worship: no more processions, religious marriages or funerals, no more ringing of bells. Montgelas did not imagine how deep the religious feelings of the very Catholic Tyrolese people could go. They sent polite petitions to the king of Bavaria, asking that the "wicked and liberticide decree" be revoked. In vain. Then there was a mass insurrection. As the bells rang furiously and their sound spread from valley to valley, peasants were seen running from every "*maso*" (farmhouse), from every village, some armed with scythes, some with pitchforks, some with old muskets. Your gigantic figure dominated them, your powerful and determined voice, your impressive black beard.

Twice the Bavarian army was defeated; but when, by the tens of thousands, the French and the Saxons came as reinforcements, inevitably your men had to disperse and turn to guerrilla fighting. Then, too, as during the Italian Resistance, they "went into the mountains." Unfortunately, two wretches betrayed you for the usual "thirty pieces of silver." Discovered by the French in the hut where you were hiding, you said: "Do what you like with me; only respect the innocence of my wife and my children." Viceroy Eugene wanted to spare you; Napoleon ordered that you be shot.

At Mantua, before the execution, like a patriarch you blessed the companions kneeling around you, and refusing the blindfold, you stood and awaited the volley. On the Iselberg, near Innsbruck, they have erected a statue. On the pedestal is written: *For God, for the Emperor, for the Fatherland.*

* * *

Leaving the emperor out of it, I would like your heroism, gentle and Christian at once, to inspire people, within and beyond the Tyrol. Mind you: I am not hoping for any guerrilla fighting; I am convinced that will not be needed, especially in democratic Italy. But your Christian faith, all of a piece, the union with your people which, thanks also to Haspinger, you were able to achieve in the hour of danger: these, yes, I would wish for with all my heart.

The prophet Elijah said to the people: "How long will you go limping with two different opinions? If the Lord is God, follow him; but if Baal, follow him!" He wanted a serious choice to be made; he implied that one cannot go to God if he has not freed himself from evil, if he is trying to sit on two stools, if he is wavering. Our own Trilussa said the same thing:

> I believe in God the Father Almighty. But . . .
> Have you some doubt? Keep it to yourself.
> Faith is beautiful without any "who knows?"
> Without the "hows" and without the "whys."

"Who knows?" and "how?" and "why?" were not what your Tyrolese wanted. Up there, in your humble inn, "am Sand," they played cards, drank, had fun, argued. But when they returned home, they recited evening prayers with their families; going to Sunday Mass, they would stop for a while at the graves of their dead in the little cemetery nestled around the church. The surroundings, the devout traditions, the time available fostered reflection: reflection developed that conviction, which the painter Egger Lienz has effectively expressed, painting the Tyrolese partisans collected ready for battle, with Haspinger at their head, holding up the Crucifix.

For us, today, overwhelmed as we are by the frenzied pace of life, silence and the possibility of reflecting are wanting; this perhaps is one of the reasons why many waver. Haspinger, the old-style preacher, recalling us roughly to the eternal truths, is not accepted today: a more discreet, persuasive voice would be needed. The great bell, ringing solemnly, is something we will not bear; we accept the little bell at home.

This little bell, this discreet voice, was represented, for example, by Brother Candido of the Christian Schools. Living a century after you, Hofer, he was traveling one day in a train. A railway timetable was on his lap; he was consulting it. A boy nearby peeked curiously at the book and watched the brother leaf through it. "Do you know this book?" Fratel Candido asked him. "No? You want to see what it's used for?" And he explained, showing the child how to look up schedules and calculate the most rapid route from one city to another. The boy became interested, tried it out for himself, soon learned, and was very proud; the other passengers in the compartment followed the dialogue of the two with interest and amusement.

At a certain point, casually, Brother Candido continued: "Do you want me to teach you also how to travel on the *Paradise Railroad?*" Both the boy and the passengers were taken by surprise. From his case Brother Candido took a little illustrated paper and explained: "Here is the *Paradise Railroad.* Starting station: any point of the globe. Time of departure: any time. Time of arrival: cannot be predicted for the traveler. Ticket: being in a state of grace. Conductor: your own conscience. Warnings: 1) keep your luggage of good works always ready; 2) lost baggage can be recovered through Confession." Et cetera.

When he had finished explaining, amiable and smiling, he offered the boy and the others present the curious and precious *timetable,* which may then have inspired some to repentance and to a new decision.

You will say: "This brother of yours is a very small-scale, skimpy version of my powerful Haspinger!" What can I do? Our present day, weak in religion, must be approached by the most suitable method. The method is not important: it is the final success that counts: making people reflect!

* * *

Even more important is keeping both Catholics and citizens united among themselves. We are Christians, but the preaching of the pagan consul Publius Rutilius is valid also for us. He was very fat. One day, to settle a terrible, seemingly endless quarrel between two parties, he said: "My dear friends, as you see, I am very fat and my wife is still fatter than I. And yet, when we are in agreement a little bed suffices for both of us. When we quarrel, however, the whole house seems small to us and is no longer enough."

Now I begin to wonder: The example of Rutilius fits, if the quarreling parties are two in number; but, alas!, in the country today, in our political parties, the factions are not two, but four, six, seven, twenty! You can no longer talk of a double bed! If consideration of the common good is not enough to restore us to unity, we should be induced to avoid disagreements at least by the fear of the harm they do. Voltaire used to say: Twice I found myself on the brink of ruin: the first time when I lost an argument; the second, when I won it.

Nations and political and religious factions which we have before our eyes can apply Voltaire's epigram to themselves. Moreover, it would be wise for them to give some thought to the "third person" who, in the popular saying, is the one who benefits when two people quarrel.

Bulwer-Lytton, author of *The Last Days of Pompeii*, wrote that the lawyer is a man who, when two other men quarrel over an oyster, opens it, drains its contents, then gives the two halves of the shell to the litigants: one apiece! This is a bit crude, but it is still true that always and in all fields the strength of our adversary is our own weakness, caused by divisions.

These considerations apply, in part, also to the Catholic Church. Its founder, Christ, feared divisions and laid a solid foundation for unity. He said: I want my followers to be "a sole thing," they should form "a single fold." To gain this end, from the crowd He chose the Twelve, of whom He said: "He who hears you hears me." Foreseeing divisions among the Twelve and their successors, He wanted one of them to act as head or as oldest brother, and He said to Peter: "Feed my lambs" "confirm your brothers." So the remedy is there: It is enough for the faithful, the priests, religious, bishops, to gather around the pope: no one will break up the Church.

Your Capuchin, Haspinger, dear Hofer, knew these things, indeed he had direct experience of them. At the time of your Tyrolese insurrection, several bishops, out of fear or self-interest, went over to the side of the most-powerful Napoleon. But you of the Tyrol resisted Napoleon and his friends, staying on the side of Pope Pius VII, who, in that very year of 1809, excommunicated Napoleon, then was arrested by the French and taken from Rome to exile in Savona.

These are all things to be remembered. To be put into practice. To end the countless disputes that weary and scandalize. To restore the union of spirits, the unity of the Church and of the country. *Für Gott . . . für Vaterland.* For God . . . for the Country as is written on the Iselberg!

December 1974

To Jesus

I Write in Trepidation

Dear Jesus,

I have received some criticism. "He is a bishop, a cardinal," it has been said, "and he's broken his arm writing in all directions, to Mark Twain, to Péguy, to Casella, to Penelope, to Dickens, to Marlowe, to Goldoni, and heavens knows how many others. But not one line to Jesus Christ!"

You know this. With You I try to maintain a constant conversation. But to translate it into letters is difficult: these are personal things. And besides, so little! And besides, what can I write to You, about You, after all the books that have been written on You?

And besides, there is already the Gospel. Just as lightning surpasses all fires and radium all metals; as the missile is faster than the arrow of the poor savage, so the Gospel surpasses all books.

Nevertheless, here is the letter. I write it in trepidation, in the condition of a poor deaf-mute, who makes an effort to be understood, or in the state of Jeremiah, who, sent to preach, said to You, filled with reluctance: "Ah, Lord God! Behold, I do not know how to speak, for I am only a youth."

* * *

Pilate, in presenting You to the people, said: Here is the man! He thought he knew You, but he did not know even a scrap of Your heart, whose mercifulness You revealed a hundred times, in a hundred ways.

Your mother. On the Cross, You were unwilling to leave this world without finding her a second son who would look after her and You said to John: Behold thy mother.

The Apostles. You lived night and day with them, treating them like real friends, putting up with their faults. You instructed them with unfailing patience. The mother of two of them asks a privileged position for her sons, and You say: With me there are no honors, but rather sufferings. The others also want the first places, and You say: You must instead make yourselves small, sit down in the last place, serve!

At the Last Supper You put them on their guard. They will be afraid, they will run away! They protest, Peter first and most of all; but then, he denies You three times. You forgive Peter and three times You say to him: "Feed my sheep."

As for the other Apostles, Your forgiveness shines brightest in Chapter 21 of John. They are out in a boat, and have been out all night long. You, the Resurrected One, are there on the shore of the lake, before dawn. You cook for them, serve them, lighting the fire, preparing the roast fish for them, the bread.

Sinners. The shepherd who rushes out to search for the lost sheep, rejoices in finding it, and celebrates when he brings it back to the fold: this is You. You are that good father who, at the return of the prodigal son, flings his arms around him, in a long embrace. A scene to be found on every page of the Gospel. In fact You approach sinners, men and women, You eat at their table, You invite Yourself, if they do not dare invite You. You really seem — this is my impression — to be more concerned with the sufferings that sin produces in the sinners than with the offense against God. Instilling the hope of pardon, You seem to say: You cannot even imagine the joy your conversion gives me!

Along with Your heart, Your practical intelligence shines in You.

Your aim was the inner person, for that matter. There were the Pharisees' faces, wan from long religious fasting, and You said: I do not like those faces; the heart of those men is far from God; it is the inner man who matters, the heart is the rule for judging; from within, from the heart of men come bad thoughts: dissoluteness, thefts, murders, adulteries, greed, pride, vanity.

You had a horror of futile words: "Let what you say be simply 'Yes' or 'No'; anything more than this comes from evil." "And in praying, do not heap up empty phrases."

You wanted concreteness and reserve: "But when you fast, anoint your head and wash your face." "But when you give alms, do not let your left hand know what your right hand is doing." To the healed leper You urged: "See that you say nothing to any one." To the parents of the girl raised from the dead, You gave strong instructions that they were not to go blowing the trumpet of the miracle that had taken place. You used to say: "I do not seek my own glory." My food is to do the will of my Father.

From the Cross, concluding Your life, You said: "It is finished," but You had always made a point of seeing that things were not done halfway. The Apostles had prompted You: These people have been following us for some time: let's send them home, to eat in their own houses. But You said: No, we'll give them something to eat. And when the meal of the multiplied loaves and fishes was over, You added: "Gather up the fragments left over, that nothing may be lost."

You wanted good to be done down to the least detail. When You raised the daughter of Jairus, You ordered that the child be given something to eat. People proclaimed of You: "He has done all things well!"

*   *   *

What light of intelligence glowed from Your preaching! Your adversaries send the guards from the temple to ar-

rest You and see them come back empty-handed. "Why
didn't you bring him in?" The guards answer: "No man
has ever spoken the way He does!" So You held people
spellbound, and from the very first days they said of You:
This man really speaks with authority! The scribes are
nothing like Him!

Poor scribes! Chained to the six hundred and thirty-
four precepts of the Law, they went around saying that
God Himself devoted a bit of time every day to the study
of the Law and, in Heaven, He reviewed the opinions of
the scribes to learn from their scribblings!

But You said: You have all heard that it was said . . .
but on the contrary I say to you . . . ! You claimed the
right and the power to perfect the Law as master of the
Law. With magnificent courage You declared: "Something greater than Solomon is here"; "Heaven and earth
will pass away, but my words will not pass away."

And You never tired of teaching in the synagogues, in
the temple, sitting in the squares on the meadows, walking in the streets, or staying in homes, even at table.

* * *

At this spectacle of people rushing to a Crucifix for so
many centuries and from every part of the world, a question arises: Was this only a great, beneficent man or was
He a God? You Yourself gave the answer and anyone
whose eyes are not veiled by prejudice but are eager for
the light will accept it.

When Peter proclaimed: "You are Christ, the Son of
the living God," You not only accepted this confession,
but also rewarded it. You have always claimed for Yourself that which the Jews considered reserved for God. To
their scandal You forgave sins, You called Yourself master
of the Sabbath, You taught with supreme authority, You
declared Yourself the equal of the Father.

Several times they tried to stone You as a blasphemer,
because You uttered the name of God. When they finally
took You and brought You before the high priest, he
asked You solemnly: "Are you the Christ, the Son of the

Blessed?" You answered: "I am; and you will see the Son
of man sitting at the right hand of Power and coming
with the clouds of heaven." You accepted death rather
than retract and deny this divine essence of Yours.

I have written, but I have never before been so dissat-
isfied with my writing. I feel as if I had left out the
greater part of what could be said of You, that I have said
badly what should have been said much better. There is
one comfort, however: the important thing is not that
one person should write about Christ, but that many
should love and imitate Christ.

And fortunately — in spite of everyting — this still
happens.

May 1974

Albino Luciani

The son of a socialist glassworker and a scullery maid, Albino Luciani was born on 17 October 1912, in the town of Forno di Canale in the Dolomite Alps of northeastern Italy. He attended seminary in the town of Feltre and graduated in philosophy and theology at the seminary of Belluno, the hometown of nineteenth-century Pope Gregory XVI. He then graduated in dogmatics at the Gregorian University in Rome and was ordained a priest in 1935. He returned to his home region to work as a parish assistant, a religion teacher in a mining technician's school, and a teacher of dogmatic and moral theology at the Gregorian Seminary in Belluno, the same city in the Dolomite foothills where he had been a student. In 1948, he was named by the Bishop of Belluno to oversee catechetics — the teaching of the faith — in the provincial diocese. He later recounted his thoughts and experiences in a book, *Catechism in Crumbs*. In 1958 Pope John XXIII appointed Luciani Bishop of Vittorio Veneto, a local diocese at the foot of the Alps, subject to Venice. Pope Paul VI promoted him to Patriarch of Venice in 1969 and named him a cardinal in 1973. He was elected the 263rd Pontiff of the Roman Catholic Church on 26 August 1978, in one of the shortest conclaves in Church history. The sixty-five-year-old Pope adopted the name John Paul I. Thirty-three days later he died unexpectedly in his sleep. He once said of himself: "I am only a poor man accustomed to small things and silence."